WHERE TO DRINK
COFFEE

WHERE TO DRINK
COFFEE

—

LIZ CLAYTON & AVIDAN ROSS

CONTENTS

The Big, Small
  World of Coffee   6
A Passion for Coffee   8
Glossary   10

OCEANIA
Australia   **16**
  Sydney   20
  Brisbane   24
  Melbourne   28
New Zealand   **34**

ASIA
China, Hong Kong
  & Taiwan   **40**
    Hong Kong   46
    Taipei   50
South & Southeast Asia   **54**
  Bangkok   58
Japan   **62**
  Tokyo   66
South Korea   **72**
  Seoul   74

EUROPE
Denmark, Finland, Iceland,
  Norway & Sweden   **82**
    Copenhagen   88
    Reykjavík   92
    Oslo   96
UK & Republic of Ireland   **100**
  London   104
  Glasgow   110
  Dublin   114
Belgium &
  The Netherlands   **118**
  Amsterdam   122
France   **126**
  Paris   130
Portugal & Spain   **136**
Germany   **140**
  Berlin   144
  Hamburg   148
The Czech Republic,
  Hungary & Poland   **152**
Croatia, Greece, Serbia
  & Turkey   **158**
  Zagreb   162
  Istanbul   166
The Russian Federation   **170**
  Moscow   172
Italy   **176**

AFRICA
Kenya & South Africa   **182**

WESTERN ASIA & THE MIDDLE EAST
Iran & The UAE   **188**

NORTH AMERICA
Canada   **194**
  Vancouver   202
  Toronto   206
United States   **210**
USA West   **212**
  Los Angeles   222
  San Francisco   230
  Denver   236
  Portland   240
  Austin   246
  Seattle   252
USA Midwest   **258**
  Chicago   268
USA South   **272**
USA Northeast   **280**
  Boston   286
  New York City   290

CENTRAL & SOUTH AMERICA
Central America   **302**
South America North   **310**
  Lima   312
South America South   **316**
  São Paulo   320

The Contributors   324
Index by Contributor   332
Index by Country   338
Index by Venue   344

THE BIG, SMALL WORLD OF COFFEE

A decade ago, even a handful of years ago in many cities, it was hard to know where to find a wonderful cup of coffee. It was difficult, sleuthing work, cobbled together by rumor, visual cues, and, if you had your feet on the ground already, word of mouth. In fact, in modern coffee's early days, the best way of all to locate a destination-worthy drink was surely that—a personal recommendation from someone who had been or had worked with a person who opened a great shop, or who had seen a great barista perform at a coffee competition (of all things!) and who could vouch for the operator's passion and quality.

Yet as specialty coffee's reach has evolved, hot on the sous-vide'd heels of the world's highly phone-photographed love affair with fancy food, the search for the best place to get coffee has paradoxically become more difficult. With the rise in consumer coffee literacy—even your co-worker knows what a flat white is by now—have come a surfeit of stylish additions to the coffee market, not all of them as quality focused as their neighbors. A cafe that may bear the superficial markings of a great place—it seems all a cafe owner has to do these days is throw up some reclaimed lumber and set out a few succulents on the tables with your cappuccino—might not actually serve the tastiest coffee. How can you tell the great from the good? Whose cup is truly legit around here? Just as in years before, the best way is still to ask someone in the know.

It's thrilling to those who love—and make—coffee to see how quickly the retail landscape has grown. The coffee shop explosion from Seoul to St. Louis has been part of a greater consciousness in the coffee-drinking public about the very real connections between better-tasting coffee and more environmentally and financially sustainable practices at the coffee's source (i.e., paying farmers better money to grow better coffee in better ways and to treat it with care throughout the distribution chain). As climate shifts and diseases threaten the future of Arabica coffee crops, it's the most passionate specialty coffee ambassadors and cafes that continue to reinforce the meaningfulness of growing these crops.

The process of selecting which cafes to recommend in *Where to Drink Coffee* has been an interesting journey, particularly as the population of so-called specialty cafes is only decades young in the food world, with credit due perhaps most notably to a certain green-aproned multinational chain that whetted the global palate (and wallet) for thinking of a special cup of coffee as a special treat rather than as something dull and everyday. During the years-long process of surveying experts to find the best of the best, it's true that some of the shops we wanted to include closed and some changed location—but at the same time, dozens of other exciting places opened to fill out the ranks.

In fact, the number of quality-focused coffee shops is growing so fast worldwide, it almost seems that such a survey guidebook might never be able to stay apace. But as we sought out the coffee experts worldwide whose collective wisdom makes up this book—everyone from people born into coffee-farming families to importers to roasters to the baristas who serve you the finished product—one thing became clear: quality and taste will always stand out, and the people who care about quality and taste will find them easy to recognize.

It's in that spirit that we feel this thoughtfully compiled collection of nearly six hundred of the world's best coffee shops can endure. Even as the coffee shop landscape multiplies, the craft-obsessed experts who work in all parts of its world somehow remain unshakably enthusiastic, dedicated, and knowledgeable about finding great coffee and sharing that knowledge with those around them, even if it's about their competition. I've never met a dedicated coffee person who didn't have one more great recommendation for me, and as you begin to sip your way across the world using this book, I'm confident that you won't either.

LIZ CLAYTON

A PASSION
FOR COFFEE

It all started with an unusual request: to drive a family car from Los Angeles to New York for my younger sister in medical school. With little notice and no set plan, my wife and I decided to embrace the opportunity. We'd focus the trip on what we loved—discovering great places to eat and drink—as we traveled across the country. Before we set off on our voyage, we visited our newest favorite coffee shop, Handsome Coffee Roasters in the Los Angeles Arts District. We'd befriended one of the owners, Michael Phillips, who had recently won the World Barista Championship. Handsome's arrival in the Los Angeles coffee landscape had been one of the most anticipated culinary happenings of the year, and as we were handed a few of the first bags of coffee off the line, we excitedly began our journey as amateur coffee delivery mules.

With only our first destination planned, and no particular schedule in mind, we headed off vaguely toward New York City via Phoenix, Arizona. We arrived midmorning at Cartel Coffee in Phoenix, a recommendation from Michael. We promptly started up a conversation with the head barista about our trip and shared with him some of our Handsome coffee beans. That opened a discussion about coffee in the Southwest, and we then had a fresh bag of Cartel coffee beans in our hands. Without skipping a beat, the barista gave us a list of other great shops in Phoenix and a destination in Denver, Colorado, where he said we should deliver his coffee.

Suddenly our itinerary, and the country, unfolded before us, one bag of coffee at a time. This experience continued from city to city, coffee shop to coffee shop. Of course, baristas are not just up on all the latest coffee places, but are also deeply versed in their local food and cocktail culture. With the guidance of these instant friends, we were never hungry or thirsty. We slowly compiled a stack of handwritten lists from baristas around the United States, guiding us to the best places in the country to experience an amazing cup of coffee.

We ended up visiting fifteen cities and over fifty cafes on our journey. We realized that every city has great cafes with baristas who are passionate about their craft and the unique culture of their town. They know their cities deeply, and each destination cafe became a great starting point for exploration, from which the entire city opened up before us. Our experiences on that trip inform our habits to this day—we never travel anywhere in the world without a bag of favorite coffee to share. With that basic gift, we have found the way to start a conversation about coffee—and so much more—in every city and country we visit.

When people go to unfamiliar cities, it can be difficult to discover new and unique places or to trust the recommendations of the great anonymous online masses. We've found no recommendations more persuasive than those of the experts themselves: people who have dedicated their livelihoods to the passion of their craft and who want to share their own joys and discoveries with like-minded travelers. As much as we used our stack of handwritten notes to create the waypoints of our road trip, we hope that this book provides you with the inspiration to explore, however near or far you may travel, and wherever the road takes you.

AVIDAN ROSS

GLOSSARY

AeroPress
Filter brew method invented by a sports equipment company, in which coffee is steeped in a cylindrical chamber and then expelled from the brewer by pressing down firmly. Its status as a niche brewer has earned it its own international brewing competitions.

Americano
An espresso-based drink that visually resembles drip coffee but is made with an espresso and the addition of hot water.

Barista
Any professional preparing coffee or espresso as his or her primary job function.

Cappuccino
An espresso-based drink made with textured milk or foam and served in a medium-sized cup.

Chemex
A unique style of filter brewing in a flask-shaped glass carafe of the same name. The Chemex brewer is as famous as an American houseware design icon as it is in the coffee world.

Cold brew
A style of preparing coffee for cold service, usually over ice, that involves brewing a highly concentrated dose of coarse coffee grounds steeped in water for at least twelve hours and then filtered after the brew, at least once. Cold brew results in a lower acidity brew than hotbrew methods.

Cortado
An espresso-based drink made with textured milk or foam, a little smaller than a cappuccino and with a higher ratio of espresso to milk.

Cupping
The professional practice of evaluating a coffee's quality and flavor using a standardized set of criteria and, usually, a score sheet. Cupping is typically done with more than one kind of coffee at a time, or variations on roast styles

of the same coffee, with the coffee grounds steeped in small, widemouthed bowls with no filter method. Coffee is evaluated both by smell (before as well as after making contact with water) and taste (sampled one spoonful at a time). Generally the practice is done in groups whose members will discuss their findings and tasting notes once the evaluation is complete.

Drip coffee
A casual term for non-espresso coffee made with any of a variety of methods (which need not drip per se) such as a pour-over drip coffee cone, automated filter brew, or Chemex. Other styles of non-espresso coffee that produce a brew of similar consistency are often referenced interchangeably with the terms *drip*, *filter*, or even *brewed coffee*, though the methods may vary considerably and may not technically involve dripping (e.g., French press, syphon, or AeroPress) or may use dramatically different styles of filtering (e.g., paper, cloth, metal, or even glass). It may be most useful to think of drip, filter, or brewed coffee as simply—as *The Professional Barista's Handbook* author Scott Rao put it—"everything but espresso."

Espresso
A style of coffee preparation made with a specific machine that forces heated water through a densely packed measure of fine-ground coffee at high pressure and speed. The resulting drink is a syrupy, highly concentrated "shot" of coffee at a small liquid volume. It is traditionally served in a demitasse.

Filter coffee
See: drip coffee.

Flat white
A style of coffee similar to the cappuccino (both have infinite small variations), but first popularized in the Southern Hemisphere, particularly New Zealand and Australia.

Full-immersion brew
A style of brewing drip coffee that involves steeping the coffee grounds in contact with hot water for a period of time before filtering the grounds from the coffee. Examples include French press and Clever dripper.

Gibraltar
See: cortado.

Iced coffee
Any form of coffee served cold and over ice, whether it be brewed hot onto ice or steeped in a cold-brew method for many hours.

Kyoto-style drip or Oji drip
A slow-brew method of preparing concentrated coffee one drip at a time for cold-brew preparation. The method uses a tall glass tower brewing device manufactured in Japan by the Oji corporation and popular in Kyoto.

Latte
An espresso-based drink made with a large quantity of milk, traditionally served in a large cup or glass.

Macchiato
An espresso-based drink made with a very small quantity of milk, traditionally served in a demitasse. The Starbucks brand Macchiato is a large, sugared, and flavored coffee beverage that is often confused with the traditional macchiato.

Manual brew
Any kind of nonautomated style of brewing coffee, also known as hand brew. Traditionally associated with methods where a barista must stand over a filter cone slowly pouring water into the coffee brewer, but which can include any brew made to order such as a French press or AeroPress.

Pour-over
A specific style of manual brewing where water is poured carefully into a usually conical-shaped brewer, through which the coffee drips down.

Q grader / Q
A coffee industry standard certification for professional-level coffee evaluation skills.

Roaster
A machine that turns coffee from green, unroasted beans into brown, roasted beans suitable for preparation and serving. Also the name of the woman or man who operates the coffee roasting machine. Coffee roasting companies may esteem certain highly experienced professional roasters as master roasters or, similarly, roastmasters.

Shot
A serving of espresso.

Signature drink
Any coffee beverage that involves creativity and nontraditional ingredients, usually associated with a specific barista's creative flair. Coffee shops may offer their own signature drinks on a menu alongside traditional drinks like espresso, cappuccino, and so on.

Syphon
A Japanese-style method of preparation based on heating water in a lower chamber and driving it upward where it meets ground coffee. The coffee and water steep and agitate for a period of time until the heat source is removed, causing a temperature differential that draws the coffee down rapidly through a filter due to a vacuum effect.

Third Wave
A term used to describe a specific movement in the coffee industry that signified a shift toward coffee appreciation on a deeper level, including appreciating coffee's terroir, approaching its roasting and preparation with care and craft, and conveying the meaning of these subtleties to the coffee consumer through storytelling. The term was originally coined by Trish Rothgeb in a 2003 article in the *Flamekeeper* newsletter.

World Barista Championship
An international coffee competition drawing together the top baristas in dozens of countries across the world, all of whom graduated to their nations' top ranks under the same competition format and were evaluated on both sensory quality and technical skill in the preparation of espresso. The competition has taken place annually since 2000, with the first World Barista Champion title awarded to Norwegian barista Robert Thoresen. Along with the World Barista Championship is a growing suite of companion competitions such as the World Brewer's Cup, World Cup Tasters, World Cezve/Ibrik, World Coffee in Good Spirits, World AeroPress, and World Latte Art Championships.

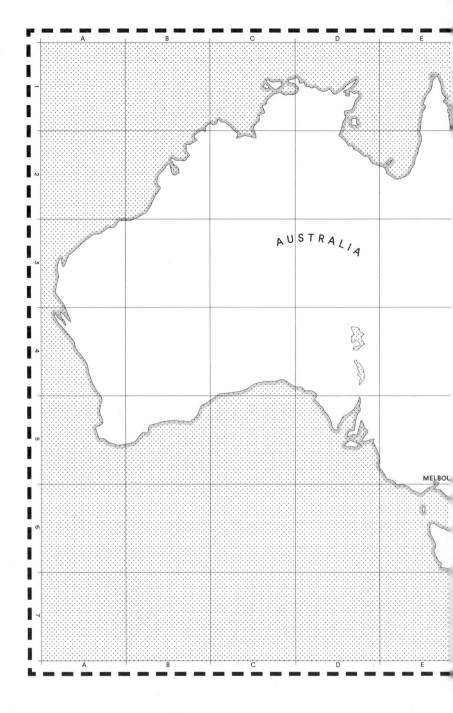

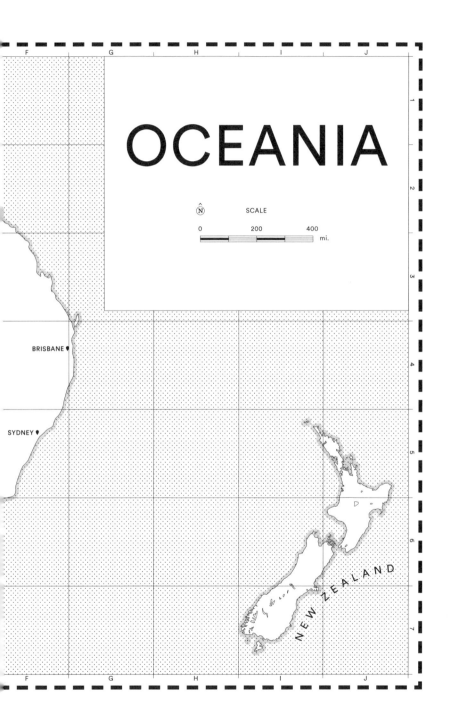

OCEANIA

$\widehat{N}$ SCALE

0   200   400
mi.

BRISBANE

SYDNEY

NEW ZEALAND

"A VIBRANT, OPEN-AIR CAFE IN THE CENTER OF BYRON, SERVING DELICIOUS FOOD AND STELLAR COFFEE."

SCOTT RAO P.18

"ABOUT THE FRIENDLIEST PEOPLE I'VE EVER MET. THEY OFFER NUMEROUS BREWING METHODS AND ROAST OUT BACK."

SCOTT RAO P.18

AUSTRALIA

"LARGE CAFE AND ROASTERY RUN BY A WELCOMING FAMILY, SERVING LOVELY FOOD AND COFFEE ROASTED ON-SITE."

SCOTT RAO P.19

"A ROASTERY AND A CAFE, SHOWCASING SCRUMPTIOUS SEASONAL COFFEES ROASTED AND BREWED UNDER ONE ROOF."

ANYA SEREDA P.18

"SIMPLE, UNASSUMING, AND VERY APPROACHABLE. THE DETAILS (BOOKS, PLANTS, GOOD TUNES) GIVE WARMTH; THE COFFEES GIVE A GOOD REASON TO COME BACK."

ANYA SEREDA P.19

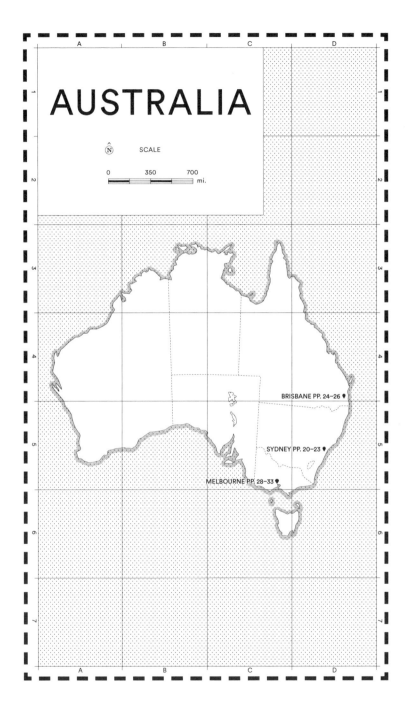

AUSTRALIA

$\hat{N}$ SCALE

0   350   700   mi.

BRISBANE PP. 24–26 ●

SYDNEY PP. 20–23 ●

MELBOURNE PP. 28–33 ●

ONA COFFEE

67 Wollongong Street
Fyshwick
Canberra
Australian Capital Territory 2609
Australia
+61 261623320
www.onacoffee.com.au

Opening hours..Mon–Fri from 7 am,
Sat–Sun from 8 am
Credit cards............................Visa, MasterCard, and Amex
Style...Coffee

"The best in the last year has been the Ona Coffee cafes
in Canberra. I think everyone knows by now Ona is an icon,
not just in Canberra but for Australian coffee in general."
—John Gordon

BAYLEAF CAFE

1 Marvell Street
Byron Bay
New South Wales 2481
Australia
+61 266858900
www.facebook.com/bayleafcoffee

Opening hours..Daily from 6:30 am
Credit cards..Visa and MasterCard
Style...Full service, with food

"A vibrant, open-air cafe in the center of Byron, serving
delicious food and stellar coffee."—Scott Rao

Sydney, see pages 20–23

IRONS AND CRAIG

29 Coldstream Street
Yamba
New South Wales 2464
Australia
+61 66461258
www.ironsandcraig.com

Opening hours..Daily from 7 am
Credit cards..Visa and MasterCard
Style...Full service, with food

"I stopped in Yamba for the charm and surf. But my favorite
part of the town was the delicious filter coffee I found in
this cafe located in a quaint house."—Scott Rao

Brisbane, see pages 24–26

CLANDESTINO ROASTERS

(inside Belmondos Organic Market)
59 Rene Street
Noosaville
Noosa
Queensland 4566
Australia
+61 1300656022
www.clandestino.com.au

Opening hours..Mon–Sat from 7 am
Credit cards..Visa and MasterCard
Style...Coffee bar with food

"About the friendliest people I've ever met. They offer
numerous brewing methods and roast out back on
a Probat P25."—Scott Rao

ELEMENTARY COFFEE

9–17 Young Street
Adelaide
South Australia 5000
Australia
www.elementarycoffee.com.au

Opening hours..Mon–Fri from 7 am
Credit cards..Visa and MasterCard
Style...Coffee and food

"A roastery and a cafe, showcasing scrumptious seasonal
coffees roasted and brewed under one roof."—Anya Sereda

EXCHANGE SPECIALTY

12–18 Vardon Avenue
Adelaide
South Australia 5000
Australia
+61 415996225
www.exchangecoffee.com.au

Opening hours..Mon–Fri from 7 am,
Sat from 8 am, Sun from 9 am
Credit cards..Visa and MasterCard
Style...Full service, with food

"Situated in a beautiful spot on a calm corner in Adelaide's
Central Business District, Exchange is a haven for delicious
Market Lane Coffee, alongside a surprisingly extensive food
menu."—Eileen P. Kenny

MONDAY'S COFFEE STORE

7/38 Gawler Place
Adelaide
South Australia 5000
Australia
www.facebook.com/mondayscoffeestore

Opening hours..Mon–Fri from 7 am,
Sat from 8 am
Credit cards..Visa and MasterCard
Style...Coffee and food

"Simple, unassuming, and very approachable. The details (books, plants, good tunes) give warmth; the coffees give a good reason to come back."—Anya Sereda

BAR 9

96 Glen Osmond Road
Parkside
Adelaide
South Australia 5063
Australia
www.bar9.com.au

Opening hours.................................Mon–Fri from 7:30 am,
Sat–Sun from 8:30 am
Credit cards..Visa and MasterCard
Style..Full service, with food

"Bar 9 set the precedent for specialty in Adelaide long before anyone else even understood how to improve service and quality."—Emily Oak

Melbourne, see pages 28–33

FIVE SENSES

3 Arkwright Road
Rockingham
Western Australia 6168
Australia
+61 895286200
www.fivesenses.com.au

Opening hours.....................................By appointment only
Credit cards..Visa and MasterCard
Style..Equipment and roasted
beans only; no showroom

"Their training and service centers are pretty lovely."
—Emily Oak

TYPIKA ARTISAN ROASTERS

331 Stirling Highway
Claremont
Perth
Western Australia 6010
Australia
+61 892846099
www.typika.com.au

Opening hours..Daily from 6:30 am
Credit cards..Visa and MasterCard
Style.....................Espresso bar and full service with food

"Large cafe and roastery run by a welcoming family, serving lovely food and coffee roasted on-site."—Scott Rao

"A MENU OF DELICIOUS FRESH FOOD IN ADDITION TO COFFEE DRINKS, SERVED WITH EFFICIENT SYSTEMS THAT APPEAL TO MY LOVE FOR CAFE ORGANIZATION."

BRENT FORTUNE P.23

SYDNEY

"A BLOCK FROM ICONIC BONDI BEACH, HARRY'S SERVES SOME OF SYDNEY'S BEST CAFE FOOD AND COFFEE WHILE BEING IMPECCABLY FRIENDLY AND BUSY. AND THE SURF IS A BLOCK AWAY."

SCOTT RAO P.22

"THEIR FOOD PROWESS MATCHES THEIR COFFEE, AND THE MENU ALWAYS HAS SOMETHING TO PIQUE YOUR INTEREST—CHEESE, SAUSAGES, CURED MEATS, AND EGG SPECIALS."

BRENT FORTUNE P.22

SYDNEY

N̂   SCALE

0   650   1300   1950
                              yd.

1. SALVAGE COFFEE (P. 22)
2. HARRY'S (P. 22)
3. EDITION COFFEE ROASTERS (P. 22)

4. COFFEE ALCHEMY (P. 22)
5. PARAMOUNT COFFEE
    PROJECT (P. 22)

6. SINGLE ORIGIN
    ROASTERS (P. 23)
7. MECCA (P. 23)

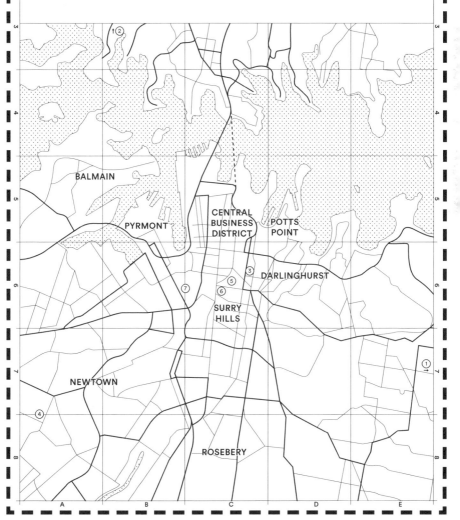

SALVAGE COFFEE

5 Wilkes Avenue
Artarmon
Sydney
New South Wales 2064
Australia
www.salvagecoffee.com

Opening hours....................................Mon–Fri from 6:30 am,
                        Sat from 7:30 am, Sun from 8 am
Credit cards...Cash only
Style..Coffee bar with food

"Their food prowess matches their coffee, and their rotating menu always has something to pique your interest—cheese, sausages, cured meats, and egg specials."—Brent Fortune

HARRY'S

Shop 2, 136 Wairoa Avenue
Bondi Beach
Sydney
New South Wales 2026
Australia
+61 291302180
www.harrysbondi.com.au

Opening hours...Daily from 7 am
Credit cards...Visa and MasterCard
Style..Full service, with food

"A block from iconic Bondi Beach, Harry's serves some of Sydney's best cafe food and coffee while being impeccably friendly and insanely busy. And the surf is a block away. Doesn't get any better."—Scott Rao

EDITION COFFEE ROASTERS

265 Liverpool Street
Darlinghurst
Sydney
New South Wales 2010
Australia
www.editioncoffeeroasters.com

Opening hours..Mon–Fri from 7 am,
                        Sat–Sun from 8 am
Credit cards...Visa and MasterCard
Style..Full service, with food

"One of the most detail-oriented cafes in the world, a standout in Sydney's awesome cafe scene."—Scott Rao

COFFEE ALCHEMY

24 Addison Road
Marrickville
Sydney
New South Wales 2204
Australia
+61 893616776
www.coffeealchemy.com

Opening hours..Mon–Fri from 7 am,
                        Sat from 8 am
Credit cards...Visa and MasterCard
Style..Coffee bar

"The care and hard work they put into roasting and brewing is evident in their beautifully crafted drinks."—Fleur Studd

PARAMOUNT COFFEE PROJECT

80 Commonwealth Street
Surry Hills
Sydney
New South Wales 2010
Australia
+61 292111122
www.paramountcoffeeproject.com.au

Opening hours..Mon–Fri from 7 am,
                        Sat from 7:30 am, Sun from 8 am
Credit cards............................Visa, MasterCard, and Amex
Style..Full service, with food

"The best filter coffee I've had recently."—Mette-Marie Hansen

SINGLE ORIGIN ROASTERS
60–64 Reservoir Street
Surry Hills
Sydney
New South Wales 2010
Australia
+61 92110665
www.singleoriginroasters.com.au

Opening hours...................................Mon–Fri from 6:30 am,
                                        Sat from 7:30 am
Credit cards..Visa and MasterCard
Style...Full service, with food

"This city and its multiplicity of roasters and coffee
professionals bleeds the meaning of specialty and a highly
developed coffee culture."—Jonathan Hutchins

MECCA
646 Harris Street
Ultimo
Sydney
New South Wales 2007
Australia
+61 292804204
www.meccacoffee.com.au

Opening hours..Mon–Fri from 7 am,
                                        Sat from 8 am
Credit cards...Cash only
Style...Full service, with food

"A menu of delicious fresh food in addition to coffee drinks,
served with efficient systems that appeal to my love for cafe
organization. Mecca Ultimo is also home to the Fermental-
ists—a new fermented and kefir beverages project—which
is one of the most exciting things happening in Australian
coffee."—Brent Fortune

"RUN BY SEBASTIAN BUTLER-WHITE, WHO WENT TO SYDNEY TO CUT HIS TEETH, THEN TOOK HIS EXPERIENCE BACK TO HIS HOMETOWN. LOVELY GUY, GOOD FOOD, AND GOOD COFFEE."

EMILY OAK P.26

BRISBANE

"LOCATED DOWN AN ALLEYWAY OFF A MAIN STRETCH IN THE CITY, STRAUSS IS A HAVEN FOR FRESH FOOD, GOOD COFFEE, AND UNIQUE NATURAL WINES."

EILEEN P. KENNY P.26

"BEAUTIFUL SPACE IN VIBRANT SOUTH BRISBANE, SERVING DELICIOUS COFFEE SUPREME COFFEE, TASTY MEALS, AND HOUSE-MADE TREATS." EILEEN P. KENNY P.26

BRISBANE

PADDINGTON

SPRING HILL

SOUTH
BRISBANE

EAST
BRISBANE

N̂   SCALE

0   525   1055   1580
yd.

1. DANDELION & DRIFTWOOD (P. 26)   4. MERRIWEATHER CAFE (P. 26)
2. BUNKER COFFEE (P. 26)   5. POURBOY (P. 26)
3. GAUGE (P. 26)   6. STRAUSS FD (P. 26)

DANDELION & DRIFTWOOD

1/45 Gerler Road
Hendra
Brisbane
Queensland 4011
Australia
+61 738684559
www.dandeliondriftwood.com

Opening hours...Daily from 8 am
Credit cards...Visa and MasterCard
Style ....Coffee and food

"A little quirky, but service and good coffee are their
absolute focus."—Emily Oak

BUNKER COFFEE

21 Railway Terrace
Milton
Brisbane
Queensland 4064
Australia
+61 422124767
www.bunkercoffee.com.au

Opening hours....................................Mon–Fri from 6:15 am
Credit cards...Visa and MasterCard
Style...Coffee

"A neat little den on an unassuming street in Milton, home
to inventive hot chocolate creations alongside well-brewed
coffee from a curated range of roasters."—Eileen P. Kenny

GAUGE

77–79 Grey Street
South Brisbane
Brisbane
Queensland 4101
Australia
+61 738526734
www.facebook.com/Gauge-876173049101227

Opening hours...Daily from 7 am
Credit cards...Visa and MasterCard
Style..Coffee and fine dining

"Multiroaster setup. Coffee and service were lovely."
—Emily Oak

MERRIWEATHER CAFE

27 Russell Street
South Brisbane
Brisbane
Queensland 4101
Australia
+61 738443609
www.merriweathercafe.com

Opening hours.......................................Mon–Sat from 7 am,
Sun from 7:30 am
Credit cards...Visa and MasterCard
Style..Coffee and food

"Beautiful space in vibrant South Brisbane, serving delicious
Coffee Supreme coffee, tasty meals, and house-made
treats."—Eileen P. Kenny

POURBOY

26 Wharf Street
Spring Hill
Brisbane
Queensland 4000
Australia
+61 731721141
www.pourboy.com.au

Opening hours...Mon–Fri from 6 am
Credit cards............................Visa, MasterCard, and Amex
Style...Full service, with food

"Run by Sebastian Butler-White, who went to Sydney to cut
his teeth, then took his experience back to his hometown.
Lovely guy, good food, and good coffee."—Emily Oak

STRAUSS FD

189 Elizabeth Street
Spring Hill
Brisbane
Queensland 4001
Australia
+61 732365232
www.straussfd.com

Opening hours....................................Mon–Fri from 6:30 am
Credit cards............................Visa, MasterCard, and Amex
Style...Coffee, food, and wine

"Located down an alleyway off a main stretch in the city,
Strauss is a haven for fresh food, good coffee, and unique
natural wines."—Eileen P. Kenny

"THE CAFE IS CALM AND LOVELY, HAS GREAT ENERGY, AND IS IN A REALLY FUN PART OF THE CITY."

JORDAN MICHELMAN P.31

"YOU WOULDN'T BE ABLE TO FIND THIS LEVEL OF CAFE ANYWHERE ELSE IN THE WORLD, IN TERMS OF QUALITY AND NUMBER OF CONSUMERS."

HIDENORI IZAKI P.31

MELBOURNE

"WONDERFUL COFFEE OFFERINGS PARTNERED WITH EQUALLY OBSESSIVE ATTENTION TO FOOD, INTERIOR, AND EXPERIENCE."

PAUL STACK P.32

"A TINY, SERENE, BEAUTIFUL, AND VERY FOCUSED SHOP THAT PREPARES EACH COFFEE WITH INCREDIBLE ATTENTION TO DETAIL."

KYLE GLANVILLE P.30

"EXACTLY WHAT I THINK A GREAT ESPRESSO BAR SHOULD BE. IT'S ONE OF THE FEW COFFEE SPACES THAT I'VE BEEN IN THAT EXECUTES AT SUCH A HIGH LEVEL WITHOUT THE ADDED NONSENSE THAT SO OFTEN FOLLOWS." LORENZO PERKINS P.31

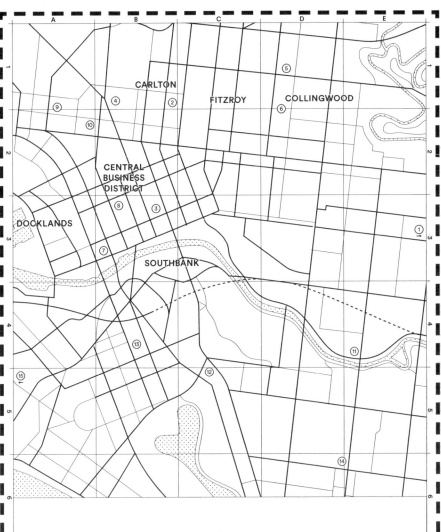

MELBOURNE

$\hat{N}$

SCALE

0   515   1035   1555
yd.

1. THE MALING ROOM (P. 30)
2. ASSEMBLY (P. 30)
3. SENSORY LAB (P. 30)
4. SEVEN SEEDS (P. 30)
5. EVERYDAY COFFEE (P. 31)

6. PROUD MARY (P. 31)
7. ALTIUS (P. 31)
8. PATRICIA COFFEE BREWERS (P. 31)
9. AUCTION ROOMS (P. 31)
10. SMALL BATCH (P. 32)

11. TOP PADDOCK (P. 32)
12. KETTLE BLACK (P. 32)
13. ST. ALI (P. 32)
14. MARKET LANE COFFEE (P. 33)
15. DUCHESS OF SPOTSWOOD (P. 33)

THE MALING ROOM

206 Canterbury Road
Canterbury
Melbourne
Victoria 3126
Australia
+61 98369889
www.malingroom.com.au

Opening hours................................Daily from 7 am
Credit cards.........................Visa and MasterCard
Style.................................Full service, with food

"They roast their coffee very well for espresso and really understand how to extract. Located in an old post office."—Sasa Sestic

ASSEMBLY

60–62 Pelham Street
Carlton
Melbourne
Victoria 3053
Australia
www.assemblystore.com

Opening hours..................................Mon–Fri from 7:30 am,
Sat from 9:00 am
Credit cards............................Visa, MasterCard, and Amex
Style...Coffee bar

"A tiny, serene, beautiful, and very focused shop that prepares each coffee with incredible attention to detail."
—Kyle Glanville

"The space is beautiful and filter coffee is their area of expertise."—Jordan Michelman

SENSORY LAB

297 Little Collins Street
Carlton
Melbourne
Victoria 3000
Australia
+61 396450065
www.sensorylab.com.au

Opening hours................................Mon–Fri from 7:30 am,
Sat from 8:30 am, Sun from 9:30 am
Credit cards.........................Visa and MasterCard
Style...Coffee bar

"The team behind these cafes share decades of industry experience and their coffees are seriously tasty. They work hard to grow their knowledge of everything coffee from a molecular level. They set industry standards and have been known to redefine how we brew and drink our coffees."
—Anya Sereda

There are four locations and one is at the entrance of a department store in the Melbourne CBD (Central Business District). So many coffees here are described as a nuance of flavors that only a genuinely trained palate can detect. There is a coffee so perfectly roasted and extracted that it even smells like fruit jam. Try the blueberry bomb.

SEVEN SEEDS

114 Berkeley Street
Carlton
Melbourne
Victoria 3053
Australia
+61 393478664
www.sevenseeds.com.au

Opening hours..Mon–Sat from 7 am,
Sun from 8 am
Credit cards............................Visa, MasterCard, and Amex
Style.................................Full service, with food

"I love the presentation—I couldn't bear to throw away the info cards served with my pour-over selections."
—Ellie Hudson

"Just bringing the best in Australia since the beginning."
—Antoine Netien

EVERYDAY COFFEE

33 Johnston Street
Collingwood
Melbourne
Victoria 3066
Australia
+61 399734159
www.everyday-coffee.com

Opening hours..................................Mon–Sat from 7 am,
Sun from 8 am
Credit cards...Visa and MasterCard
Style..Full service, with food

"The cafe is calm and lovely, has great energy, and is in a
really fun part of the city. The environment is just perfect."
—Jordan Michelman

PROUD MARY

172 Oxford Street
Collingwood
Melbourne
Victoria 3011
Australia
+61 394175930
www.proudmarycoffee.com.au

Opening hours.......................................Mon–Fri from 7 am,
Sat–Sun from 8 am
Credit cards............................Visa, MasterCard, and Amex
Style..Full service, with food

"Exceptional."—Andrew Hetzel

"There is an energy in the place that almost makes your
head spin."—Ellie Hudson

ALTIUS

517 Flinders Lane
Docklands
Melbourne
Victoria 3000
Australia
www.altiuscoffeebrewers.com.au

Opening hours...Mon–Fri from 7 am
Credit cards...Visa and MasterCard
Style...Coffee bar

"Beautiful drinks."—Fleur Studd

PATRICIA COFFEE BREWERS

Little Bourke and Little William Streets
Docklands
Melbourne
Victoria 3000
Australia
+61 396422237
www.patriciacoffee.com.au

Opening hours...Mon–Fri from 7 am
Credit cards............................Visa, MasterCard, and Amex
Style...Coffee bar

"As tiny and busy coffee bars go, this place takes the cake.
And they have the best croissants in all of Australia."
—Brent Fortune

"A buzzing, tiny, hidden shop with great music, lively
ambience, awesome pastries, and beautiful service."
—Kyle Glanville

"Exactly what I think a great espresso bar should be. It's one
of the few coffee spaces that I've been in that executes at
such a high level without the added nonsense that so often
follows."—Lorenzo Perkins

"Really good coffee menu, attention to service, a busy and
vibrant atmosphere, easy to order from a focused menu,
and great-tasting drinks."—Klaus Thomsen

AUCTION ROOMS

103–107 Errol Street
North Melbourne
Melbourne
Victoria 3051
Australia
+61 393267749
www.auctionroomscafe.com.au

Opening hours.......................................Mon–Fri from 7 am,
Sat–Sun from 7:30 am
Credit cards............................Visa, MasterCard, and Amex
Style..Full service, with food

"The design of the place is very clever and comfortable.
Beautiful cooked breakfast—eggs, avocados, and salmon
paired with coffee."—Sonja Björk Grant

"You wouldn't be able to find this level of cafe anywhere
else in the world, in terms of quality and number of
consumers."—Hidenori Izaki

SMALL BATCH

3–9 Little Howard Street
North Melbourne
Melbourne
Victoria 3051
Australia
+61 393266313
www.smallbatch.com.au

Opening hours...By appointment only
Credit cards................................Online payment via PayPal
                                         or major credit card
Style...Bean sales only

"Best espresso."—Tim Varney

TOP PADDOCK

658 Church Street
Richmond
Melbourne
Victoria 3121
Australia
+61 394294332
www.toppaddockcafe.com

Opening hours...Mon–Fri from 7 am,
                                          Sat–Sun from 8 am
Credit cards.............................Visa, MasterCard, and Amex
Style..Full service, with food

"Wonderful coffee offerings partnered with equally
obsessive attention to food, interior, and experience."
—Paul Stack

THE KETTLE BLACK

50 Albert Road
South Melbourne
Melbourne
Victoria 3205
Australia
+61 390880721
www.thekettleblack.com.au

Opening hours...Mon–Fri from 7 am,
                                          Sat–Sun from 8 am
Credit cards.............................Visa, MasterCard, and Amex
Style..Full service, with food

"I liked the space, the neighborhood, the vibrancy, the
energy, the design, and the coffee. No question that
they are executing coffee and food at a superhigh level."
— Tyler J. Wells

ST. ALI

12–18 Yarra Place
South Melbourne
Melbourne
Victoria 3205
Australia
+61 396862990
www.stali.com.au

Opening hours...Daily from 7 am
Credit cards.............................Visa, MasterCard, and Amex
Style..Full service, with food

"Sal is a business savant, raising the bar for coffee in each
city he touches."—Tracy Allen

MARKET LANE COFFEE

Shop 13, Prahran Market, 163 Commercial Road
(Elizabeth Street entrance)
South Yarra
Melbourne
Victoria 3141
Australia
+61 398047434
www.marketlane.com.au

Opening hours	Mon from 7 am (for bean and equipment sales only), Tue–Sat from 7 am, Sun from 8 am
Credit cards	Visa, MasterCard, and Amex
Style	Coffee bar

"You just can't compete with perfect control of the entire production chain, from sourcing the best beans, importing them, roasting them perfectly, and then extracting the coffee in the best possible way at their cafes."—Nico Alary

"Beautiful atmosphere, settings, and a presentation fully focused on coffee."—Masahiro Onishi

DUCHESS OF SPOTSWOOD

87 Hudsons Road
Spotswood
Melbourne
Victoria 3015
Australia
+61 393916016
www.facebook.com/duchessofspotswood

Opening hours	Mon–Fri from 7 am, Sun from 8 am
Credit cards	Visa and MasterCard
Style	Full service, with food

"Best breakfast in town—fresh, delicious, creative food paired with top coffee."—Nico Alary

"NEW ZEALAND'S PROGRESSIVE COFFEE BARS OFFER SOME OF THE MOST INTERESTING CAFE DESIGN IN THE WORLD—A COMBINATION OF ANTIPODEAN CONTEMPORARY COOL WITH AN UNSHAKABLE KIWI REVERENCE FOR ALL THINGS RETRO AND MID-CENTURY IN THEIR CORNER OF THE WORLD."

JORDAN MICHELMAN P.36

NEW ZEALAND

"THE MOST SKILLFULLY MADE COFFEE IN NEW ZEALAND, SERVED IN A TINY CAFE AT THE BOTTOM OF A HIGH-RISE OFFICE BUILDING."

SCOTT RAO P.36

"A VARIETY OF HAND-BREWED COFFEE METHODS, AN APPROPRIATELY UNDERSTATED SLAYER ESPRESSO MACHINE ANCHORING THE BAR."

JORDAN MICHELMAN P.36

"A FRIENDLY PLACE WITH GREAT COFFEE, RUN BY JASON MOORE, ONE OF THE BEST BARISTAS I'VE EVER WORKED WITH."

SCOTT RAO P.36

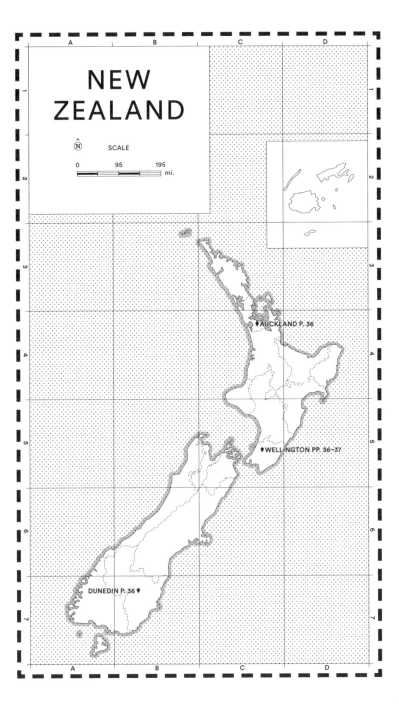

NEW ZEALAND

N̂ SCALE

0   95   195 mi.

AUCKLAND P. 36

WELLINGTON PP. 36–37

DUNEDIN P. 36

KOKAKO ORGANIC COFFEE

537 Great North Road
Grey Lynn
Auckland 1021
New Zealand
+64 93792868
www.kokako.co.nz

Opening hours...Daily from 7:30 am
Credit cards ....Visa and MasterCard
Style ....Full service

"New Zealand's progressive coffee bars offer some of the
most interesting cafe design in the world—a combination
of antipodean contemporary cool with an unshakable
Kiwi reverence for all things retro and mid-century in their
corner of the world (Kiwiana). Kokako inhabits a disused
post office in the Auckland suburb of Grey Lynn. A roaster,
cold brew bottler, and coffee bar with great healthful food,
featuring table service as is local custom for cafe/restaurant
hybrids of this type. The design here is clean and beautiful.
Think of it as a New Zealand version of wabi-sabi. It makes
for beguiling coffee bars, and Kokako is one of the best."
—Jordan Michelman

BE SPECIALTY

57 Fort Street
Parnell
Auckland 1010
New Zealand
+64 210302217
www.bespecialty.co.nz

Opening hours..Mon–Fri from 7 am
Credit cards.............................Visa, MasterCard, and Amex
Style..Coffee bar

"The most skillfully made coffee in New Zealand, served in
a tiny cafe at the bottom of a high-rise office building."
—Scott Rao

VANGUARD SPECIALTY COFFEE CO.

329 Princes Street
Otago
Dunedin 9016
New Zealand
+64 34779511
www.vanguardcoffeeco.com

Opening hours.......................................Mon–Fri from 7 am,
Sat–Sun from 8 am
Credit cards..Visa and MasterCard
Style..Coffee and food

"I like Vanguard because it's a friendly place with great
coffee, run by Jason Moore, one of the best baristas I've
ever worked with."—Scott Rao

CUSTOMS

39 Ghuznee Street
Te Aro
Wellington 6011
New Zealand
+64 43852129
www.coffeesupreme.com

Opening hours..................................Mon–Fri from 7:30 am,
Sat–Sun from 8:30 am
Credit cards..Visa and MasterCard
Style..Coffee and food

"Part mid-century airport lounge, part Peter Brady's
rumpus room from *The Brady Bunch*, but with clever modern
flourishes. A variety of hand-brewed coffee methods,
an appropriately understated Slayer espresso machine
anchoring the bar, and an iPad at the front counter open to
Supreme's website. Oh, right—this is a Coffee Supreme
cafe, although in the Australasian style it's not identified as
such by name. Supreme's a Wellington institution—the
third wave of coffee arguably started here in the early 1990s,
and though many brands played a part, Supreme's is one
of the few that remained independent and has continued
to push quality over the last several decades. Today they are
roasters, green coffee importers, and cafe creators across
New Zealand and Australia. All of their cafes are worth
visiting, but Customs is perhaps the best, evoking the deeply
felt Kiwi sensibility of conquering isolation through the
internationalism of travel and flavor."—Jordan Michelman

FLIGHT COFFEE

119 Dixon Street
Te Aro
Wellington 6011
New Zealand
+64 48300909
www.flightcoffee.co.nz

Opening hours	Mon–Fri from 7 am, Sat–Sun from 8 am
Credit cards	Visa and MasterCard
Style	Coffee and food

"Welly's next generation of coffee lovers—and leaders—hang out at the Flight Coffee 'Hangar' space on Dixon Street, a block removed from the nightly madness of Wellington's busiest high street. The Hangar hosts DJs, turns into a cocktail bar by night, and is a playground for Flight's take on coffee sourcing and roasting, including coffees from their own proprietary farm project in Colombia. Food here is a serious part of the offer and shouldn't be missed. Flight's formidable and growing wholesale program echoes back to the appeal and renown of this place, and it's easy to see why."—Jordan Michelman

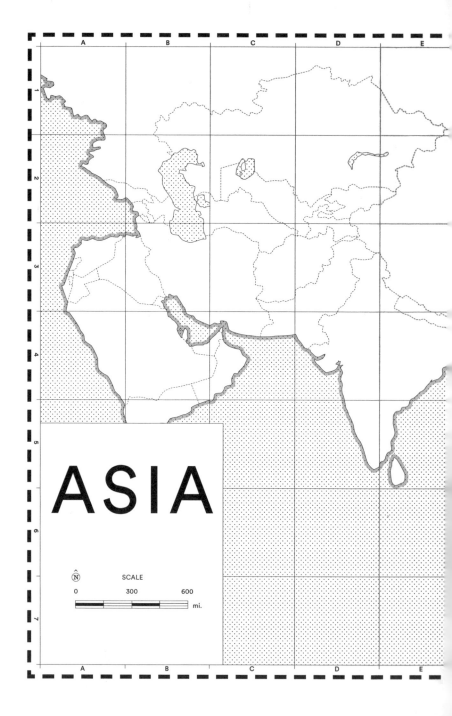

ASIA

N

SCALE

0   300   600   mi.

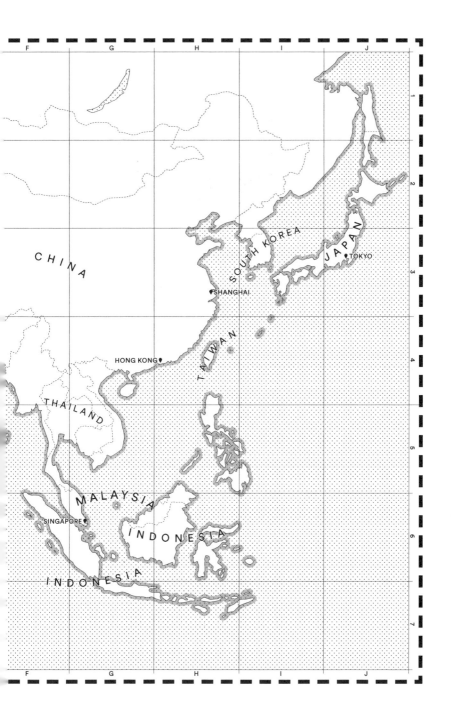

"MANY CRAFTSMEN GATHER HERE, MAKING HANDMADE BARISTA APRONS, CUPS, AND SO ON."

ECHO LOU P.43

CHINA, HONG KONG & TAIWAN

"EACH DRINK WAS INDIVIDUALLY AND CAREFULLY PREPARED WITH TIME."

CYNTHIA LUDVIKSEN P.43

"THIS MIGHT BE THE MOST PROFESSIONAL FILTER-COFFEE STORE IN BEIJING."

ECHO LOU P.42

"THIS IS THE OLDEST COFFEE STORE IN GUANGZHOU, SERVING HOME-ROASTED COFFEE. THEY PROVIDE MORE THAN FORTY SPECIALTY COFFEES EACH MONTH, INCLUDING SOME MICROLOTS."

ECHO LOU P.42

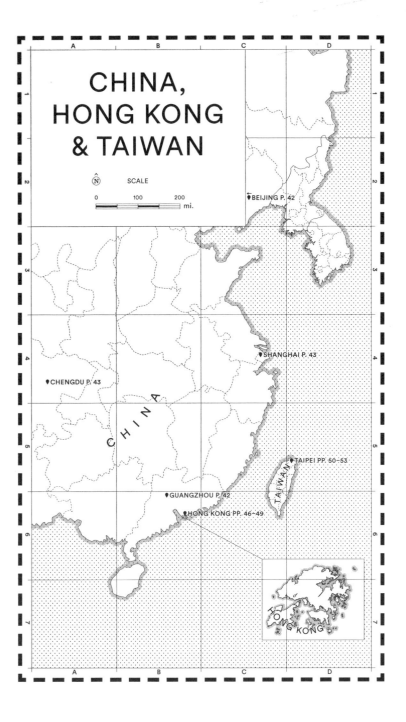

CHINA, HONG KONG & TAIWAN

N SCALE

0   100   200
mi.

BEIJING P. 42

SHANGHAI P. 43

CHENGDU P. 43

CHINA

TAIPEI PP. 50-53

TAIWAN

GUANGZHOU P. 42

HONG KONG PP. 46-49

HONG KONG

REAL COFFEE

#12, west end of Tang Gong Hutong
Dongcheng District
Beijing
China
+86 13301062580

Opening hours..Daily from 11 am
Credit cards...Cash only
Style..Coffee bar

"This might be the most professional filter-coffee store in Beijing. It's also the first cafe in Beijing to use a handcrafted Kees van der Westen espresso machine. They have some foreign beans of famous brands."—Echo Lou

VOYAGE COFFEE

80 Beiluoguxiang
Dongcheng District
Beijing
China
+86 11322067

Opening hours..Daily from 9 am
Credit cards...Cash only
Style..Coffee bar

"The design of the store is quite good. They provide filter coffee and AeroPress."—Echo Lou

ROSE CAFE

F1, #29 Huiji Xilu, Zhongshan Liu Road
Yuexiu District
Guangzhou
Guangdong
China
+86 2088900899

Opening hours..Tue–Sun from 10 am
Credit cards...Cash only
Style..Coffee and food

"This is the oldest coffee store in Guangzhou, open for eight years, serving home-roasted coffee. They provide more than forty specialty coffees each month, including some microlots. The owner is a good talker, very willing to share her experience with customers."—Echo Lou

UNI-UNI

#68 Changjiang Road
Xuanwu District
Nanjing
Jiangsu
China
+86 02585439800

Opening hours..Daily from 10 am
Credit cards...Cash only
Style..Coffee bar

"Owned by the 2014 Chinese National Barista Champion, Jeremy Zhang. His store has wonderful home-roasted coffee. He and his team are now competing in different championships and do some professional training courses. Jeremy is also one of the most influential baristas in the China coffee world." —Echo Lou

CAFÉ BINTINO

Yan An Lu 55-1
Zhongshan District
Dailan
Liaoning
China
+86 41182647551
www.caffebintino.com

Opening hours..Daily from 9:30 am
Credit cards...Cash only
Style..Coffee bar

"A successful store in Dalian, open for years. The baristas are always full of passion. The design is quite impressive." —Echo Lou

Hong Kong, see pages 46–49

CAFÉ MINGQIAN

218 Fengxian Lu, Near Nanhui Lu
Jingan District
Shanghai
200041
China
+86 52735855

Opening hours	Daily from 8 am
Credit cards	Cash only
Style	Coffee and food

"They have home-roasted beans and do some training. Few Chinese cafes are willing to pay money to single-origin farms; Mingqian is one of the exceptions. And they are quite pleased to share their knowledge with others."—Echo Lou

SEESAW COFFEE

433 YuYuan Road
Jingan District
Shanghai
200040
China
+86 2152047828
www.seesawcoffee.com

Opening hours	Daily from 10 am
Credit cards	Cash only
Style	Roastery cafe

"This is an up-and-coming independent chain in China. The original space is set off a courtyard behind a shopping street, where the ambience is clean and contemporary, with nice tile work and a hint of modern high-class sophistication. It's definitely a local neighborhood hangout. The other locations are all unique spaces built into high-end shopping malls. Seesaw serves great-tasting quality coffee prepared by a conscientious staff without pretentiousness. Many of their baristas can also be found competing in the Chinese Barista Competitions, and the shops support active coffee community events."—Cynthia Ludviksen

"In the world's largest country the coffee scene is just starting, and this roastery cafe is doing a great job of focusing on quality."—Kris Schackman

China's coffee scene is relatively new but, like everything in China, growing quickly. It's clear the team at Seesaw is committed to bringing the global coffee experience to a new audience. Most of the Seesaw crew has trained in Australia, and they have developed a fantastic roasting program as well. Chinese coffee drinkers embrace an afternoon ritual rather than the typical Western morning coffee. Come by any day at 3 pm to see the young and hip of Shanghai.

CAFÉ DEL VOLCÁN

80 Yong Kang Lu
Xuhui District
Shanghai
200031
China
+86 15618669291
www.cafevolcan.com

Opening hours	Mon–Fri from 8 am, Sat–Sun from 10 am
Credit cards	Cash only
Style	Coffee bar

"It was a surprise to find this in the French Quarter of Shanghai. The tiny little boutique cafe has a small bar with one barista on staff and seating for about ten people. They had a small selection of single-origin coffees that they would brew by hand per order. Each drink was individually and carefully prepared with time. It was a nice departure from the busy hustle and bustle of Shanghai."
—Cynthia Ludviksen

MONDOLI STUDIO

3 Da Ci Si Road, Lang Yu-1 Dan Yuan #4604
Jinjiang District
Chengdu
Sichuan
610000
China
+86 83373738
www.mondoli.co

Opening hours	By appointment only
Credit cards	Cash only
Style	Coffee and housewares

"They lead the coffee culture in Chengdu; it is a must-go place. They provide foreign-brand beans and many vintage items. Many craftsmen gather here, making handmade barista aprons, cups, and so on."—Echo Lou

HOMERUN ROASTERS

82, Ren 2 Road
Ren'ai District
Keelung 206
Taiwan
+886 224254663
www.facebook.com/homerunroasters

Opening hours..Daily from 10 am
Credit cards...Cash only
Style...Coffee bar

CAFÉ LULU

#217, Wu-Chang Street
North District
Taichung 404
Taiwan
+886 422066866
www.cafelulu.com.tw

Opening hours.......................................Mon–Wed from 1 pm,
Fri–Sun from 1 pm
Credit cards...Cash only
Style...Coffee bar

RETRO/MOJOCOFFEE

#116, Section 1, Wuquan West Road
West District
Taichung 403
Taiwan
+886 423755592
www.mojocoffee.com.tw

Opening hours.......................................Mon–Sat from 8 am,
Sun from 9 am
Credit cards...Cash only
Style...Coffee bar

Taipei, see pages 50–53

"BEST FILTER COFFEE."
RANUT KONGPICHAYANOND P.48

"WORLD BARISTA CHAMPIONSHIP JUDGES. REALLY GOOD FOOD AND COFFEE."
DAWN CHAN P.48

HONG KONG

"SUCH GOOD SINGLE-ORIGIN FILTER COFFEE. AND THE WAFFLES ARE AMAZING."
DAWN CHAN P.49

"THE MOST MEMORABLE ESPRESSO I HAD IN HONG KONG WAS AT THE CUPPING ROOM. THE STAFF HE WORKS WITH HAVE SUCH AN INFECTIOUS ENTHUSIASM FOR WHAT THEY DO."
COLIN HARMON P.49

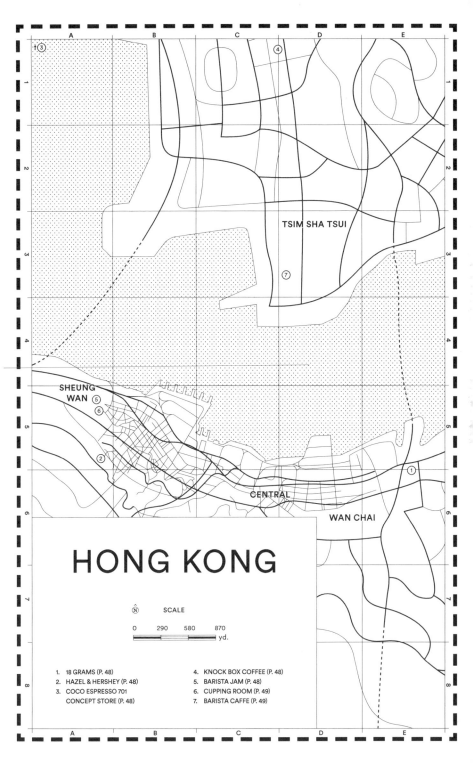

HONG KONG

0   290   580   870
yd.

1. 18 GRAMS (P. 48)
2. HAZEL & HERSHEY (P. 48)
3. COCO ESPRESSO 701
   CONCEPT STORE (P. 48)
4. KNOCK BOX COFFEE (P. 48)
5. BARISTA JAM (P. 48)
6. CUPPING ROOM (P. 49)
7. BARISTA CAFFE (P. 49)

TSIM SHA TSUI

SHEUNG WAN

CENTRAL

WAN CHAI

18 GRAMS

Unit C, G/F, 15 Cannon Street
Causeway Bay
Hong Kong Island
Hong Kong S.A.R., China
+852 28938988
www.18grams.com

Opening hours...Daily from 8 am
Credit cards...Cash only
Style..Coffee and food

"World Barista Championship judges. Really good food and coffee."—Dawn Chan

HAZEL & HERSHEY

Shop 3, 69 Peel Street
HKG Central District
Hong Kong Island
Hong Kong S.A.R., China
+852 31060760
www.hazelnhershey.com

Opening hours...Daily from 10 am
Credit cards....................................Visa and MasterCard
Style...Coffee and equipment

"They sell a lot of coffee equipment in the shop. Coffee lovers must go shopping here."—Dawn Chan

COCO ESPRESSO 701 CONCEPT STORE

Unit 1, 7/F Vanta Centre, 21–23 Tai Lin Pai Road
Kwai Chung
Hong Kong Island
Hong Kong S.A.R., China
+852 24997255
www.cocobarista.com

Opening hours......................................Mon–Fri from 9 am,
Sat–Sun from 10 am
Credit cards..Cash only
Style...Coffee bar

"There are three shops in Hong Kong and they are very good at latte art. Barista Kim Yeung is the 2012 Coffee Fest Latte Art Champion."—Dawn Chan

KNOCK BOX COFFEE

21 Hak Po Street, ground floor
Mong Kok, Kowloon
Hong Kong Island
Hong Kong S.A.R., China
+852 27810363
www.knockboxcoffee.hk

Opening hours..Daily from 11 am
Credit cards...Cash only
Style..Coffee and food

"Best filter coffee."—Ranut Kongpichayanond

BARISTA JAM

Shop D, G/F, 126–128 Jervois Street
Sheung Wan
Hong Kong Island
Hong Kong S.A.R., China
+852 28542211
www.baristajam.com.hk

Opening hours..Mon from 10 am,
Tue–Fri from 8 am,
Sat from 10 am, Sun from 11 am
Credit cards....................................Visa and MasterCard
Style..Coffee and food

"There are La Marzocco Strada EP and GB5 espresso machines in the shop. They are really good at filter coffee."—Dawn Chan

THE CUPPING ROOM

Shop LG/F, 287–299 Queen's Road Central
Sheung Wan
Hong Kong Island
Hong Kong S.A.R., China
+852 27993398

Opening hours..Mon–Fri from 8 am,
Sat–Sun from 9 am
Credit cards..Cash only
Style..Coffee and food

"The most memorable espresso I had on my travels in
Hong Kong was at the Cupping Room. I have so much
respect for what Kapo is doing there, and the staff he works
with have such an infectious enthusiasm for what they do.
The coffee was roasted by Andy Sprenger at Sweet Bloom,
a roaster who to my mind deserves a lot more attention than
he gets."—Colin Harmon

"Best espresso."—Ranut Kongpichayanond

Hong Kong has quite a bit of great coffee, but the Cupping
Room truly stands out. Home of the two-time Hong Kong
Barista Champion, Kapo Chiu, its coffee is always on point.
In addition to great coffee, the food is also worth the trip.

BARISTA CAFFE

3/F, 18 Ashley Road
Tsim Sha Tsui
Hong Kong Island
Hong Kong S.A.R., China
+852 25110998
www.facebook.com/baristacaffehk

Opening hours..Mon–Fri from 8 am,
Sat from noon
Credit cards..Cash only
Style..Coffee and food

"Such good single-origin filter coffee. And the waffles are
amazing."—Dawn Chan

"IT'S A PLACE THAT IS ALWAYS INNOVATING AND WAS DESIGNED TO BE A LAB, FOR THE CREATION OF BEVERAGES AND NEW CONCEPTS IN COFFEE THAT CHALLENGE ME EVERY TIME—FROM BREWING METHODS AND THE WAY WE APPLY COFFEE AS A BEVERAGE OR AN ELEMENT OF TASTE."

JOSUE MORALES P.52

TAIPEI

"IF I HAVE A FREE TICKET TO FLY OUT FOR A COFFEE NOW, I WILL GO TO EITHER COFFEE LAB IN SÃO PAULO, BRAZIL, OR FIKA FIKA IN TAIPEI, TAIWAN."

KYONGHEE SHIN P.52

"HAVE A SEAT AT THE SIPHON BAR AND WATCH THE METICULOUS PREPARATION LEAD UP TO A DELICIOUS CUP."

SCOTT CONARY P.52

"AN AIRY AND SUPREMELY SCANDINAVIAN SPACE IN A QUIET, LEAFY POCKET OF TAIPEI. DELICIOUSLY FRUITY AND LIGHT COFFEES ARE ROASTED EXTREMELY WELL. PLENTY OF DIVERSE SEATING OPTIONS AND ELEVATIONS HELP SPEAK TO ONE'S MOOD. I WISH THIS PLACE WERE MY OFFICE."

MATT PERGER P.52

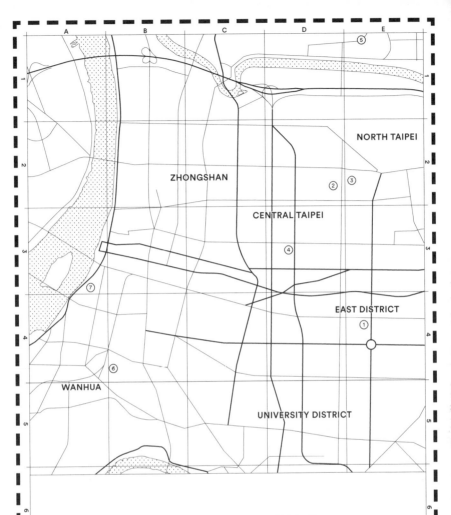

NORTH TAIPEI

ZHONGSHAN

CENTRAL TAIPEI

EAST DISTRICT

WANHUA

UNIVERSITY DISTRICT

TAIPEI

SCALE

0   485   970   1455
yd.

1. COFFEE LOVER'S PLANET (P. 52)
2. UGLY DUCKLING COFFEE BAR (P. 52)
3. GABEE (P. 52)
4. FIKA FIKA (P. 52)
5. RAHDESIGN CAFÉ (P. 52)
6. PELOSO COFFEE ROASTERS (P. 53)
7. WOW (WOOLLOOMOOLOO OUT WEST) (P. 53)

COFFEE LOVER'S PLANET

#B4, 246 Dunhua South Road, Section 1
Da'an District
Taipei 106
Taiwan
+886 227524157
www.coffee-lovers-planet.com.tw

Opening hours..Daily from 11 am
Credit cards.............................Visa, MasterCard, and Amex
Style...Coffee bar

UGLY DUCKLING COFFEE BAR

#8, Lane 73, Section 1F, Hejiang Street
Jhongshan District
Taipei
Taiwan
+886 225060239
www.ud-baristatraining.com

Opening hours..Mon–Fri from 8 am
Credit cards.............................Visa, MasterCard, and Amex
Style...Coffee and barista training

"Silence Huang opened this combo cafe and training space
in a great little neighborhood, catering to business folks
and locals alike. Have a seat at the siphon bar and watch the
meticulous preparation lead up to a delicious cup. There
is a convenient takeaway window on one side facing a
pedestrian alley for those needing a quick coffee, with
beautiful latte art in the shape of a swan. Silence is known
for his educational programs and the amazing books he has
published on many aspects of coffee."—Scott Conary

GABEE

#21, Lane 113, Section 3, Min Sheng East Road
Songshan District
Taipei 105
Taiwan
+886 227138772
www.gabee.cc

Opening hours..Daily from 9 am
Credit cards..Cash only
Style..Coffee and food

"It's a place that is always innovating and was designed to
be a lab, for the creation of beverages and new concepts
in coffee that challenge me every time—from brewing
methods to the way we apply coffee as a beverage or an
element of taste."—Josue Morales

FIKA FIKA

#33 Yitong Street
Zhongshan District
Taipei 104
Taiwan
+886 225070633
www.fikafikacafe.com

Opening hours...Mon from 10:30 am,
Tue–Fri from 8 am, Sat–Sun from 9 am
Credit cards..Visa and MasterCard
Style..Coffee and food

"An airy and supremely Scandinavian space in a quiet, leafy
pocket of Taipei. Deliciously fruity and light coffees are
roasted extremely well. Plenty of diverse seating options
and elevations help speak to one's mood. I wish this place
were my office."—Matt Perger

"They have a bunch of fancy single-origins there, and when
you order one they serve it to you as an AeroPress and then
do an iced version, too. The cafe is pretty and all the baristas
were supernice. Packaging is adorable, too."—Esther Shaw

"If I have a free ticket to fly out for a coffee now, I will go to
either Coffee Lab in São Paulo, Brazil, or Fika Fika in Taipei,
Taiwan. The beverages, atmosphere, customer service, and
food pairings are all beyond your expectations. Both places
are very modern but have some green surroundings, making
you want to stay longer. Every single drink is prepared to its
best presentation."—Kyonghee Shin

RAHDESIGN CAFÉ

#1, Lane 9, Dazhi Street
Zhongshan District
Taipei 104
Taiwan
+886 225327778

Opening hours..Daily from 11 am
Credit cards..Cash only
Style..Coffee and food

PELOSO COFFEE ROASTERS

#40, Lane 75, Section 2, Zhonghua Road
Zhongzheng District
Taipei 100
Taiwan
+886 2 23122955

Opening hours...Daily from noon
Credit cards...Cash only
Style..Roastery cafe

"Peloso Coffee Roasters is in the Xiaonanmen neighborhood
of Taipei, where my dad grew up. My family has spent a lot
of time visiting there over the years and I taught at a school
in that neighborhood. It was a pleasant surprise to be
wandering around the neighborhood with my parents and
to find this charming coffee shop, run by a bunch of young
Taiwanese hipster types who are super enthusiastic about
coffee and do a great job."—Esther Shaw

WOW (WOOLLOOMOOLOO OUT WEST)

#2, Lane 120, Section 2, Wuchang Street
Zhongzheng District
Taipei 108
Taiwan
+866 0223888180
www.woolloomooloo.tw

Opening hours...Daily from 10 am
Credit cards............................Visa, MasterCard, and Amex
Style..Coffee bar

"TINY BUT INCREDIBLY LIGHT-FILLED AND OPEN ESPRESSO BAR/ ROASTERY BENEATH A HOUSING COMPLEX IN KANTONMENT. THEIR SCANDINAVIAN-STYLE ROASTING IS ON POINT."

MATT PERGER P.57

"A BUNCH OF CAFFEINE DEALERS IS A TRENDSETTER AND ONE OF JAKARTA'S HIPPEST CAFES. IF YOU'RE LOOKING FOR NEW WAVE COFFEE IN JAKARTA, THIS IS A GREAT PLACE TO START."

EVAN GILMAN P.56

SOUTH & SOUTHEAST ASIA

"BEST QUALITY, BEST VARIETY, SMALL AND COMFORTABLE."

RANUT KONGPICHAYANOND P.57

"FOR THE AUSTRALIAN, THIS CAFE CAN BE A SLICE OF HOME; FOR THE COFFEE GEEK, IT CAN BE A HAVEN."

EVAN GILMAN P.56

SOUTH & SOUTHEAST ASIA

N   SCALE

0   65   135
mi.

THAILAND
♦BANGKOK PP. 58-60

MALAYSIA
♦KUALA LUMPUR P. 56

SINGAPORE P. 57 ♦

INDONESIA

INDONESIA

♦JAKARTA P. 56

♦BALI P. 56

MANGSI

Jalan Hayam Wuruk #195
Panjer
Denpasar
Bali 80235
Indonesia
+62 81805533847
www.facebook.com/mangsicoffee

Opening hours...Daily from 11 am
Credit cards..Cash only
Style..Full service

"A truly Indonesian cafe, Mangsi offers everything from kopi tubruk to the standard espresso fare—and all the coffee is locally grown in Bali. If you want to get a good idea of what Bali nightlife is like, try Mangsi."—Evan Gilman

REVOLVER

Jalan Kayu Aya, Gang 51
Seminyak
Kuta
Bali 80361
Indonesia
+62 85100884968
www.revolverespresso.com

Opening hours...Daily from 7 am
Credit cards..Visa and MasterCard
Style..Full service

"If you're looking for a well-prepared espresso beverage, Revolver never fails. For the Australian, this cafe can be a slice of home; for the coffee geek, it can be a haven."—Evan Gilman

SENIMAN COFFEE STUDIO

Jalan Sriwedari #5
Banjar Taman Kelod
Ubud
Bali 80561
Indonesia
+62 361972085
www.senimancoffee.com

Opening hours...Daily from 8 am
Credit cards..Visa and MasterCard
Style...Coffee and food

"The company does it all—sourcing beans, processing, roasting, and brewing, from bean to cup."—Khalid Al Mulla

"A great place that pairs funky design (coffee is served in glassware made from upcycled bottles) with great coffee."
—Anna Brones

ABCD (A BUNCH OF CAFFEINE DEALERS)

Pasar Santa, Level 1, Block AL.01-BKS #75–77,
Jalan Cipaku 1
Kebayoran Baru
Jakarta 2170
Indonesia
www.abunchofcaffeinedealers.wordpress.com

Opening hours...No set hours
Credit cards..Cash only
Style...Coffee bar

"A Bunch of Caffeine Dealers is a trendsetter and one of Jakarta's hippest cafes. If you're looking for New Wave coffee in Jakarta, this is a great place to start."
—Evan Gilman

ABCD, a workshop for baristas and coffee enthusiasts, pops up at weekends without a set schedule.

TANAMERA

Thamrin City Office Park Block AA07, Jalan Kebon
Kacang Raya
Tanah Abang
Jakarta 10230
Indonesia
+62 2129625599
www.tanameracoffee.com

Opening hours...Daily from 7 am
Credit cards..Visa and MasterCard
Style...Coffee bar

"I wasn't sure what I would experience in Indonesia, but finding one of the best naturally processed coffees I've had anywhere threw me for a loop!"—Pete Licata

VCR

2 Jalan Galloway
Bukit Bintang
Kuala Lumpur 50150
Malaysia
+60 321102330
www.vcr.my

Opening hours..Daily from 8:30 am
Credit cards..Visa and MasterCard
Style...Coffee bar

NYLON

4 Everton Park #01-40
Bukit Merah
Singapore
80004
+65 62202330
www.nyloncoffee.sg

Opening hours...............................Mon–Sat from 8:30 am,
Sun from 9 am
Credit cards..Cash only
Style...Coffee bar

"Best quality, best variety, small and comfortable."
—Ranut Kongpichayanond

"Supersmall shop with only a two-group vintage La
Marzocco espresso machine out on the front counter.
They roast in the back on a tiny Probat."—Scott Lucey

"Tiny but incredibly light-filled and open espresso bar/
roastery beneath a housing complex in Kantonment. Their
focus is on bright, light, interesting African and Central
American coffees. Their Scandinavian-style roasting is
on point."—Matt Perger

NANYANG OLD COFFEE

268 South Bridge Road
Outram
Singapore
58817
+65 6221 6973
www.nanyangoldcoffee.com

Opening hours...Daily from 7 am
Credit cards...Credit cards, Cash
Style...Coffee bar

"My love and I were vacationing and stumbled across this
place in Chinatown while exploring temples. The coffee
here is traditional style, served with sweetened condensed
milk and evaporated milk. The bonuses: it also boasts a
small coffee museum documenting Malay coffee history
and serves delicious kaya toast."—Bronwen Serna

Bangkok, see pages 58–60

"THE OWNER OF THIS CAFE IS THE 2014 THAILAND BARISTA CHAMPION."

BODIN AMORNPAHTTHANAKUUN P.60

BANGKOK

"A NEW-GENERATION CAFE AND ROASTER."

BODIN AMORNPAHTTHANAKUUN P.60

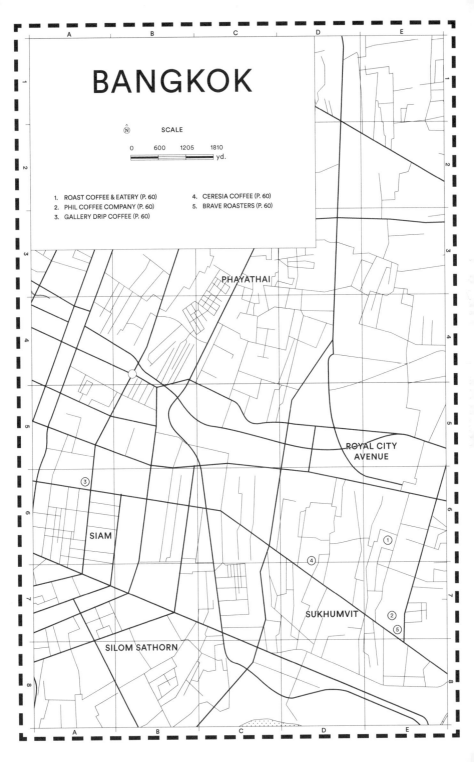

BANGKOK

N

SCALE

0   600   1205   1810
yd.

1. ROAST COFFEE & EATERY (P. 60)
2. PHIL COFFEE COMPANY (P. 60)
3. GALLERY DRIP COFFEE (P. 60)

4. CERESIA COFFEE (P. 60)
5. BRAVE ROASTERS (P. 60)

PHAYATHAI

ROYAL CITY
AVENUE

SIAM

SUKHUMVIT

SILOM SATHORN

ROAST COFFEE & EATERY

335 Thonglor Soi 17, Sukhumvit 55
Khlong Nuea, Watthana
Bangkok 10110
Thailand
+66 21852865
www.roastbkk.com

Opening hours.....................................Mon–Thu from 10 am,
Fri–Sun from 9 am
Credit cards...........................Visa, MasterCard, and Amex
Style..Coffee and food

"The owner of this cafe is the 2014 Thailand Barista
Champion."—Bodin Amornpahtthanakuun

PHIL COFFEE COMPANY

Inside Sukhumvit 61, left side
Klong Tan Nuea
Bangkok 10110
Thailand
+66 20015850
www.philscoffeecompany.com

Opening hours...Tue–Sun from 9 am
Credit cards...Cash only
Style...Coffee bar

GALLERY DRIP COFFEE

Bangkok Art & Culture Centre, 1st floor,
939 Rama 1 Road
Pathum Wan
Bangkok 10330
Thailand
+66 0819895244

Opening hours...Tue–Sun from 11 am
Credit cards...Cash only
Style...Coffee bar

CERESIA COFFEE

593/29-41 Sukhumvit Soi 33/1
Thung Maha Mek
Bangkok 10500
Thailand
+66 982514327
www.facebook.com/pg/ceresia-coffee-roast-
ers-431787946917113

Opening hours...Daily from 8 am
Credit cards...Cash only
Style...Coffee and bar

BRAVE ROASTERS

19/12 Ekkamai 12, Sukhumvit 63 Road,
Klongton Nua
Wattana
Bangkok 10110
Thailand
+66 800466885

Opening hours...Daily from 9 am
Credit cards...Cash only
Style...Coffee bar

"A new-generation cafe and roaster."
—Bodin Amornpahtthanakuun

"ORGANIC HIGH-QUALITY FOODS AND BEVERAGES. THEY UNDERSTAND WHAT SPECIALTY COFFEE IS."

YUKO ITOI P.64

"THEIR ESPRESSO AND CAPPUCCINO ARE REALLY NICE."

YUKO ITOI P.64

JAPAN

"TYPICAL EXAMPLE OF JAPANESE THIRD-WAVE CAFE."

HIDENORI IZAKI P.68

"BEST HOSPITALITY, AMAZING COFFEE, BEAUTIFUL SHOP."

HIDENORI IZAKI P.68

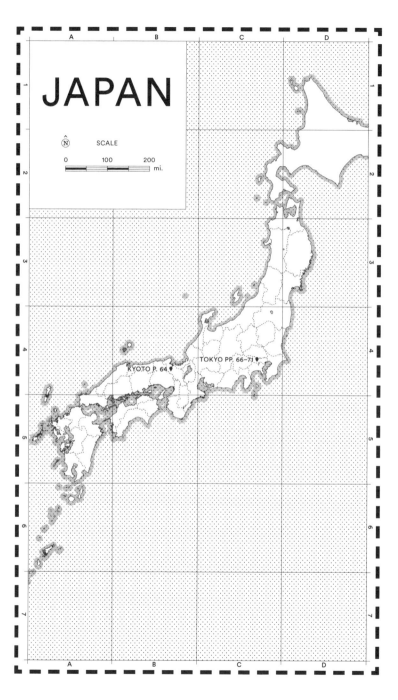

JAPAN

N   SCALE

0   100   200 mi.

KYOTO P. 64

TOKYO PP. 66–71

CAFÉ PHALAM
24 Nishinokyo Hokuseicho
Nakagyo-ku
Kyoto
Kyoto 604-8382
Japan
+81 754964843
www.phalam.jp

Opening hours..Mon–Fri from 8 am,
Sat–Sun from 9 am
Credit cards..Cash only
Style..Coffee and food

"Organic high-quality foods and beverages. They
understand what specialty coffee is."—Yuko Itoi

SENTIDO
1F Nippo Karasuma Building, 445 Sasaya-cho
Nakagyo-ku
Kyoto
Kyoto 604-8187
Japan
+81 757417439

Opening hours.......Mon–Fri from 7:30 am, Sat from 8 am
Credit cards..Cash only
Style..Coffee and food

"Their espresso and cappuccino are really nice."—Yuko Itoi

Tokyo, see pages 66–71

"MY ABSOLUTE FAVORITE PLACE TO GO FOR COFFEE IN THE ENTIRE WORLD IS CAFÉ DE L'AMBRE IN TOKYO. IT HAS SUCH A SENSE OF HISTORY AND PLACE WITH COFFEE IN JAPAN."

BRONWEN SERNA P.68

"IT'S REALLY EASY TO JUST WALK ON BY IT, BUT IF YOU HEAD UP THOSE STAIRS AND INSIDE, IT'S LIKE DISAPPEARING INTO A POCKET-SIZED FILM NOIR EXPERIENCE."

HENGTEE LIM P.69

TOKYO

"AMAZING—BUT YOU'D BETTER FOLLOW THEIR RULES." NATHAN MYHRVOLD P.69

"UNDER THE NEARLY TWO-THOUSAND-FOOT-HIGH SKYTREE TOWER IN EAST TOKYO, THIS COFFEE BAR AND TRAINING CENTER HAS AMAZINGLY WELL-ROASTED COFFEE, USED IN DRINKS AND COCKTAILS."

SCOTT CONARY P.70

TOKYO

N   SCALE

0   585   1170   1755
                            yd.

1. GLITCH COFFEE (P. 68)
2. SARUTAHIKO COFFEE ATELIER SENAGWA (P. 68)
3. CAFÉ DE L'AMBRE (P. 68)
4. ARISE COFFEE ROASTERS (P. 68)
5. SWITCH COFFEE (P. 69)
6. CAFÉ LES JEUX (P. 69)
7. MARUYAMA COFFEE (P. 69)
8. BEAR POND ESPRESSO (P. 69)
9. FUGLEN (P. 70)
10. ABOUT LIFE COFFEE BREWERS (P. 70)
11. THE LOCAL COFFEE STAND (P. 70)
12. UNLIMITED COFFEE BAR (P. 70)
13. BE A GOOD NEIGHBOR (SKYTREE TOWN) (P. 71)

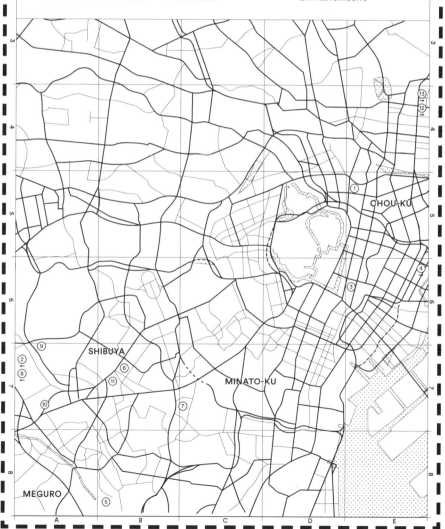

GLITCH COFFEE

1F 3-16 Kanda-Nishikicho
Chiyoda-ku
Tokyo 101-0054
Japan
+81 352445458
www.glitchcoffee.com

Opening hours	Mon–Fri from 7:30 am,
	Sat–Sun from 9 am
Credit cards	Cash only
Style	Coffee and food

"Typical example of Japanese third-wave cafe."
—Hidenori Izaki

SARUTAHIKO COFFEE ATELIER SENAGWA

1-48-3 Sengawacho
Chofu-shi
Tokyo 182-0002
Japan
+81 369090922
www.sarutahiko.co

Opening hours	Mon–Fri from 7 am,
	Sat–Sun from 10 am
Credit cards	Cash only
Style	Coffee

"Best hospitality, amazing coffee, beautiful shop."
—Hidenori Izaki

CAFÉ DE L'AMBRE

8-10-15 Ginza
Chuo
Tokyo 104-0061
Japan
+81 0335711551
www.h6.dion.ne.jp/~lambre

Opening hours	Daily from noon
Credit cards	Cash only
Style	Coffee bar

"My absolute favorite place to go for coffee in the entire world is Café de L'Ambre in Tokyo. It has such a sense of history and place with coffee in Japan. They do very traditional-style brewed coffee (with cloth) with a vast menu of single-origin coffees. They create their own coffee elixirs, and the owner, Ichiro Sekiguchi, still roasts (he's over 100 years old). It's a magical place and I can spend many hours there."—Bronwen Serna

ARISE COFFEE ROASTERS

1-13-8 Hirano
Koto-ku
Tokyo 135-0023
Japan
+81 336433601
www.arisecoffee.jp

Opening hours	Tue–Sun from 9:30 am
Credit cards	Cash only
Style	Coffee bar

"Arise Coffee Roasters in Tokyo served me a wine-barrel-aged, single-origin-pulp natural Dominican coffee that blew me away. The gentleman who made my coffee was a beautiful example of an occurrence I describe to people often. My contemporaries and I can get pretty nerdy about numbers associated with water-to-weight ratios, temperature, and extraction percentages. This guy used no thermometers, no scales, and no timers while prepping a surprisingly inspirational cup. It felt like years of experience guided his hands through the process and it looked like a calamity of impossibilities. I really figured there was little chance of it being enjoyable. It was awesome."
—Christopher Alameda

"My favorite filter coffee thus far."—Hengtee Lim

"The owner is super awesome and creates a really great vibe. He's genuinely nice, polite, chill, and passionate about coffee. I like his efficient use of a small space (which is common in Tokyo). He roasts in there, stores his green coffee, and has a simple pour-over setup. Nice neighborhood feel as well—an older gentleman came in with his cute dog."—Esther Shaw

SWITCH COFFEE

1-17-23 Meguro
Meguro-ku
Tokyo 153-0063
Japan
+81 364203633
www.switchcoffeetokyo.com

Opening hours..Daily from 10 am
Credit cards...Cash only
Style...Coffee and bar

"Masahiro Onishi of Switch Coffee was really open to sharing with me his ideas of coffee, and I love that he's all about a high-quality experience but in a simple way. Sure, he wants to source, roast, and serve the best-quality coffee he can, but he does that simply as a way to share it with the local neighborhood. I feel we can all learn a little from that kind of humility."—Hengtee Lim

CAFÉ LES JEUX

5-9-5 Minamiaoyama
Minato
Tokyo 107-0062
Japan
+81 334996297
www.sites.google.com/site/lesjeuxgrouniet

Opening hours......................................Mon–Fri from 10 am,
Sat–Sun from noon
Credit cards...Cash only
Style...Coffee bar

"Aoyama is well-known as a place for expensive fashion brands and shopping, but down a side street among all of these big-name brands there's a small sign and a staircase leading up to an old coffeehouse called Café Les Jeux. It's really easy to just walk on by it, but if you head up those stairs and inside, it's like disappearing into a pocket-sized film noir experience. It's very different from the rest of Aoyama, with a coffee that matches the environment."
—Hengtee Lim

MARUYAMA COFFEE

Yubinbango, 3-13-3 Nishiazabu
Minato-ku
Tokyo 106-0031
Japan
+81 0368045040
www.maruyamacoffee.com

Opening hours...Daily from 8 am
Credit cards...........................Visa, MasterCard, and Amex
Style...Coffee bar

"Best filter coffee."—Jamie Jessup

BEAR POND ESPRESSO

2-36-12 Kitazawa
Setagaya-ku
Tokyo 155-0031
Japan
+81 3354542486
www.bear-pond.com

Opening hours...Mon from 11 am,
Wed–Sun from 11 am
Credit cards...Cash only
Style...Coffee bar

"Amazing—but you'd better follow their rules."
—Nathan Myhrvold

Bear Pond is the epitome of serious coffee in Japan. While there is a Shibuya location, the true experience is in the original shop on the outskirts of Tokyo. Tanaka takes a level of pride in his craft that seems obsessive even by Japanese standards. You'll notice a small book beside the espresso machine, where every shot is logged in great detail. If he's taking a break, don't expect an espresso shot; only the legend himself is allowed to work behind the machine.

FUGLEN

1-16-11 Tomigaya
Shibuya
Tokyo
151-0063
Japan
+81 334810884
www.fuglen.com

Opening hours..................................Mon–Sat from 8 am,
Sun from 9 am
Credit cards...........................Visa, MasterCard, and Amex
Style..Coffee and cocktails

"I drank the best cold press ever at Fuglen in Tokyo."
—Esther Shaw

"If I could only go to one coffee shop for the rest of my life,
I would choose Fuglen Tokyo without much hesitation.
It's the Japanese outpost of an Oslo cafe, and it combines
everything that I love about a cafe: Scandinavian aesthetics
(warm, stylish, functional), a very approachable bar and
knowledgeable staff, excellent coffees (both locally roasted
and imported from a rotating cadre of reputed Norwegian
roasters), skillful preparation, a lovely outdoor bench and
patio area, direct access to both a beautiful serene park
(Yoyogikoen) as well as the glittering skyscrapers (and
shopping districts) in Shibuya and Shinjuku, and finally an
evening transition to a cocktail bar that incorporates coffee
and coffee techniques into their drinks. Everything in the
space is done with purpose in mind as well as with an eye
for design—from glassware and furniture to the eclectic
selection of home furnishings and accessories available for
purchase."—Mike Yung

ABOUT LIFE COFFEE BREWERS

1-19-8 Dōgenzaka
Shibuya-ku
Tokyo 150-0043
Japan
+81 368090751
www.about-life.coffee

Opening hours..Daily from 8:30 am
Credit cards..Cash only
Style..Coffee bar

"About Life is a rare place to get proper coffee in the
morning. Only a few coffee spots open in early morning
in Japan. I would also mention the baristas there are really
nice guys."—Masahiro Onishi

THE LOCAL COFFEE STAND

2-10-15 Shibuya
Shibuya-ku
Tokyo 150-0002
Japan
+81 334091158
www.thelocal2016.com

Opening hours.......................................Mon–Fri from 8 am,
Sat–Sun from 9 am
Credit cards.......................................Visa and MasterCard
Style...Coffee and bar

"Local is curating coffee from all over Japan and showcasing
their diversity."—Hidenori Izaki

UNLIMITED COFFEE BAR

1-18-2 Narihira
Sumida
Tokyo 130-0002
Japan
+81 366588680
www.unlimitedcoffeestore.com

Opening hours.....................................Tue–Fri from 11 am,
Sat–Sun from 9 am
Credit cards...........................Visa, MasterCard, and Amex
Style..Coffee bar

"Newly opened under the nearly two-thousand-foot-high
Skytree tower in East Tokyo, this coffee bar and training
center has it all: amazingly well-roasted coffee, used in
drinks and cocktails that are thoroughly explained and
assembled by a knowledgeable staff. Three floors take you
from the cafe on the first floor to the beautiful training room
on the second, complete with sample roaster and espresso/
brewing equipment, all the way to the third floor where
focused cuppings are held. Both Daichi Matsubura and his
wife, Rena, are well accredited with multiple certifications,
and Daichi is also a World Barista Championship–certified
judge. All this knowledge is transferred in a setting that
will make you relax among locals and tourists alike at their
seated slow bar, well-appointed with wood and images
of their logo: a stag head and antlers."—Scott Conary

"I recently had a delightful visit to Unlimited Coffee Bar
in Tokyo, where a cold Ethiopian and tonic was prepared
and presented to the high standards one would expect
of a master chef. Wow, that was cool."—Andrew Hetzel

BE A GOOD NEIGHBOR (SKYTREE TOWN)

Solamachi 2F, 1 Chome-1-2 Oshiage
Sumida-ku
Tokyo 131-0045
Japan
+81 356191692
www.beagoodneighbor.net/soramachi

Opening hours .... Daily from 10 am
Credit cards .... Visa and MasterCard
Style .... Coffee kiosk

"Best coffee in a random place . . . espresso and filter coffee
at Be a Good Neighbor coffee kiosk in Tokyo Skytree
Town."—Matt Lee

"CALM AND CLASSIC. SOLID AND STEADY. YOU CAN GO BACK FROM FANCY SPECIALTY COFFEE. IT FEELS LIKE HOME ALWAYS."

BK KIM P.78

SOUTH KOREA

"BEAUTIFUL COFFEE WITH OUTSTANDING DEDICATION."

STEPHEN ROGERS P.78

"A UNIQUE SPACE THAT LOOKS LIKE IT WAS FASHIONED FROM AN OLD LOADING BAY, WITH AN OLD WAREHOUSE ATMOSPHERE WITH SOME FUNKY CHARM."

CYNTHIA LUDVIKSEN P.76

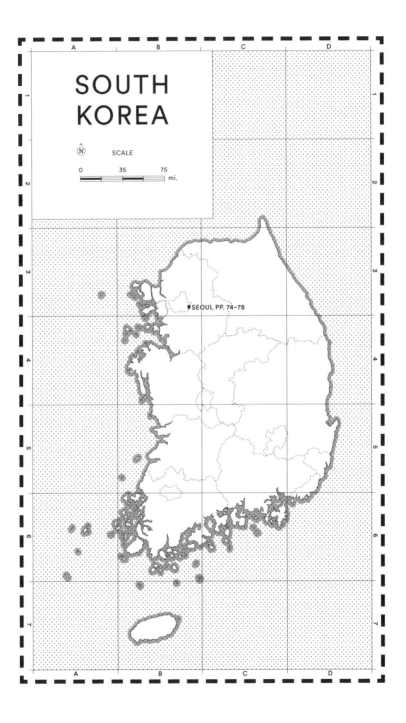

SOUTH
KOREA

N
SCALE
0   35   75
━━━━━━━━━━━ mi.

▼SEOUL PP. 74–78

"**MY FAVORITE CAFE IN THE WORLD.**"

STEPHEN ROGERS P.76

"THERE IS A SINCERITY IN BEING A LOCALLY OWNED BUSINESS THAT TAKES PRIDE IN ITS YEARS OF ESTABLISHMENT."

CYNTHIA LUDVIKSEN P.76

SEOUL

"THE FEEL OF THIS SHOP IS LIKE VISITING YOUR FRIEND'S HOUSE: YOU CAN SIT AND ENJOY A STAY AND NEVER FEEL RUSHED TO LEAVE."

CYNTHIA LUDVIKSEN P.77

"I HAVEN'T SEEN A VIBE SIMILAR TO THIS PLACE ANYWHERE ELSE IN THE WORLD."

SANG HO PARK P.77

SEOUL

N   SCALE

0   875   1750   2620
yd.

1. CLUB ESPRESSO (P. 76)
2. COFFEE LIBRE (P. 76)
3. 5 BREWING (P. 76)
4. ANTHRACITE (P. 76)

5. COFFEE SEED (P. 77)
6. COFFEE TEMPLE (P. 77)
7. FRITZ COFFEE COMPANY (P. 77)
8. 2FFECT COFFEE (P. 78)

9. BOHEMIAN (P. 78)
10. HELL CAFE (P. 78)

SAMCHEONG-DONG

SEODAEMUN-GU

MYEONG-DONG

HONGDAE

ITAEWON

YEONGDEUNGPO-GU

DONGJAK-GU

SEOCHO-GU

CLUB ESPRESSO

132 Changuimun-ro
Jongno-gu
Seoul
South Korea
+82 27648719
www.clubespresso.co.kr

Opening hours..Daily from 10 am
Credit cards............................Visa, MasterCard, and Amex
Style...Coffee bar

"I recall visiting this establishment a few years ago and being pleasantly surprised by its unique character. Club Espresso first opened in 1990, well in advance of the boom in the specialty coffee scene in Seoul. The shop looks like it was built by hand, with wonderfully warm wooden beams all around the walls and ceilings, and it had cozy wooden tables and chairs. There was a quaint coziness to the ambience. It felt like a place that invited you to sit and enjoy. Behind the counter was an impressive display of high-end modern equipment and a sophisticated variety of coffee offerings that expressed that the staff took coffee quite seriously. There were a number of espresso grinders to allow the option of sampling a wide variety of their coffees at any time. The coffee is wellcrafted and you get the feeling that it's a very professional establishment but far from corporate. There is a sincerity in being a locally owned business that takes pride in its years of establishment. Club Espresso seemed a bit off the beaten path but was definitely well worth a visit."—Cynthia Ludviksen

COFFEE LIBRE

227-15 Yeonnam
Mapo
Seoul
South Korea
+82 23340615
www.coffeelibre.kr

Opening hours...Tue–Sun from 1 pm
Credit cards............................Visa, MasterCard, and Amex
Style...Coffee bar

"Coffee Libre may feel more like a roastery than a coffee shop, but they do welcome visitors who are just looking to stop by for a drink or to buy a bag of coffee. The location is set inside an old marketplace, so it's a very unique space that looks like it was fashioned from an loading bay, with a warehouse atmosphere with some funky charm. If the shop could reflect a persona, it would be a character that shouts, 'I'm authentic and I make my own rules.' The coffee I had here was outstanding and the whole experience was made more enjoyable because the owner, Pil Hoon, was there to share his company's story."—Cynthia Ludviksen

5 BREWING

446-297 Yeonhui-dong
Seodaemun-gu
Seoul
South Korea
+82 23245815

Opening hours..Daily from 11 am
Credit cards............................Visa, MasterCard, and Amex
Style..Roastery cafe

"This shop was opened by past Korean barista champion Cho Hyun Sun. What I appreciated about this coffee shop is its fun vintage-meets-industrial kind of atmosphere. There was a nice characteristic of the shop's individualism. The roaster can be seen on-site and the menu was filled with a lot of creative signature drinks that champions have used in competitions."—Cynthia Ludviksen

"Its quirky interior and chilled service belie a very precise and considered coffee experience. The decor is right up my alley: funky, minimalist retro—if that's a thing."
—Candice Madison

ANTHRACITE

357-6 Hapjeong-dong
Mapo-gu
Seoul
South Korea
+82 23220009
www.anthracitecoffee.com

Opening hours..Daily from 11 am
Credit cards......................................Visa and MasterCard
Style..Roastery cafe

"My favorite cafe in the world."—Stephen Rogers

COFFEE SEED

24-7 Dongmak-ro 3-gil
Mapo-gu
Seoul
South Korea
+82 23266230

Opening hours................................Daily from 10 am
Credit cards............................Visa, MasterCard, and Amex
Style..Coffee bar

"Coffee Seed is situated in the popular Hongdae area of Seoul that is close to a university and bursting with food establishments. The shop is off a side street that only subtly shows the name Coffee Seed. Upstairs from the shop is the CBSC training school. The shop and school were started by Youngmin Lee (Barista Champion and Latte Art Champion from Korea) and his partner Sunny Yoon (editor of *Coffee, Tea & Ice Cream Korea*). The space is very unique, with a large outdoor patio and cozy decor. There is a distinctive homemade feel to the space, which is decorated with tables and benches strewn with wool blankets and pillows. The mismatched chairs, independent arts and crafts, and small display of collectibles and awards from the owners showcase the charm and cuteness of this shop. Behind the bar is a simple printed menu, which changes frequently, based on daily offerings. There is a small bar area with usually only one or two baristas on staff. Just ask for their suggestions or let them surprise you with what they are happy to serve. The feel of this shop is like visiting your friend's house: you can sit and enjoy a stay and never feel rushed to leave."—Cynthia Ludviksen

"Probably the Americoke at Coffee Seed is my favorite signature coffee drink so far. It is a very accessible and flavorful summer drink that will make you happily chilled." —Kyonghee Shin

COFFEE TEMPLE

396 World Cup Buk-ro
Mapo-gu
Seoul
South Korea
+82 221328051

Opening hours................................Daily from 9 am
Credit cards............................Visa, MasterCard, and Amex
Style..Coffee bar

"Great espresso."—Stephen Rogers

"Recently I had a memorable shot of espresso at Coffee Temple. Tropical fruit and caramel were nicely combined, and the acidity and sweetness were well balanced with a clean finish."—Kyonghee Shin

FRITZ COFFEE COMPANY

68 Mapo-daero
Mapo-gu
Seoul
South Korea
+82 232752045
www.fritz.co.kr

Opening hours........................Mon–Fri from 8 am,
                                                   Sat–Sun from 10 am
Credit cards............................Visa, MasterCard, and Amex
Style..Coffee bar

"My absolute favorite is Fritz Coffee Company in Seoul. And the reasons are many but mostly the thoughtful design (though the coffee and service are nothing to fault)—from the considered old architecture to the cafe layout, the reclaimed vintage ceramic light fittings, cups and saucers, the dark wood, the stepped entrance to the shop, the on-site bakery that you see and smell the instant you arrive, and even down to the brand design itself. Owner BK Kim has an eye for uniqueness in an industry where many copy. There is thoughtfulness behind all the details. And his team, with their energy and service, create an environment you want to go back to time and time again."—Jamie Jessup

"I love the atmosphere, the interior design, and the people who work behind the bar. Their 'feel' is unique. I haven't seen a vibe similar to this place anywhere else in the world." —Sang Ho Park

"Manned by the current wunderkinds of Korean Specialty Coffee. A three-story complex of specialty coffee and similarly in-vogue fusion-style baked goods."—Matt Perger

"Wonderful hand drip." —Stephen Rogers

"The old three-story building is full of cheap vintage furniture from a traditional market, which sets the tone of this cafe beautifully. Their completely open bar run by well-known baristas amazes customers by showing how much care they put into every single beverage." —Kyonghee Shin

2FFECT COFFEE

38 Hwarang-ro 32-gil
Seongbuk-gu
Seoul
South Korea
+82 1025330214

Opening hours	Mon–Fri from 11 am
Credit cards	Visa, MasterCard, and Amex
Style	Coffee bar

BOHEMIAN

22-3 Gaeunsa-gil
Seongbuk-gu
Seoul
South Korea
+82 29277949
www.cafebohemian.co.kr

Opening hours	Mon–Fri from 10 am
Credit cards	Visa, MasterCard, and Amex
Style	Coffee bar

"Calm and classic. Solid and steady. You can go back from
fancy specialty coffee. It feels like home always."—BK Kim

HELL CAFE

76 Bogwang-ro
Yongsan-gu
Seoul
South Korea
+82 1048064687

Opening hours	Mon–Fri from 8 am,
	Sat–Sun from noon
Credit cards	Visa, MasterCard, and Amex
Style	Roastery cafe

"Yo-Sep Kwon roasts all his coffee on a stovetop burner
in a drum, which he turns by hand. Beautiful coffee with
outstanding dedication."—Stephen Rogers

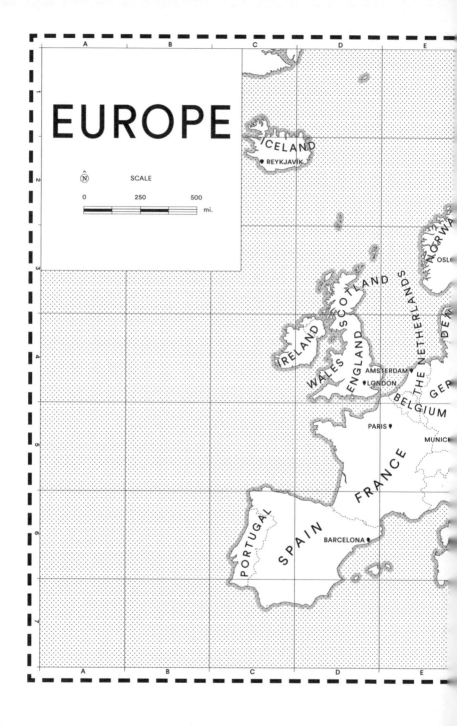

EUROPE

N

SCALE

0   250   500

mi.

ICELAND

• REYKJAVIK

NORWAY

OSLO

SCOTLAND

IRELAND

WALES

ENGLAND

THE NETHERLANDS

AMSTERDAM

LONDON

BELGIUM

GER

PARIS

MUNICH

FRANCE

PORTUGAL

SPAIN

BARCELONA

"THE PLACE IS IN THE MIDDLE OF NOWHERE, AND IF YOU COME THERE ON A HORSE, THERE ARE PLACES FOR YOU TO KEEP IT WHILE DRINKING BEAUTIFUL COFFEE." SONJA BJÖRK GRANT P.84

"EXCELLENT FILTER COFFEE DELIVERED WITHOUT FUSS." PAUL STACK P.86

DENMARK, FINLAND, ICELAND, NORWAY & SWEDEN

"THEY LOVE WHAT THEY DO AND DO IT WITH STYLE. THEY ROAST THEIR COFFEES AND SOURCE WORLDWIDE." NICHOLAS CHISTYAKOV P.84

"THE COFFEE IS SERVED IMPECCABLY." EILEEN P. KENNY P.91

"THE HIGH, VAULTED CEILINGS AND FLICKERING CANDLES MAKE FOR A UNIQUE ATMOSPHERE, ALMOST AS IF YOU WERE DRINKING COFFEE IN AN OLD CATHEDRAL." ANNA BRONES P.85

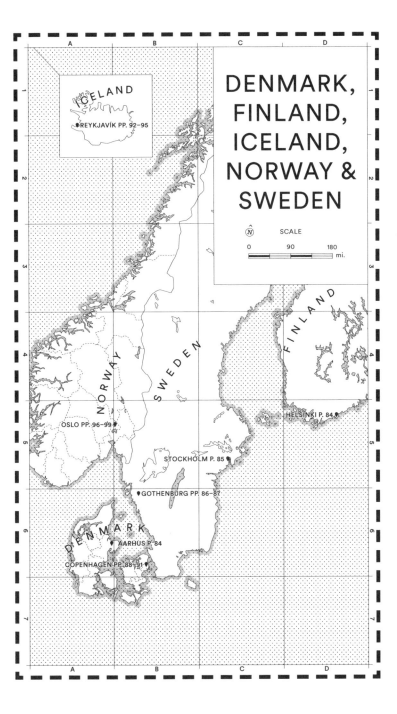

A 1

B 1

C 1

D 1

A 2

B

SWEDEN

NORWAY

FINLAND

ICELAND
REYKJAVÍK PP. 92–95

DENMARK,
FINLAND,
ICELAND,
NORWAY &
SWEDEN

N

SCALE

0   90   180
mi.

HELSINKI P. 84

OSLO PP. 96–99

STOCKHOLM P. 85

GOTHENBURG PP. 86–87

DENMARK

AARHUS P. 84

COPENHAGEN PP. 88–91

LA CABRA
Graven 20
Aarhus C
Aarhus 8000
Denmark
+45 42924925
www.lacabra.dk

Opening hours................................Tue–Sat from 8 am,
Sat–Sun from 10 am
Credit cards.........................Visa, MasterCard, and Amex
Style...Roastery Cafe

Copenhagen, see pages 88-91

PALLETT KAFFIKOMPANÍ
Strandgata 75
Hafnarfjörður 220
Iceland
+354 5714144
www.facebook.com/pg/pallettkaffi

Opening hours................................Mon–Fri from 7:30 am,
Sat–Sun from 8 am
Credit cards..........................Visa, MasterCard, and Amex
Style...Coffee and breakfast

"The best Irish coffee (the oldest coffee cocktail) is for sure
at Pallett Kaffikompaní in Iceland, where former Icelandic
barista champion Pálmar Þór Hlöðversson is running his
small coffee bar."—Sonja Björk Grant

GOOD LIFE COFFEE
Kolmas Linja 17
Kallio
Helsinki
Uusimaa FI-00530
Finland
www.goodlifecoffee.fi

Opening hours................................Mon–Fri from 8:30 am,
Sat from 10 am
Credit cards.................................Visa and MasterCard
Style...Coffee bar

"A small but very important coffee place in Helsinki. They
love what they do and do it with style. A very cozy and
friendly place. They roast their coffees and source
worldwide."—Nicholas Chistyakov

"A wonderful cold brew with craft tonic."—Felipe Croce

KAHVILA SIILI
Ilmattarentie 8C
Käpylä
Helsinki
Uusimaa 00610
Finland
+358 405228401
www.kahvilasiili.com

Opening hours..May–August
Credit cards.........................Visa, MasterCard, and Amex
Style.............................Seasonal outdoor cafe, with food

BRAGGINN—CLAY AND COFFEE
Birtingaholt 3
Flúðir
Hrunamannahreppur 845
Iceland
+354 8979923
www.bragginnstudio.is

Opening hours....................Daily in the summer from 11 am
Credit cards.................................Visa and MasterCard
Style...Coffee and food

"This is a workshop where ceramic artist Erna Elinbjörg
Skúladóttir is working with her art and she has a few tables.
The place is open during the summer and some special
weekends during the winter. Her parents are vegetable
farmers, so all the food and raw cakes are organic. They
serve V60-brewed pour-over coffee and used to have coffee
from Kaffismiðjan and now from Reykjavík Roasters. The
place is in the middle of nowhere, and if you come there on
a horse, there are places for you to keep it while drinking
beautiful coffee." —Sonja Björk Grant

Reykjavík, see pages 92–95

Oslo, see pages 96–99

KOPPI

Norra Storgatan 16
Helsingborg
Skåne 252 20
Sweden
+46 42133033
www.koppi.se

Opening hours.................................Mon–Fri from 9 am,
Sat from 10 am
Credit cards.................................Visa and MasterCard
Style...Roastery cafe

"Best espresso."—David Latourell

"I have a special place in my heart for Koppi. The decor, the
unfussy and unpretentious service, and the space allowed
me to relax, read, and enjoy my coffee. The roasting area is
on an elevated platform behind glass walls, so if you're
interested—and I always am—you can have a gander while
you sit."—Candice Madison

KAFFEVERKET/SNICKARBACKEN 7

Snickarbacken 7
Norrmalm
Stockholm 111 39
Sweden
+46 868429009
www.snickarbacken7.se

Opening hours.................................Mon–Fri from 8 am,
Sat from 9 am, Sun from 10 am
Credit cards.................................Visa and MasterCard
Style...Coffee bar

"Kaffeverket wins points not only for its coffee but for its
space. Part cafe, part gallery, part clothing store, it's all
housed in a building dating back to the early 1800s that was
then used as stables. The high, vaulted ceilings and
flickering candles make for a unique atmosphere, almost as
if you were drinking coffee in an old cathedral. There are
freshly baked sandwiches and iconic Swedish coffee buns,
and espresso drinks are made on a Synesso machine."
—Anna Brones

DROP COFFEE

Wollmar Yxkullsgatan 10
Södermalm
Stockholm 118 50
Sweden
+46 841023363
www.dropcoffee.com

Opening hours.................................Mon–Fri from 8 am,
Sat–Sun from 10 am
Credit cards.................................Visa, MasterCard, and Amex
Style...Coffee and food

"Sweden coffee pioneers and provocateurs. This is an
innovative and rapidly changing coffeeplace. Small,
hipster-looking, and crowded with great baristas and
an award-winning roaster. A must-visit place while you
are in Stockholm."—Nicholas Chistyakov

JOHAN & NYSTROM CONCEPT STORE

Swedenborgsgatan 7
Södermalm
Stockholm 118 48
Sweden
+46 087022040
www.johanochnystrom.se

Opening hours.................................Mon–Fri from 7:30 am,
Sat from 10 am, Sun from 11 am
Credit cards.................................Visa and MasterCard
Style...Coffee bar

DA MATTEO

Vallgatan 5
Inom Vallgraven
Gothenburg
Västra Götaland 411 16
Sweden
+46 31130609
www.damatteo.se

Opening hours	Mon–Fri from 8 am, Sat–Sun from 10 am
Credit cards	Visa and MasterCard
Style	Coffee and food

"Da Matteo's roastery café in Gothenburg oozes style with substance to match. Excellent filter coffee delivered without fuss."—Paul Stack

"The batch brew (Ethiopian Yirgacheffe Gedeb) at da Matteo was impressive—dialed in with a very good balance of flavor, and texture with consistency cup after cup."
—Mike Yung

SYSTER MARMELAD

Mariagatan 16
Kungsladugård
Gothenburg
Västra Götaland 414 71
Sweden
+46 31141160
www.systermarmelad.se

Opening hours	Mon–Fri from 5pm, Sat–Sun from 11 am
Credit cards	Visa and MasterCard
Style	Restaurant

"In the popular neighborhood of Majorna sits Syster Marmelad, a vegetarian and vegan restaurant that just so happens to have a solid coffee service. Here you will find unique uses for fresh produce, like pickled carrots, which have in turn been roasted. If food isn't what you're in the mood for, head across to their more casual cafe, Kafe Marmelad, where you can sit down for an iconic Swedish fika."—Anna Brones

KALE'I KAFFEBAR

Kyrkogatan 13
Inom Vallgraven
Gothenburg
Västra Götaland 411 15
Sweden
+46 723500013
www.kaleikaffebar.se

Opening hours	Mon–Fri from 7:30 am, Sat from 8 am
Credit cards	Visa and MasterCard
Style	Coffee and food

"Hidden in a courtyard, Kale'i is the definition of the Swedish word *mysig*, often translated as 'cozy' in English. The space is simple yet inviting, and the comfortable atmosphere makes you feel right at home—except that the coffee and food are better than what you would have made yourself. Of note is the brunch spread, a lovely Scandinavian assortment of sweet and savory that's a perfect way to kick off your day."—Anna Brones

VIKTORS KAFFE

Geijersgatan
Lorensberg
Gothenburg
Västra Götaland 411 34
Sweden
+46 762686867
www.viktorskaffe.se

Opening hours	Mon–Fri from 7:30 am, Sat–Sun from 10 am
Credit cards	Visa, MasterCard, and Amex
Style	Coffee bar and food

"Just off Kungsportsavenyn lies Viktors, a small coffee bar that's dedicated to good service. You'll find some of the best cinnamon rolls in town here, perfect to pair with a pour-over for an afternoon fika. When the it's bright, there are a couple of tables placed outside so you can soak up the Swedish sun."—Anna Brones

ALKEMISTEN

Gustaf Dalénsgatan 14
Gothenburg
Västra Götaland 417 05
Sweden
+46 700522928
www.alkemistenkaffebar.se

Opening hours................................Tue–Fri from 7 am,
Sat–Sun from 10 am
Credit cards............................Visa, MasterCard, and Amex
Style..Coffee bar

"HAVING GREAT COFFEE IN RESTAURANTS IS ALWAYS VERY UNEXPECTED! THE BEST EXPERIENCE HAS BEEN AT AMASS." JENNI BRYANT P.90

"THEIR FRIENDLY SERVICE, THE ATMOSPHERE OF THEIR CAFES, AND THE QUALITY OF THEIR COFFEE ARE STILL TOP IN THE WORLD IN MY OPINION."
BENJAMIN PUT P.90

COPENHAGEN

"I WAS BLOWN AWAY THE FIRST TIME I WENT TO COFFEE COLLECTIVE IN DENMARK."
FABRIZIO SENCIÓN RAMÍREZ P.90

"WHETHER I SIT IN THE BAR FOR A QUICK ESPRESSO OR READ THE PAPER AT A TABLE, EUROPA MAKES ME FEEL LIKE I AM AT THE HUB OF THE UNIVERSE."
BJÖRG BREND LAIRD P.90

"CONSISTENTLY EXQUISITE COFFEE AND ESPRESSO, KNOWLEDGEABLE AND FRIENDLY STAFF, AND BEAUTIFULLY DESIGNED CAFES, PACKAGING, AND ROASTED COFFEE."
ANDREW BARNETT P.90

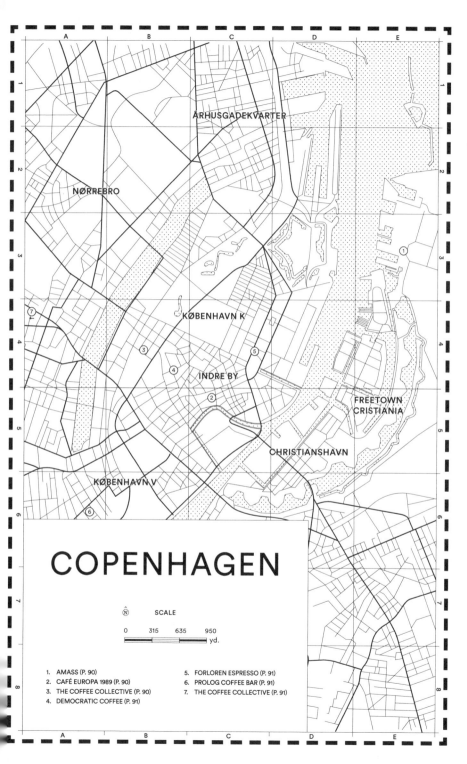

COPENHAGEN

N̂   SCALE

0   315   635   950
                    yd.

1. AMASS (P. 90)
2. CAFÉ EUROPA 1989 (P. 90)
3. THE COFFEE COLLECTIVE (P. 90)
4. DEMOCRATIC COFFEE (P. 91)

5. FORLOREN ESPRESSO (P. 91)
6. PROLOG COFFEE BAR (P. 91)
7. THE COFFEE COLLECTIVE (P. 91)

ÅRHUSGADEKVARTER

NØRREBRO

KØBENHAVN K

INDRE BY

FREETOWN CRISTIANIA

CHRISTIANSHAVN

KØBENHAVN V

AMASS

Refshalevej 153
Refshaleøen
Copenhagen 1432
Denmark
+45 43584330
www.amassrestaurant.com

Opening hours..Tue–Sat from 6 pm,
Fri–Sat from noon
Credit cards............................Visa, MasterCard, and Amex
Style...Fine dining

"Having great coffee in restaurants is always very
unexpected! The best experience has been at Amass."
—Jenni Bryant

CAFÉ EUROPA 1989

Amagertorv 1
Copenhagen 1160
Denmark
+45 33142889
www.europa1989.dk

Opening hours...................................Mon–Sat from 7:45 am,
Sun from 9 am
Credit cards............................Visa, MasterCard, and Amex
Style...Full service, Coffee and food

"Whether I sit in the bar for a quick espresso or I read the
paper at a table, Europa makes me feel like I am at the hub
of the universe. The setting on Amagertorv with the
fishbowl-like windows gives you an overview of the world.
The table service is a factor, too – there is no bus bin, where
I am supposed to take my dishes? Oh, America, you got it all
wrong!" —Björg Brend Laird

THE COFFEE COLLECTIVE

Vendersgade 6D
Copenhagen 1363
Denmark
+45 60151525
www.coffeecollective.dk

Opening hours..Mon–Fri from 7 am,
Sat–Sun from 8 am
Credit cards..Visa and MasterCard
Style..Coffee kiosk in food hall

"When I'm in transit in Copenhagen Airport, I usually go
to their place in Torvehallerne by taking the metro, which
is very easy to do. The Coffee Collective in Torvehallerne
is in a food market where you can buy everything you need
for your dinner parties. The design of the place is a long
and open bar, with an espresso machine and brew bar."
—Sonja Björk Grant

"Consistently exquisite coffee and espresso, knowledgeable
and friendly staff, beautifully designed cafes and packaging,
and beautifully roasted coffee from some of my favorite
coffee farms."—Andrew Barnett

"The best filter coffee was in Copenhagen at Coffee
Collective. The coffees there were so clean and crisp."
—Robert Dan Griffin

"Anytime anyone mentions Copenhagen I immediately
think of Coffee Collective. When I started in coffee and
learned about Klaus Thomsen (2006 World Barista
Champion), I knew I wanted to visit. They were famous for
their lighter-style roasting, and they had the World Barista
Champion and the World Cupping Champion! It wasn't
until 2012 that I finally got to go there, and I was not
disappointed. Their friendly service, the atmosphere of their
cafes, and the quality of their coffee are still top in the world
in my opinion. If they have Panama Hacienda La Esmeralda
on the menu, get it!"—Benjamin Put

"I was blown away the first time I went to Coffee Collective
in Denmark. Everything from the setting to the roasting
facilities was fantastic. The coffees they serve are amazing."
—Fabrizio Sención Ramírez

DEMOCRATIC COFFEE

Krystalgade 15
Copenhagen 1172
Denmark
+45 40196237

Opening hours.................................Mon–Fri from 8 am,
Sat from 9 am
Credit cards...Accepted
Style...Coffee and food

FORLOREN ESPRESSO

Store Kongensgade 32
1264 Copenhagen
Denmark
www.forlorenespresso.dk

Opening hours.................................Mon–Fri from 8 am,
Sat from 9 am, Sun from 10 am
Credit cards...Accepted
Style...Coffee bar

PROLOG COFFEE BAR

Høkerboderne 16
1712 Copenhagen
Denmark
+45 31255675

Opening hours.................................Mon–Fri from 7 am,
Sat–Sun from 9 am
Credit cards...Accepted
Style...Coffee and food

THE COFFEE COLLECTIVE

Godthåbsvej 34B
Frederiksberg
Frederiksberg 2000
Denmark
+45 60151525
www.coffeecollective.dk

Opening hours.........................Mon–Fri from 7:30 am,
Sat from 9 am, Sun from 10 am
Credit cards.............................Visa and MasterCard
Style...Coffee and food

"A big space that's separated into a long serving bar, cupping area, and seating area. On the other side of a very nice glass wall is their roaster and production and offices. I really enjoy this place for meeting people when I'm staying for short visit in Copenhagen. The Coffee Collective has beautiful coffees, directly trade from farmers. I always drink their filter coffee and sometimes I'm there at cupping time and they always invite you to cup with them."
—Sonja BjörkGrant

"The venue itself is stunning—set back from an unassuming street, it's a long space with windows covering nearly every wall and beautiful Danish furniture everywhere. The coffee is served impeccably, with interesting side offerings like cascara soda in summer, or delicious food. It's the sort of place where you can settle in for hours with a book or some work and feel totally at home (if your home were beautifully styled and incredibly Danish)." —Eileen P. Kenny

There's no "best" Coffee Collective shop to choose because they're each so excellent in their own distinct ways. But most will find the soothing tone at the company's Godthåbsvej roastery-cafe to be the just the Scandinavian fantasy they've always dreamed of. There's ample space to enjoy the cafe's coffee and the small, exquisite food selection. There are plenty of opportunities to fly one's coffee geek flag at full mast, be it through cuppings, tours of the adjacent roastery, or just that in-depth conversation with your barista as you sample brew after brew.

> # "IT WAS TRULY CONSIDERED, DELIGHTFUL, AND A LONG-REMEMBERED EVENING."
> JAMIE JESSUP P.94

REYKJAVÍK

> # "THIS IS A HIDDEN GEM IN A BEAUTIFUL COUNTRY AND OOZES THAT REYKJAVÍK SPIRIT."
> KLAUS THOMSEN P.94

> # "CO-OWNER SONJA BJÖRK GRANT HAS FOR A LONG TIME MADE A HUGE IMPACT—BOTH IN ICELAND, TRAINING A GENERATION OF PASSIONATE BARISTAS, AND IN THE GLOBAL BARISTA COMMUNITY, JUDGING BARISTA COMPETITIONS, AMONG MANY THINGS."
> TUMI FERRER P.94

REYKJAVÍK

N

SCALE

0   265   530   805
                       yd.

1. DILL (P. 94)   4. KAFFIBRUGGHÚISÐ (P. 94)
2. REYKJAVÍK ROASTERS (P. 94)   5. KAFFIHÚS VESTURBÆJAR (P. 95)
3. KAFFISLIPPUR (P. 94)

VESTURBÆR

DOWNTOWN

101 AUSTURBÆR

HOLT

ÖSKJUHLÍÐ

DILL

Hverfisgata 12
Reykjavík 101
Iceland
+353 5521522
www.dillrestaurant.is

Opening hours...Wed–Sat from 7 pm
Credit cards............................Visa, MasterCard, and Amex
Style...Fine dining

"We were served a seasonal tasting menu that finished with a coffee course pairing, leaning on the tasting notes of a selection of coffees to complement the dessert plates. It was truly considered, delightful, and a long-remembered evening."—Jamie Jessup

REYKJAVÍK ROASTERS

Kárastígur 1
Reykjavík 101
Iceland
+354 5175535
www.reykjavikroasters.is

Opening hours.......................................Mon–Fri from 8 am,
Sat–Sun from 9 am
Credit cards............................Visa, MasterCard, and Amex
Style..Coffee bar

"Reykjavík Roasters in Iceland is a place special to me. It was opened under the name Kaffismiðjan by a good friend of mine, Sonja Björk Grant, and later one of our former baristas at the Coffee Collective took over together with three other passionate coffee people. This is a hidden gem in a beautiful country and oozes that Reykjavík spirit." —Klaus Thomsen

This roastery-cafe in a house downtown is all you'd want on a cold — or warm! — Iceland day. It is designed like a living room, staffed with thoughtful, down-to-earth coffee people, and serves delightful house-roasted coffees. Warning: it may be hard to believe you're not living inside a fairy tale while you're there.

KAFFISLIPPUR

Myrargata 2
Old West Side
Reykjavík 101
Iceland
+354 5608060
www.kaffislippur.is

Opening hours.......................................Mon–Sun from 7 am
Credit cards............................Visa, MasterCard, and Amex
Style...Coffee and food

"This shop is within the Icelandair Hotel at the harbor. They also run an amazing restaurant and one of the most popular cocktail bars. This cafe is their newest project, run by an amazing barista, Vala Stefánsdóttir, who has been a Coffee in Good Spirits national champion and Latte Art national champion."—Sonja Björk Grant

KAFFIBRUGGHÚISÐ

Fiskislóð 57-59
Vesturbær
Reykjavík 101
Iceland

Opening hours.......................................Mon–Sat from 8 am
Credit cards............................Visa, MasterCard, and Amex
Style...Roastery cafe

"Co-owner Sonja Björk Grant has for a long time made a huge impact—both in Iceland, training a generation of passionate baristas, and in the global barista community, judging barista competitions, among many things. Her business partner, Njáll Björgvinsson (you can call him "Njalli"), has been working in coffee since 2000, and over the years he has done his fair share of competing, training, and consulting. He is the current head of the Specialty Coffee Association of Europe chapter of Iceland, which successfully broke the three-year silence in Icelandic barista competitions, sending competitors to represent Iceland in the World Brewers Cup for the first time since 2013." —Tumi Ferrer

KAFFIHÚS VESTURBÆJAR

Melhaga 20-22
Vesturbær
Reykjavík 107
Iceland
+354 5510623
www.kaffihusvesturbaejar.is

Opening hours	Mon–Fri from 8 am, Sat–Sun from 9 am
Credit cards	Visa, MasterCard, and Amex
Style	Coffee and food

"They have a simple kitchen, but a good one, and do filter and espresso drinks. This cafe is very popular because it is not downtown but is opposite one of our great swimming pools, so families go there for coffee. I go there when I'm home to meet with friends who live around this area. It is still only a fifteen-minute walk to downtown. I like it."
—Sonja Björk Grant

"BEAUTIFUL DESIGN, WITH BEAUTIFUL COFFEES."

SCOTT LUCEY P.99

"REMARKABLE—ONE OF THE GREAT COFFEE PLACES ON EARTH, IN A VERY UNASSUMING NEIGHBORHOOD IN OSLO."

NATHAN MYHRVOLD P.98

OSLO

"THE DRINKS ARE ALMOST ALWAYS IMPECCABLE, AND THE SERVICE FRIENDLY AND PROFESSIONAL. IT'S BEAUTIFUL AND COZY."

DAVID LATOURELL P.98

"THERE'S NOTHING PRETENTIOUS, ONLY GREAT COFFEE AND AN EXCEPTIONAL FEELING OF BEING APPRECIATED AS A CUSTOMER, AND I LOVE THAT!"

METTE-MARIE HANSEN P.98

"EVERY DETAIL IS IMPOSSIBLY CONSIDERED—A SLEEK JUGGERNAUT OF NORDIC COFFEE TRIUMPHALISM, AND HOME TO ONE OF THE BEST COFFEE DESSERTS ON THE PLANET: THE ICED CAPPUCCINO."

ALEX BERNSON P.98

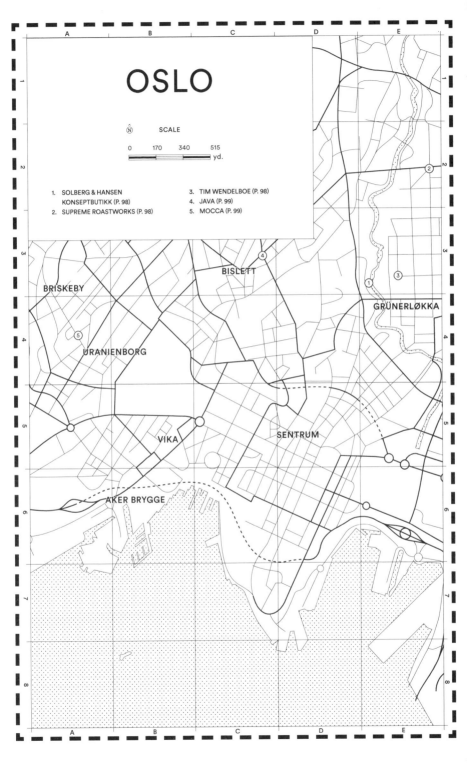

OSLO

N   SCALE

0   170   340   515
━━━━━━━━━━━━━ yd.

1. SOLBERG & HANSEN
   KONSEPTBUTIKK (P. 98)
2. SUPREME ROASTWORKS (P. 98)
3. TIM WENDELBOE (P. 98)
4. JAVA (P. 99)
5. MOCCA (P. 99)

BISLETT

BRISKEBY

GRÜNERLØKKA

URANIENBORG

VIKA

SENTRUM

AKER BRYGGE

SOLBERG & HANSEN KONSEPTBUTIKK
Maridalsveien 17
Grünerløkka
Oslo 0175
Norway
+47 91127856
www.solberghansen.com

Opening hours................................Mon–Sat from 10 am,
                                                         Sun from 11 am
Credit cards.....................................Visa and MasterCard
Style..Coffee bar

"When a 135-year-old company plans to launch its first retail space, a lot of thought needs to go into it. But how do you create a coffee space that sells and serves coffee but does so in a way that is totally different from anyone else in your market? First and foremost, you devote the space to the sale of whole-bean coffee. You also create a set of spaces built on the premise of public education around home brewing. Then you clarify your intent to remain a neutral provider of roasted coffee by not serving milk in your space. No milk! If you want an espresso-based beverage, you get espresso. If you want filter coffee, you get black coffee. It's about the coffee! You also have to ensure the staff is knowledgeable enough to handle the most arcane, coffee-nerd questions around but is also keenly interested in helping the average consumer 'get it.' I've definitely had some of the best coffee of my life served to me by kind and knowledgeable Norwegians here."—David Latourell

SUPREME ROASTWORKS
Thorvald Meyers Gate 18A
Grünerløkka
Oslo 0474
Norway
+47 22714202
www.srw.no

Opening hours...Mon–Fri from 7 am,
                                                                 Sat from 10 am
Credit cards.............................Visa, MasterCard, and Amex
Style...Coffee and food

"As a native Norwegian, I always go to Norway for holidays, and I just love coming home and seeing familiar faces and enjoying great coffee. Supreme Roastworks embraces their customers like nowhere else. I feel like they are just genuinely excited to greet every single customer. There's nothing pretentious, only great coffee and an exceptional feeling of being appreciated as a customer, and I love that!"
—Mette-Marie Hansen

TIM WENDELBOE
Grünersgate 1
Grünerløkka
Oslo 0552
Norway
+47 40004062
www.timwendelboe.no

Opening hours................................Mon–Fri from 8:30 am,
                                                         Sat–Sun from 11 am
Credit cards.............................Visa, MasterCard, and Amex
Style...Coffee and bar

"Every detail is impossibly considered—a sleek juggernaut of Nordic coffee triumphalism, the canonical place to go and learn just what all the fuss is about light roasting and AeroPresses, but also home to one of the best coffee desserts on the planet: the iced cappuccino. They found a vintage blender that gives this treat this most delightfully fluffy texture—refined and refreshing, yet willing to have some fun, much like the eponymous Wendelboe himself."
—Alex Bernson

"The drinks are almost always impeccable, and the service friendly and professional. It's beautiful and cozy."
—David Latourell

"Remarkable—one of the great coffee places on earth, in a very unassuming neighborhood in Oslo. I wonder if many of their customers realize how special it is. I have talked to many Oslo residents who have no idea their city has one of the best coffee shops in the world."—Nathan Myhrvold

"Tim Wendelboe, as a shop, has an amazing story. Wendelboe designed and built it himself, which no one really talks about, despite the fact that it's a beautiful bar. The drop ceiling (made out of amazing wood, because it's Scandinavian) of the former space was repurposed as the bar itself. He sands down and restains the floors black every Easter simply because it's the right thing to do to make the shop look perfect. The fact that the business has just never had to make a qualitative sacrifice is a product of the fact that he has deep-pocket investors who believe in him (and his marketing value) and also that Tim as a person is so well reflected in the shop. He constantly says, 'Well, it's my name on the shop, so I'm accountable if it's not excellent.' We'll probably never see another shop like it, and as he will tell you himself, there will never be another shop (in Norway, at least)."—Ben Kaminsky

"I had my mind reset by Tim Varney at Tim Wendelboe in 2010 when I clicked from ristretto to true espresso—being able to enjoy a properly balanced extraction rather than an intense salty double that was so in vogue in Australia. That absolutely reinvigorated my ability to drink espresso coffee again."—Emily Oak

"I find Tim's light roasts to be among the best in the world, especially when brewed with Oslo water."
—Sebastian Sztabzyb

"The world's best coffee roaster/buyer is Tim Wendelboe."
—Tim Varney

JAVA

Ullevålsveien 47
St. Hanshaugen
Oslo 171
Norway
+47 22460800
www.javaoslo.no

Opening hours..................................Mon–Fri from 7 am,
Sat from 8 am, Sun from 9 am
Credit cards..........................Visa, MasterCard, and Amex
Style...Coffee bar

"I can't put my finger on exactly what it is about Java that I like so much. Aside from the delicious coffee from Kaffa roastery and a bar design that has aged incredibly well considering how long Java has been around, I find it a very enjoyable place to just have a coffee. Working in the specialty coffee industry often turns every coffee shop experience into work (it's too easy to find yourself approaching having a coffee somewhere as research or quality control). But for some reason I always feel like I can just have a great coffee at Java and not need to worry about anything else."—David Nigel Flynn

"Beautiful design, with beautiful coffees."—Scott Lucey

MOCCA

Niels Juels Gate 70B
Uranienborg
Oslo 0259
Norway
+47 22555518
www.moccaoslo.no

Opening hours..................................Mon–Fri from 7 am,
Sat from 9 am, Sun from 10 am
Credit cards..........................Visa, MasterCard, and Amex
Style...Coffee bar

"The best filter coffee I've had was at Mocca, a Kenyan Tegu from Kaffa brewed on a V60."—Nicolas Clerc

"ONE OF THOSE GREAT AND RARE PLACES WHERE YOUR COFFEE IS GENERALLY MADE BY THE CAFE OWNER—ADD TO THAT SKILL, CRAFT, CARE, AND WHAT RESULTS IS A CONSISTENTLY EXCELLENT CUP."

JON SHARP P.103

UK & REPUBLIC OF IRELAND

"IT WAS THE MOST ELEGANT ESPRESSO I'VE EVER HAD. SOFT, BALANCED, AND FRUITY WITHOUT ANY OF THE FUNK."

MIKE YUNG P.102

"THEY KNOCK IT OUT OF THE PARK ALL THE TIME IN A VERY UNDERDEVELOPED MARKET. THEY LEAD EASILY."

STEPHEN LEIGHTON P.102

"THEY HAVE A UNIQUE APPROACH TO SERVICE, COMMUNICATION, AND MENU STRUCTURE, BREWING TASTY COFFEE OUTSIDE OF THE NORMAL PARAMETERS THAT OUR INDUSTRY USES AND KILLING IT."

JOHN GORDON P.102

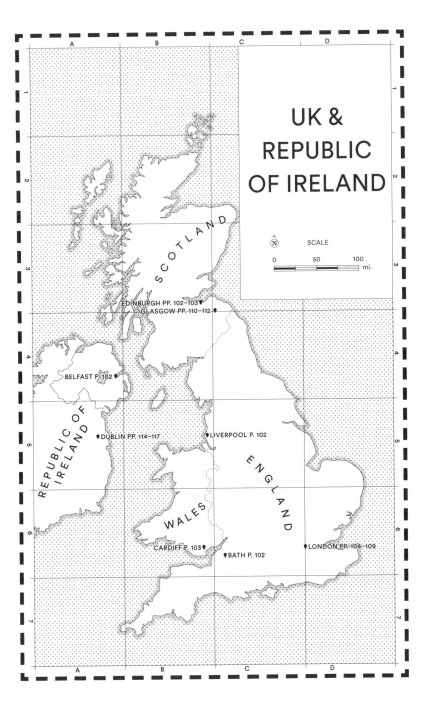

UK &
REPUBLIC
OF IRELAND

N̂   SCALE

0   50   100
                    mi.

SCOTLAND

EDINBURGH PP. 102–103
GLASGOW PP. 110–112

BELFAST P. 102

REPUBLIC OF IRELAND

DUBLIN PP. 114–117

LIVERPOOL P. 102

ENGLAND

WALES

CARDIFF P. 103

BATH P. 102

LONDON PP. 104–109

COLONNA & SMALLS

6 Chapel Row
Bath BA 1HN
England
+44 7766808067
www.colonnaandsmalls.co.uk

Opening hours...................................Mon–Fri from 8 am,
Sat from 8 am, Sun from 10 am
Credit cards...Visa and MasterCard
Style..Coffee bar

"They have a unique approach to service, communication, and menu structure, brewing tasty coffee outside of the normal parameters that our industry uses and killing it. It's a huge accomplishment for Maxwell, Leslie, and their staff, and they have created a comfortable and humble, yet super-educational environment for the specialty coffee industry."—John Gordon

"Best espresso."—Candice Madison

"Three-time UK barista champion Maxwell Colonna-Dashwood prepared an espresso lungo for me at Colonna & Smalls using a natural processed Limoncello Red Pacamara from Nicaragua, roasted by Has Bean. It was the most elegant espresso I've ever had. Soft, balanced, and fruity without any of the funk. As baristas, we usually have strong feelings about natural coffees as single-origin espresso (or even filter for that matter), but this coffee, prepared the way it had been, would win over any person for natural coffee."
—Mike Yung

BOLD STREET

89 Bold Street
Ropewalks
Liverpool L1 4HF
England
+44 1517070760
www.boldstreetcoffee.co.uk

Opening hours...................................Mon–Fri from 7:30 am,
Sat from 8 am, Sun from 9:30 am
Credit cards...Visa and MasterCard
Style...Coffee and breakfast

"They knock it out of the park all the time in a very underdeveloped market. They lead easily."
—Stephen Leighton

London, see pages 104–109

HARRIS AND HOOLE

Stansted Airport
Stansted CM24 1QW
England
www.harrisandhoole.co.uk

Opening hours...................................Daily from 3:30 am
Credit cards.........................Visa, MasterCard, and Amex
Style..Coffee bar

ESTABLISHED COFFEE

54 Hill Street
Cathedral Quarter
Belfast BT1 2LB
Northern Ireland
+44 2890319416
www.established.coffee

Opening hours...................................Mon–Fri from 7 am,
Sat from 8 am, Sun from 9 am
Credit cards.........................Visa, MasterCard, and Amex
Style...Coffee and food

ARTISAN COFFEE

57 Broughton Street
New Town
Edinburgh EH1 3RJ
Scotland
+44 7858884756
www.artisanroast.co.uk

Opening hours...................................Mon–Fri from 8 am,
Sat–Sun from 9 am
Credit cards..Cash only
Style...Coffee and food

"Opened by Kiwi and Chilean business partners Mike and Gustavo in 2005, this cafe was one of the first wave of great coffee shops that can now be found across Edinburgh. Originally roasting and serving only in this tiny shop, operations now extend to a warehouse and multiple cafes."
—Jon Sharp

FORTITUDE COFFEE
3C York Place
New Town
Edinburgh EH1 3EB
Scotland
+44 1315573063
www.fortitudecoffee.com

Opening hours.....................................Mon–Fri from 8 am,
                              Sat from 10 am, Sun from 11 am
Credit cards............................Visa, MasterCard, and Amex
Style...Coffee bar

"A relatively new small coffee bar run by partners (in both
senses) Matt and Helen. One of those great and rare places
where your coffee is generally made by the cafe owner—
add to that skill, craft, care, and what results is a
consistently excellent cup. Great choice of espresso and
filter coffees from selected roasters."—Jon Sharp

Glasgow, see pages 110–112

THE PLAN
28-29 Morgan Arcade
Cardiff CF10 1AF
Wales
+44 2920398764
www.theplancafe.co.uk

Opening hours.................................Mon–Sat from 8:30 am,
                                          Sun from 10 am
Credit cards............................Visa, MasterCard, and Amex
Style...Coffee and food

"The Plan was a pioneer in the area. The barista, Trevor, has
a blog and has been a force for good since before there were
sufficient people to care."—James Hoffmann

Dublin, see pages 114–117

"THE BEST FILTER COFFEE I EVER HAD WAS AT PRUFROCK IN LONDON ON LEATHER LANE—A FLIGHT OF SQUARE MILE COFFEES ALL PREPARED DIFFERENTLY."

ANTHONY BENDA P.107

"IT'S A TINY CORRIDOR OF A SPACE, BUT THE LIGHTISH FOOTFALL MAKES FOR A COZY RATHER THAN A CRAMPED EXPERIENCE."

CANDICE MADISON P.108

LONDON

"WHEN I THINK ABOUT A FAVORITE PLACE, IT STARTS TO HAVE AS MUCH TO DO WITH THE COFFEE AS THE PLACE ITSELF AND THE EXPERIENCE IT ENCOMPASSES."

JOANNE BERRY P.109

"THE BEST ESPRESSO I'VE EVER HAD WAS AT PRUFROCK."

RYAN FISHER P.107

"CONSISTENCY AND TOP QUALITY IN A RESIDENTIAL PART OF LONDON."

DEREK LAMBERTON P.106

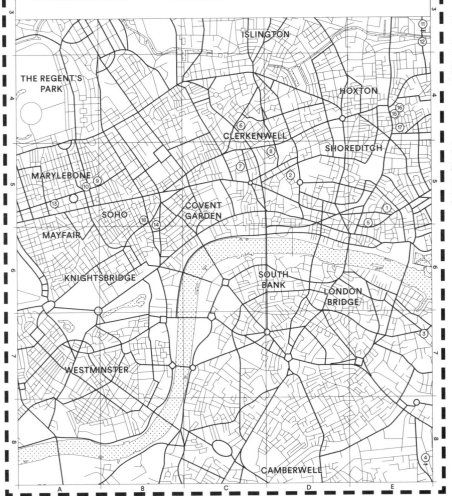

LONDON

SCALE

N̂

0   465   930   1405
yd.

1. ASSOCIATION COFFEE (P. 106)
2. DOSE ESPRESSO (P. 106)
3. CRAFT (P. 106)
4. BROWNS OF BROCKLEY (P. 106)
5. CURATOR'S COFFEE STUDIO (P. 106)
6. CARAVAN ROASTERS (P. 106)

7. PRUFROCK COFFEE (P. 107)
8. WORKSHOP (P. 107)
9. KAFFEINE (P. 107)
10. WORKSHOP (FITZROVIA) (P. 108)
11. 46B ESPRESSO HUT (P. 108)
12. CLIMPSON & SONS (P. 108)

13. WORKSHOP (MARYLEBONE) (P. 108)
14. TIMBERYARD UK (SEVEN DIALS) (P. 108)
15. BULLDOG EDITION (P. 109)
16. LEILA'S SHOP (P. 109)
17. LYLE'S (P. 109)
18. BAR TERMINI (P. 109)

ASSOCIATION COFFEE

10–12 Creechurch Lane
Aldgate
London EC3A 5AY
England
+44 2078231155
www.associationcoffee.com

Opening hours...................................Mon–Fri from 7:30 am
Credit cards...Visa and MasterCard
Style...Coffee and food

"I really like the muted aesthetic of Association, to say nothing of the excellent service and tasty coffees I experienced there."—Cory Andreen

DOSE ESPRESSO

70 Long Lane
Barbican
London EC1A 9EJ
England
+44 2076000382
www.dose-espresso.com

Opening hours..Mon–Fri from 7 am
Credit cards...Visa and MasterCard
Style...Coffee and food

CRAFT

41 Maltby Street
Bermondsey
London SE1 3PA
England
+44 2086167676
www.craft-coffee.co.uk

Opening hours....................Sat from 9 am, Sun from 11 am
Credit cards..Cash only
Style..Mobile cart

BROWNS OF BROCKLEY

5 Coulgate Street
Brockley
London SE4 2RW
England
+44 2086920722
www.brownsofbrockley.com

Opening hours................................Mon–Fri from 7:30 am,
Sat–Sun from 9 am
Credit cards...Visa and MasterCard
Style...Coffee and food

"Consistency and top quality in a residential part of London."—Derek Lamberton

CURATOR'S COFFEE STUDIO

9A Cullum Street
City of London
London EC3M 7JJ
England
+44 2072834642
www.curatorscoffee.com

Opening hours...............................Mon–Fri from 7:30 am
Credit cards..........................Visa, MasterCard, and Amex
Style...Coffee and food

"Best filter coffee." —Derek Lamberton

CARAVAN ROASTERS

11–13 Exmouth Market
Clerkenwell
London EC1R 4QD
England
+44 2071017663
www.caravanonexmouth.co.uk

Opening hours.......................................Mon–Fri from 8 am,
Sat–Sun from 10 am
Credit cards...........................Visa, MasterCard, and Amex
Style...Restaurant

"High marks for food and coffee pairings go to Caravan Roasters in London. Their Kings Cross store is one of my favorite haunts on my way home or into London. Evenings are as delicious as brunch."—Stephen Leighton

PRUFROCK COFFEE

23–25 Leather Lane
Clerkenwell
London EC1N 7TE
England
+44 2072420467
www.prufrockcoffee.com

Opening hours..................................Mon–Fri from 8 am,
Sat–Sun from 10 am
Credit cards..Visa and MasterCard
Style..Coffee and food

"The best filter coffee I ever had was at Prufrock in London on Leather Lane—a flight of Square Mile coffees all prepared differently. It was the first time I really understood the advantages of a brew bar to an uninitiated coffee drinker. It opened my eyes to the possibilities of being able to engage with a customer about the intricacies of brewing, without the condescension or pompousness that is often so hard to avoid."—Anthony Benda

"The best espresso I've ever had was at Prufrock."
—Ryan Fisher

"One of the best espressos I've had was from Prufrock Coffee in London—Square Mile's blend, pulled off a Victoria Arduino lever machine."—Sebastian Sztabzyb

WORKSHOP

27 Clerkenwell Road
Clerkenwell
London EC1M 5RN
England
+44 2072535754
www.workshopcoffee.com

Opening hours................................Mon–Sat from 7:30 am,
Sun from 8 am
Credit cards...........................Visa, MasterCard, and Amex
Style..Coffee and food

"Workshop on Clerkenwell Road is consistently among my favorites for best espresso."—Joanne Berry

"London's Workshop Coffee could be a textbook on how to marry a food-and-coffee program. Breakfast at Workshop was a highlight of a recent trip to London. It started with a slow-braised pork shank and poached egg over caramelized sweet potato served with an AeroPress of a deeply fruit-forward Kenyan coffee, and it finished with a perfect shot of Rwandan espresso. It was a perfect balance of food and coffee, executed at the highest levels."—Anthony Rue

"Workshop Coffee has built a really wonderful family of coffee bars that deliver excellent coffee and food. The spaces are well curated and comfortable. When I think of what kind of coffee business I might want to open someday, Workshop comes to mind."—Ryan Willbur

KAFFEINE

66 Titchfield Street
Fitzrovia
London NW8 7LD
England
+44 2075806755
www.kaffeine.co.uk

Opening hours................................Mon–Fri from 7:30 am,
Sat from 9 am, Sun from 9:30 am
Credit cards...........................Visa, MasterCard, and Amex
Style..Coffee and food

"Best espresso has to go to Kaffeine in London, just nailed perfectly. This is the best shot of Red Brick from Square Mile I have ever had."—Stephen Leighton

WORKSHOP (FITZROVIA)

80A Mortimer Street
Fitzrovia
London W1W 7FE
England
+44 2072535754
www.workshopcoffee.com

Opening hours................................Mon–Fri from 7 am,
Sat–Sun from 9 am
Credit cards............................Visa, MasterCard, and Amex
Style..Coffee bar

"Intimate, nicely done, easy to interact with baristas."
—Kalle Freese

46B ESPRESSO HUT

46B Brooksby's Walk
Homerton
London E9 6DA
England
+44 7702063172
www.46b-espressohut.co.uk

Opening hours................................Mon–Fri from 7 am,
Sat from 9 am, Sun from 10 am
Credit cards............................Visa, MasterCard, and Amex
Style...Coffee and food

"It's a tiny corridor of a space, but the lightish footfall makes
for a cozy rather than a cramped experience. When I first
visited they had a three-piece jazz band playing on the tiny
platform above the prep area. It was just lovely."
—Candice Madison

CLIMPSON & SONS

67 Broadway Market
London Fields
London E8 4PH
England
+44 2072547199
www.climpsonandsons.com

Opening hours................................Mon–Fri from 7:30 am,
Sat from 8:30 am, Sun from 9 am
Credit cards....................................Visa and MasterCard
Style...Coffee and food

"The music, the atmosphere, and the vibes of the staff make
me feel like I'm at home in London. Of course they
make an excellent coffee!"—Santiago Rigoni

WORKSHOP (MARYLEBONE)

1 Barrett Street
Marylebone
London W1U 1AX
England
+44 2072535754
www.workshopcoffee.com

Opening hours................................Mon–Fri from 7 am,
Sat–Sun from 9 am
Credit cards............................Visa, MasterCard, and Amex
Style...Coffee and food

"My most memorable espresso shot was at Workshop
Coffee in London at their Marylebone location. It was a
Costa Rican, which tasted like biting into an unsweetened
dried cherry, mouthfeel and all. It was tart but syrupy,
just beautiful."—Seanna Forey

TIMBERYARD UK (SEVEN DIALS)

7 Upper St. Martin's Lane
Seven Dials
London WC2H 9DL
England
www.tyuk.com

Opening hours................................Mon–Fri from 8 am,
Sat–Sun from 10 am
Credit cards....................................Visa and MasterCard
Style...........................Coffee and food in a working space

"Timberyard is a rare third-wave cafe that cares about
customer service and comfort and also happens to brew
some of the most consistently good drip coffee in London."
—Scott Rao

BULLDOG EDITION
(Ace Hotel)
100 Shoreditch High Street
Shoreditch
London E1 6JQ
England
+44 2076138900
www.acehotel.com/london

Opening hours..Daily from 6:30 am
Credit cards............................Visa, MasterCard, and Amex
Style..Coffee bar

"When I think about a favorite place, it starts to have as much to do with the coffee as the place itself and the experience it encompasses. Right now I would have to say Bulldog Edition in London. I like how I can sit and enjoy the coffee and watch people coming and going or read the paper. It's a moment to myself."—Joanne Berry

LEILA'S SHOP
15–17 Calvert Avenue
Shoreditch
London E2 7JP
England
+44 2077299789

Opening hours....................................Wed–Sun from 10 am
Credit cards...Visa and MasterCard
Style...Coffee and grocery shop

"I've only ever wanted coffee to be as good as everything else in a space. There are so many places with great cakes, great pastries, great sandwiches, and just miserably poor coffee. When I lived in East London, I used to love the short walk to Leila's just off Arnold Circus. It's a general store of sorts, with very few tables and a setup that feels like you're sitting in the pantry of someone's country kitchen. Incredible custard tarts, hot skillets of eggs and ham, baskets of warm toast wrapped in a blanket, solid coffee, and pleasant staff. It wasn't a spot for the cerebral coffee experience—it's a spot where everything's solid, which isn't too common."—Stephen Morrissey

LYLE'S
Tea Building, 56 Shoreditch High Street
Shoreditch
London E1 6JJ
England
+44 2030115911
www.lyleslondon.com

Opening hours..Mon–Fri from 8 am,
Sat from 6 pm
Credit cards............................Visa, MasterCard, and Amex
Style...Restaurant

"The only way to survive London's long gray winters is with an occasional slice of Lyle's warm ginger loaf with a generous pad of butter melting across it. Pair with a frothy flat white or a fruity filter and you won't be stuck wondering why on earth you came to this country or why you've never left."—Derek Lamberton

If London's coffee scene didn't seem quite fancy enough for you already, enter Lyle's, a fine-dining establishment with one of the city's most esteemed coffee programs in a genteel, sunny dining room on Shoreditch High Street. Whether you come for a meal or just coffee and cake, your inner aficionado will feel right at home any time of day.

BAR TERMINI
7 Old Compton Street
Soho
London W1D 5JE
England
+44 7860945018
www.bar-termini.com

Opening hours....................................Mon–Sat from 10 am,
Sun from 11 am
Credit cards............................Visa, MasterCard, and Amex
Style.............................Coffee, cocktails, and charcuterie

"I love the simplicity of the biscotti served at Bar Termini in the heart of Soho. It is a classic recipe created by nuns in sixteenth-century Novara, Italy. I enjoy the way the malliard flavors of the roast mix with the baked biscuit as I suck it dry."—Gwilym Davies

"VERY HIP ARTS COLLECTIVE/ FURNITURE AND DESIGN SHOP WITH A COFFEE BAR INSIDE."

JORDAN MICHELMAN P.112

"COOL LOCAL ROASTER WITH GLOBAL INFLUENCES... AN IMPORTANT PART OF THE GLASGOW COFFEE SCENE."

JORDAN MICHELMAN P.112

GLASGOW

"TINY, LASER-FOCUSED COFFEE BAR IN THE GLASGOW CENTRAL BUSINESS DISTRICT... WHEN YOU TALK TO GLASWEGIAN COFFEE PROS THIS IS THE SPOT THEY RECOMMEND AND GO TO ON THEIR DAYS OFF."

JORDAN MICHELMAN P.112

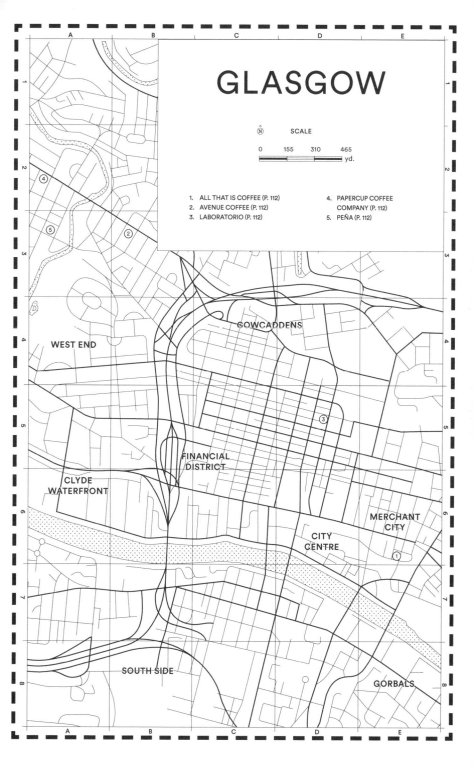

GLASGOW

N

SCALE

0   155   310   465
                              yd.

1. ALL THAT IS COFFEE (P. 112)
2. AVENUE COFFEE (P. 112)
3. LABORATORIO (P. 112)

4. PAPERCUP COFFEE
   COMPANY (P. 112)
5. PEÑA (P. 112)

GOWCADDENS

WEST END

FINANCIAL
DISTRICT

CLYDE
WATERFRONT

MERCHANT
CITY

CITY
CENTRE

SOUTH SIDE

GORBALS

ALL THAT IS COFFEE

60 Osbourne Street
Glasgow G1 5QH
Scotland
+44 1412714777

Opening hours..Mon–Fri from 9 am
Credit cards..Visa and MasterCard
Style...Coffee bar

"Very hip arts collective/furniture and design shop with
a coffee bar inside."—Jordan Michelman

AVENUE COFFEE

321 Great Western Road
Glasgow G4 9HR
Scotland
+44 1413391334
www.avenue.coffee

Opening hours................................Mon–Fri from 9:30 am,
Sat–Sun from 9 am
Credit cards............................Visa, MasterCard, and Amex
Style...Coffee and food

"Cool local roaster with global influences (Scandinavia,
Canada, etc.)—an important part of the Glasgow coffee
scene. Their Great Western Road location is just down the
street from Papercup, and it's a nice walk between the two."
—Jordan Michelman

LABORATORIO

93 West Nile Street
Glasgow G2 1RW
Scotland
+44 1413531111
www.laboratorioespresso.com

Opening hours................................Mon–Fri from 7:30 am,
Sat from 9 am, Sun from 11 am
Credit cards..Visa and MasterCard
Style...Coffee bar

"Tiny, laser-focused coffee bar in the Glasgow Central
Business District. On our visit they served Coffee Collective
and Has Bean. When you talk to Glaswegian coffee pros this
is the spot they recommend and go to on their days off."
—Jordan Michelman

PAPERCUP COFFEE COMPANY

603 Great Western Road
Glasgow G12 8HX
Scotland
+44 7719454376
www.papercupcoffeecompany.bigcartel.com

Opening hours................................Mon–Fri from 8:30 am,
Sat–Sun from 9 am
Credit cards...Cash only
Style...Coffee and food

"A favorite on our trip to Glasgow last year, lots of hand-built
charm paired with tasty coffee and good food. They roast
in-house. It reminded us of cafes in the Pacific Northwest
that we grew up with, but with much, much better coffee."
—Jordan Michelman

PEÑA

5 Elton Lane
Glasgow G12 8NX
Scotland
www.penaglasgow.co.uk

Opening hours................................Mon–Sat from 8:30 am
Credit cards...Cash only
Style...Coffee and food

"A charming hideaway. A youthful, hip, international coffee
bar just off Great Western, near the university. Design-wise
it could be in Echo Park if it weren't so rainy outside. Good
food. On our visit they served Workshop from London and
the Barn from Berlin."—Jordan Michelman

> **"ONE OF MY FAVORITE CAFES IN DUBLIN AND THE FIRST PLACE I USUALLY VISIT WHEN HOME."**
>
> BRIAN Ó CAOIMH P.117

DUBLIN

> **"THE INTERIOR ARCHITECTURE, COFFEE PREPARATION, AND SERVICE BESTOW A TOUCH OF UNOSTENTATIOUS LUXURY WHILE CENTERING THE EXPERIENCE AROUND THE CUSTOMER."**
>
> PAUL STACK P.116

> **"SQUARE MILE PROVIDES STAPLES, BUT MOST WEEKS THEY HAVE A RANGE OF COFFEES FROM ROASTERS ALL OVER EUROPE AND FURTHER AFIELD."**
>
> COLIN HARMON P.116

DUBLIN

N   SCALE

0   210   420   630
                        yd.

1. PROPER ORDER (P. 116)
2. 3FE (P. 116)
3. FUMBALLY CAFE (P. 116)
4. COFFEEANGEL (SAS) (P. 116)

5. KAPH (P. 117)
6. ROASTED BROWN
    COFFEE COMPANY (P. 117)
7. TAMP AND STITCH (P. 117)

8. VICE (INSIDE WIGWAM) (P. 117)
9. LOVE SUPREME (P. 117)

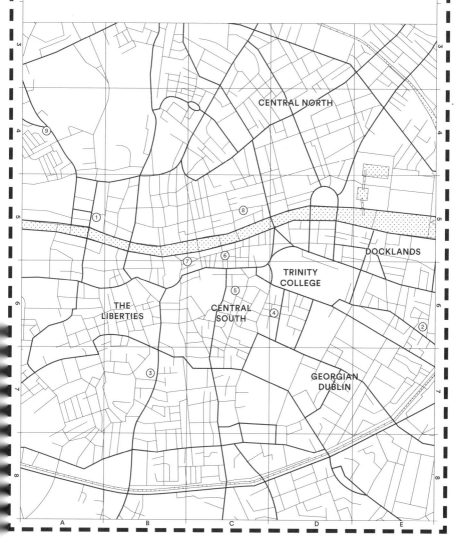

CENTRAL NORTH

DOCKLANDS

TRINITY
COLLEGE

THE
LIBERTIES

CENTRAL
SOUTH

GEORGIAN
DUBLIN

PROPER ORDER
7 Haymarket
Arran Quay
Dublin
Republic of Ireland
www.properordercoffeeco.com

Opening hours...................................Mon–Fri from 7 am,
Sat–Sun from 10 am
Credit cards.........................Visa, MasterCard, and Amex
Style..Coffee bar

"Run by Niall Wynn (formerly of Coffeeangel) and Dave Regan (formerly of Vice, Prufrock, 3fe), Proper Order opened in 2016 in a beautiful old building in an old but up-and-coming part of Dublin. Square Mile provides staples, but most weeks they have a range of coffees from roasters all over Europe and further afield. Dave and Niall are two of the best baristas in the city and have a range of awards and achievements between them."—Colin Harmon

3FE
32 Grand Canal Street Lower
Grand Canal Dock
Dublin
Republic of Ireland
+353 16619329
www.www.3fe.com

Opening hours.................................Mon–Fri from 7:30 am,
Sat–Sun from 9 am
Credit cards...Visa and MasterCard
Style...Coffee and food

"When I think of Dublin and coffee, I actually think of the Twisted Pepper nightclub on Middle Abbey Street. The now world-famous 3fe started here as a small coffee corner when Colin Harmon was given the opportunity to use the space during the daytime. A friend had told me about Harmon, this barista champion of Ireland, who was doing the best coffee in Dublin, and so I wandered down to see what was really going on there. My first experience was very confusing. I thought something had been put in my espresso to flavor it, that some kind of foul play was afoot. And so I returned whenever I was in Dublin, trying to get my head around what was going on in the cup. Later, when Colin moved 3fe to Grand Canal Street Lower and started running barista classes, I quickly signed up. I wanted to know the secrets." —Brian Ó Caoimh

FUMBALLY CAFE
Fumbally Lane
Merchants Quay
Dublin
Republic of Ireland
+353 15298732
www.thefumbally.ie

Opening hours...Tue–Fri from 8 am,
Sat from 10 am
Credit cards...Visa and MasterCard
Style...Cafe and restaurant

"The space is huge and used to be some kind of industrial location. It is very raw, with secondhand tables and chairs. OMG, really good eggs and such great vegetables. They also sell vegetables and some organic wine, so the place is full of different corners where you can sit and enjoy either coffee brewed in Chemex or espresso. Since the space is so big and the ceilings so high, there are many interesting paintings, posters, and kitschy pictures on the walls."
—Sonja Björk Grant

COFFEEANGEL (SAS)
16 South Anne Street
Dublin D02 VF29
Republic of Ireland
+353 19696001
www.coffeeangel.com

Opening hours.................................Mon–Fri from 7:30 am,
Sat from 9 am, Sun from 10 am
Credit cards...Visa and MasterCard
Style...Coffee and food

"While being quietly insistent on excellent coffee, Coffeeangel manages to serve you efficiently while enabling that most precious of sensations—some quality me time. The interior architecture, coffee preparation, and service bestow a touch of unostentatious luxury while centering the experience around the customer, not the excellent beverage."—Paul Stack

KAPH

31 Drury Street
Dublin
Republic of Ireland
+353 16139030
www.kaph.ie

Opening hours............................Mon–Sat from 8 am,
Sun from noon
Credit cards..Visa and MasterCard
Style...Coffee bar

"Chris Keegan's Kaph is located on Drury Street in the heart
of Dublin's cultural quarter and close to Grafton Street, the
main shopping district. Kaph is mostly take-away oriented and
has a wonderful pace and atmosphere that has made it an
institution in the city despite its young age." —Colin Harmon

ROASTED BROWN COFFEE COMPANY

Filmbase, Level 1, 2 Curved Street, Temple Bar
Dublin
Republic of Ireland
www.roastedbrown.com

Opening hours................................Mon–Fri from 10:30 am,
Sat from 11 am
Credit cards.........................Visa, MasterCard, and Amex
Style...Roastery cafe

"Roasting out of Delany, County Wicklow, Fergus Brown's
Temple Bar cafe is a welcome retreat. Ferg has built a
reputation over the years as an early driver of specialty
coffee in Ireland and is building a strong wholesale presence
throughout the country."
—Colin Harmon

TAMP AND STITCH

Unit 3 Scarlet Row, Essex Street West, Temple Bar
Dublin
Republic of Ireland
+353 15154705
www.facebook.com/TampandStitch

Opening hours.....................................Mon–Fri from 10 am,
Sat from 11 am, Sun from 1 pm
Credit cards...Visa and MasterCard
Style...Coffee and clothing

"An interesting development internationally where an
excellent coffee is provided to add to the customer's core
experience, be it buying clothes or browsing housewares.
When offered in this environment, the coffee program is a
value-add to the customer experience and not a strict profit
center, which almost enables a better coffee." —Paul Stack

VICE (INSIDE WIGWAM)

54 Middle Abbey Street
Dublin
Republic of Ireland
www.vicecoffeeinc.com

Opening hours...Daily from 11 am
Credit cards..Cash only
Style..Coffee and food

"Definitely one of my favorite cafes in Dublin and the first
place I usually visit when home. It really gets you thinking
of all the wasted daytime space around the city and how
people can enjoy a space in very different ways at different
times of the day. I am probably not the only one who has
been there for an afternoon espresso only to find themselves
back again at midnight with a stronger drink in their hand."
—Brian Ó Caoimh

LOVE SUPREME

57 Manor Street
Stoneybatter
Dublin
Republic of Ireland
www.lovesupreme.ie

Opening hours..Mon–Fri from 10 am
Credit cards...Visa and MasterCard
Style..Coffee and food

"A boutique cafe in what is one of Dublin's trendiest districts,
Love Supreme have built an incredible reputation over the
years with coffees roasted by Roasted Brown Coffee
Company. Head barista Craig Andrew keeps everything
rolling along and the cafe is conveniently located to
L. Mulligan Grocer, probably the best craft beer and
whiskey bar in the city."—Colin Harmon

"THIS CAFE AND ROASTER SEEMS TO BE LEADING ROTTERDAM'S NEW-WAVE COFFEE SCENE AND DOING SO WITHOUT COMPROMISING ITS QUALITY STANDARDS."

KARINA HOF P.120

BELGIUM & THE NETHERLANDS

"THIS IS A FAMILY COMPANY: THE FATHER HAS BEEN ROASTING FOR THIRTY YEARS, AND HIS TWO SONS AND MOTHER WORK THERE."

SONJA BJÖRK GRANT P.120

"IT IS A LITTLE GUEST HOUSE RUN BY A GUY CALLED SIMON WHO SERVES GREAT COFFEE." JAMES HOFFMANN P.120

BELGIUM
& THE
NETHERLANDS
N
SCALE
0
250
500
mi.
A
B
C
D
1
2
3
4
5
6
7
AMSTERDAM PP. 122–125
THE NETHERLANDS
ROTTERDAM P. 120
GHENT P. 120
KORTRIJK P. 120
MAASTRICHT P. 120
BELGIUM

SIMON SAYS

Sluizeken 8
Ghent 9000
Belgium
+32 92330343
www.simon-says.be

Opening hours................................Tue–Fri from 9 am,
Sat–Sun from 10 am
Credit cards..Visa and MasterCard
Style...Coffee and food

"It is a little guest house run by a guy called Simon who serves great coffee."—James Hoffmann

VIVA SARA KAFFÉE

Grote Markt 33
Kortrijk 8500
Belgium
+32 56217270
www.vivasara.be

Opening hours....................................Mon–Fri from 8 am,
Sat from 9 am
Credit cards..Visa and MasterCard
Style...Full service, with food

"This place is amazing. It is seven hundred square meters and a mix of the old-fashioned European cafes, but with a brew bar where they serve syphon, V60, and Chemex. And it has one of the best kitchens I have seen in a cafe. Because the town is very small, this is the only real cafe, so that is why they focus not only on coffee. This is a family company: the father has been roasting for thirty years, and his two sons and mother work there. The sons are former Belgium champions. They are buying good coffees, sometimes Cup of Excellence. This is a good business but also good quality."
—Sonja Björk Grant

Amsterdam, see pages 122–125

MAISON BLANCHE DAEL

Wolfstraat 28
Centre
Maastricht 6211 GN
The Netherlands
+31 433213475
www.blanchedael.nl

Opening hours..Mon from 1pm,
Tue–Fri from 9:30am,
Sat from 9:30 am, Sun from noon
Credit cards..........................Visa, MasterCard, and Amex
Style...Coffee and tea

MAN MET BRIL KOFFIE

Vijverhofstraat 70
Agniesebuurt
Rotterdam 3032SN
The Netherlands
www.manmetbrilkoffie.nl

Opening hours....................................Mon–Fri from 8 am,
Sat–Sun from 9 am
Credit cards...........Visa, MasterCard, and Amex; no cash
Style...Roastery cafe

"This cafe and roaster seems to be leading Rotterdam's new-wave coffee scene and is doing so without compromising its quality standards. They have fully embraced the bean-to-brew process. You can see it in owner Paul Sharo's priority on firsthand sourcing, his employment of really gifted roaster Jelle van Rossum, and the commitment to serve Rotterdam first and foremost. Man Met Bril seems really dedicated to helping uplift the community. Sharo is especially enjoyable to talk with because he's self-aware enough to know that not everybody wants to nerd out on coffee talk!"—Karina Hof

> "THE SCANDINAVIAN EMBASSY MAKES THE MOST INNOVATIVE FOOD PAIRING."
>
> KLAUS THOMSEN P.124

> "TO SAY THAT ANYTHING HAS TAKEN A SCENE BY STORM OFTEN SOUNDS HYPERBOLIC, BUT WHITE LABEL COFFEE HAS DONE JUST THAT."
>
> KARINA HOF P.125

AMSTERDAM

> "THE BEST FILTER COFFEE I'VE HAD WAS AT THE SCANDINAVIAN EMBASSY."
>
> ZACHARY CARLSEN P.124

> "THE LAST TIME I WAS HERE THEY SERVED US THIS OYSTER DISH CONSISTING OF THREE OYSTERS AND A SHOT OF ESPRESSO."
>
> JORDAN MICHELMAN P.124

A B C D E

WESTERPARK

JORDAAN
②

DE BAARSJES

①
CENTRUM

④

OUD WEST

OUD ZUID

③

AMSTERDAM

N̂ SCALE

0   500 1000 1500
├──┼──┼──┼──┤ yd.

1. KOKO COFFEE & DESIGN (P. 124)   3. SCANDINAVIAN EMBASSY (P. 124)
2. HEADFIRST COFFEE ROASTERS (P. 124)   4. WHITE LABEL COFFEE (P. 125)

KOKO COFFEE & DESIGN

Oudezijds Achterburgwal 145
Burgwallen Oude Zijde
Amsterdam 1012 DG
The Netherlands
+31 206264208
www.ilovekoko.com

Opening hours	Mon from 10 am, Tue–Fri from 9 am, Sat from 10 am, Sun from noon
Credit cards	Visa and MasterCard
Style	Coffee and fashion

"Koko is a shotgun cafe down a side street in Amsterdam's rightly infamous red-light district, and you would be hard pressed to find a cafe with more dramatic difference between the scene outside and the scene inside. Many clothing boutiques in Europe are serving something approximating espresso, but this may be the best hybrid fashion and coffee bar in the world, because they take both parts equally seriously. The coffee is meticulously prepared, sourced from Belgium's Caffenation, and prepared by some of Amsterdam's best baristas; the fashion comes from Dutch and Nordic brands like Wood Wood, Stutterheim Raincoats, and Monique Poolmans. A shop like this in the red-light district of Amsterdam isn't just unexpected; it's subversive." —Jordan Michelman

HEADFIRST COFFEE ROASTERS

Westerstraat 150
De Jordaan
Amsterdam
North Holland 1015 MP
The Netherlands
www.headfirstcoffeeroasters.com

Opening hours	Mon–Fri from 8 am, Sat–Sun from 9 am
Credit cards	Visa and MasterCard
Style	Roastery cafe

"Best filter coffee." —Anna Brones

SCANDINAVIAN EMBASSY

Sarphatipark 34
Oude Pijp
Amsterdam 1072 PB
The Netherlands
+31 619518199
www.scandinavianembassy.nl

Opening hours	Mon–Fri from 7:30 am, Sat–Sun from 9 am
Credit cards	Cash or debit card only
Style	Full service, with food

"The best filter coffee I've had was at the Scandinavian Embassy. Light-roast coffee, to me, has a one-in-ten chance of turning out delicious. Maybe the odds are a little higher and I'm just cynical, but I've had enough sour coffee in my life to feel justified in saying so."—Zachary Carlsen

"The last time I was here they served us this oyster dish consisting of three oysters and a shot of espresso. You consume the dish in stages: sip of espresso, slurp the first oyster; take another sip of espresso, slurp the second oyster. Then one more big sip of espresso, and for the last oyster, the chef has topped it with clarified butter infused with cascara—heated tableside using a spoon and blowtorch. You slurp that last buttery, sweet, ridiculous oyster, and then finish the espresso shot, getting all the sweetness in the last sip. It is an absolutely outstanding, mind-blowing, best-ever coffee pairing dish." —Jordan Michelman

"The Scandinavian Embassy makes the most innovative food pairing."—Klaus Thomsen

WHITE LABEL COFFEE

Jan Evertsenstraat 136
Van Galenbuurt
Amsterdam 1056 EK
The Netherlands
+31 207371359
www.whitelabelcoffee.nl

Opening hours	Mon–Fri from 8 am, Sat–Sun from 9 am
Credit cards	Visa and MasterCard
Style	Coffee bar

"To say that anything has taken a scene by storm often sounds hyperbolic, but White Label Coffee has done just that. Co-founders Elmer Oomkens and Francesco Grassotti make excellent coffee—and employ baristas who do so as well—and have become one of the country's leading indie roasters. Their coffee is served in cafes and restaurants across Amsterdam, and Elmer is one of the kindest coffee professionals I've encountered in these parts. He's always happy to share information and help fellow baristas who are starting out. The cafe itself is pleasant to be in, simply designed with raw industrial touches that are just as functional as they are cool looking."—Karina Hof

"I REMEMBER WELL DRINKING GREAT FILTER COFFEE AND ENJOYING EGGS OVER EASY WITH BLOOD SAUSAGE."

RYAN WILLBUR P.133

"THIS IS THE PLACE IN TOWN TO EAT WELL AND DRINK GOOD COFFEE, PARTICULARLY FOR BREKKIE."

ANNA BRONES P.133

FRANCE

"BRINGING A NEW COFFEE DYNAMIC INTO THE CITY BY FEATURING A ROTATING LIST OF FRENCH SPECIALTY COFFEE ROASTERS AND CREATING A FAVORITE NEIGHBORHOOD SPOT IN THE PROCESS."

ANNA BRONES P.128

"IT'S THE FRENCH INTERPRETATION OF AN AMERICAN COFFEE BAR. THE BEST OF BOTH WORLDS."

EILEEN HASSI RINALDI P.134

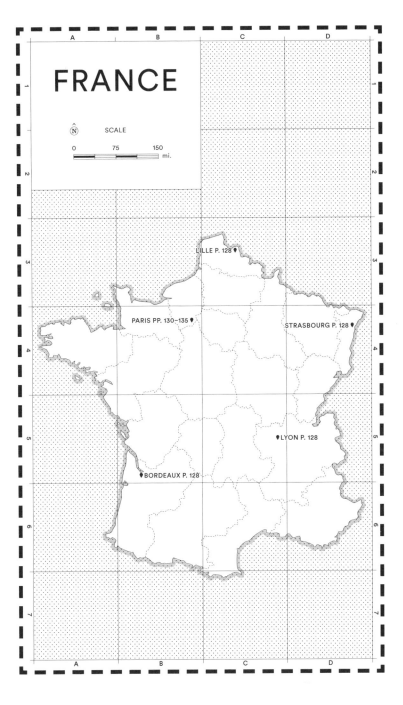

FRANCE

SCALE

0   75   150
mi.

L'ILLE P. 128 ♥

PARIS PP. 130–135 ♥

STRASBOURG P. 128 ♥

♥ LYON P. 128

♥ BORDEAUX P. 128

ALCHIMISTE

87 Quai de Queyries
La Bastide
Bordeaux 33100
France
+33 0665052591
www.alchimiste-cafes.com

Opening hours...Mon–Sat from 9 am
Credit cards...Visa and MasterCard
Style...Roastery cafe

BLACKLIST

27 Place Pey Berland
Downtown
Bordeaux 33000
France
+33 689918265
www.blacklistcafe.com

Opening hours............Mon–Fri from 8 am, Sat from 9 am
Credit cards...Visa and MasterCard
Style...Coffee bar

TAMPER ESPRESSO BAR

10 Rue des Vieux Murs, Vieux-Lille
Lille
Nord 5900
France
+33 320392821
www.tamperlille.fr

Opening hours.......................................Wed–Sat from 9 am,
                                                                    Sun from 11:30 am
Credit cards...Visa and MasterCard
Style...Coffee and breakfast

LA BOÎTE À CAFÉ

3 Rue de L'Abbé Rozier
1st Arrondissement
Lyon
Metropole de Lyon
69001
France
+33 427014871
www.cafemokxa.com

Opening hours................................Mon–Fri from 7:30 am,
                                                Sat from 9 am, Sun from 11 am
Credit cards...Visa and MasterCard
Style...Coffee and food

Paris, see pages 130–135

CAFÉ BRETELLES

47 Rue de Zurich
Krutenau
Strasbourg 67000
France
+33 388232096
www.cafe-bretelles.fr

Opening hours...Mon–Fri from 8 am,
                                                                          Sat from 9 am
Credit cards...Visa and MasterCard
Style...Coffee bar

"Coffee roasting has a tradition in Alsace, the region in the northeastern part of France. But much like in other parts of northern Europe, that has often meant overroasted beans and overextracted espresso shots. Café Bretelles in Strasbourg is trying to change that, bringing a new coffee dynamic into the city by featuring a rotating list of French specialty coffee roasters and creating a favorite neighborhood spot in the process. There's a box with punch cards for regulars, which sits atop the coffee bar, and exposed, dark wooden beams hint to the traditional Alsatian architecture of the building."— Anna Brones

"THE COFFEE WAS BREWED TO BE LIGHT, BUT VIBRANT."

RYAN WILLBUR P.132

PARIS

"AFTER A FEW TIMES YOU GET TO KNOW THE FACES AND EVENTUALLY YOU BECOME A FACE YOURSELF. IF YOU SIT THERE LONG ENOUGH, SOMEBODY WILL SAY SOMETHING TO YOU; THE SPACE LENDS ITSELF TO CONVERSATION."

BRIAN Ó CAOIMH P.132

"HOUSED IN A COURTYARD, HONOR CAFE'S STRUCTURE LOOKS ALMOST LIKE A GREENHOUSE." ANNA BRONES P.133

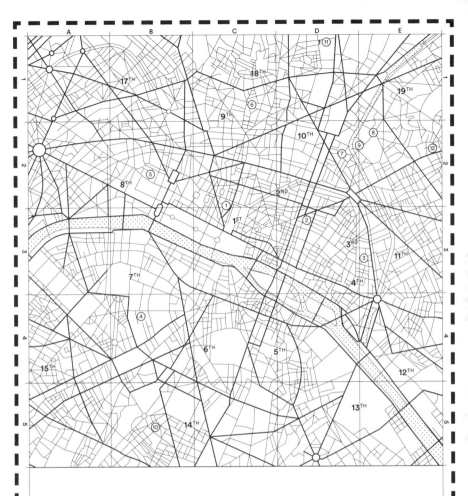

PARIS

SCALE

0   500   1000   1500
                              yd.

1. TÉLESCOPE (P. 132)   5. HONOR CAFE (P. 133)   9. TEN BELLES (P. 134)
2. LOUSTIC (P. 132)   6. KB CAFESHOP (P. 133)   10. HEXAGONE CAFÉ (P. 134)
3. FRAGMENTS (P. 132)   7. HOLYBELLY (P. 133)   11. CAFÉ LOMI (P. 134)
4. COUTUME (P. 133)   8. LA FONTAINE DE BELLEVILLE (P. 134)   12. CREAM (P. 135)

TÉLESCOPE

5 Rue Villedo
1st Arrondissement
Paris 75001
France
www.telescopecafe.com

Opening hours.............................Mon–Fri from 8:30 am,
Sat from 9:30 am
Credit cards.............................Visa, MasterCard, and Amex
Style...Coffee bar

"It's tucked away and has a quiet location on Rue Villedo.
Owner Nicolas Clerc is a great host and incredibly
passionate about his work and all things food related.
And the olive financier with an espresso is a perfect balance
of sweet and savory."—Alice Quillet

"The best filter coffee I've experienced was from Télescope.
The coffee was brewed to be light, but vibrant. It was more
tealike in body, but the delicate flavors made for a kind
of coffee I could drink all day."—Ryan Willbur

A great hip coffee shop, which is unexpected this close to the
Louvre, started by a photographer with a passion for coffee.

LOUSTIC

40 Rue Chapon
3rd Arrondissement
Paris 75003
France
+33 980310706
www.cafeloustic.com

Opening hours..Mon–Fri from 8 am,
Sat from 9 am, Sun from 10 am
Credit cards...Visa and MasterCard
Style...Coffee and food

"Since opening in 2013, Loustic has established itself as an
espresso bar par excellence. Using beans from Caffenation
in Antwerp, Belgium, Loustic plays an active role in
supporting and advancing the overall Parisian specialty-
coffee community. On the wall behind the coffee bar hangs
a poster with the slogan 'Make coffee, not war.' Its prime
location in the 3rd arrondissement makes Loustic a hot spot
during Paris Fashion Week, but the team at Loustic is always
happy to serve up coffee for any visitor, whether they want
to stay and enjoy a baked good or grab the coffee to go and
explore the Parisian streets."—Anna Brones

FRAGMENTS

76 Rue de Tournelles
4th Arrondissement
Paris 75003
www.facebook.com/fragments-paris-515511241861260

Opening hours.............................Mon, Wed–Sun from 9 am
Credit cards...Cash only
Style...Coffee bar

"I have a friend making coffee in Paris; his name is Youssef,
and he has this place called Fragments. He is a one-man
band. He has this chef who always rotates, because they
never get along. Youssef is very special. He actually hates
me a lot, but I love him with all my life. I sit right next to his
coffee machine in the window on a little bench they have.
He can take ten minutes to make an espresso, make it three
times, but when it's right it's bam! He hasn't got a lot of
customers because people know he's going to take ten to
fifteen minutes to serve a coffee, but that coffee's incredible.
And Youssef is the right kind of freak as well. That's the one
who makes me the most comfortable."—Marcos Bartolomé

"My favorite place to get coffee is Fragments in Paris.
After a few times you get to know the faces and eventually
you become a face yourself. If you sit there long enough,
somebody will say something to you; the space lends itself
to conversation and interaction. Lots of people come here
alone and then just keep coming back once they see how it
goes and how welcoming it can be. I first started going
because of the coffee. I was one of the guys showing up
asking all kinds of questions, and in return I left with all
kinds of other questions. It was here that many of my ideas
about coffee were challenged, where I cut my teeth, and
was really exposed to a different way of coming at coffee.
For many, coffee can be a cup of caffeine, but for some time
now I've understood that it can resonate in us somewhere
else, tell a story, and for the romantics among us, it can set
the tone and play with our nostalgic side. Before Fragments,
I hadn't seen this side of coffee." —Brian Ó Caoimh

Parisians are obsessed with their coffee, but much of it is
uninspired. Thankfully, folks like Yousef are out there breaking
the mold. In Paris, this is a standout.

COUTUME

47 Rue de Babylone
7th Arrondissement
Paris 75007
France
+33 145515047

Opening hours..Mon—Fri from 8 am,
Sat—Sun from 10 am
Credit cards............................Visa, MasterCard, and Amex
Style...Coffee and food

"Antoine Netien is one of the most inspirational people for me in the coffee industry. He has a different, not really freaky and geeky way of thinking about coffee. He's really calm."—Marcos Bartolomé

HONOR CAFE

54 Rue du Faubourg Saint-Honoré
8th Arrondissement
Paris 75008
France
+33 782529363
www.honor-cafe.com

Opening hours...Mon—Fri from 9 am,
Sat from 10 am
Credit cards...Visa and MasterCard
Style.................................Outdoor coffee kiosk, with food

"If there is one entirely unique cafe in Paris, it is Honor Cafe. Housed in a courtyard, Honor Cafe's structure looks almost like a greenhouse. From this building, its owners, the English-Australian couple Angelle Boucher and Daniel Warburton, have built a devoted neighborhood following, as well as established Honor as one of the top specialty cafes in the city. Their attention to detail served in a distinct atmosphere makes it well worth a visit."—Anna Brones

KB CAFÉSHOP

53 Avenue Trudaine
9th Arrondissement
Paris 75009
France
+33 156921241
www.kbcafeshop.com

Opening hours ....Mon—Fri from 7:30 am,
Sat—Sun from 9 am
Credit cards..Visa and MasterCard
Style..Coffee and food

"Opened in 2010, KB Cafe was one of the first Anglo-style coffee shops in Paris and has been a go-to for Parisians and tourists alike. Offering a rotating selection of European roasters, in the fall of 2015 KB Cafe also began roasting its own beans at the collaborative roasting space, the Beans on Fire. Inspired by typical Australian cafes, at KB Cafe you'll find the usual Aussie offerings like flat whites and carrot cake, as well as an assortment of freshly pressed juices, sandwiches, and salads. A stone's throw from Montmartre, it's the perfect spot for an afternoon refuel."—Anna Brones

HOLYBELLY

19 Rue Lucien Sampaix
10th Arrondissement
Paris 75010
France
www.holybel.ly

Opening hours...............................Mon, Thu—Fri from 9 am,
Sat—Sun from 10 am
Credit cards..Visa and MasterCard
Style..Coffee and food

"This is the place in town to eat well and drink good coffee, particularly for brekkie."—Anna Brones

"One of my favorite coffee experiences ever was a breakfast I had at Holybelly in Paris. I had fantastic coffee and an excellent breakfast. Though there are not necessarily specific pairings, the coffee and food are both excellent, and you can't go wrong with anything on the menu. I remember well drinking great filter coffee and enjoying eggs over easy with blood sausage."—Ryan Willbur

This popular breakfast and lunch spot in Canal Saint-Martin focuses on inspired, luscious food —pancakes topped with eggs, bacon, and bourbon butter and fresh daily specials— that pair beautifully with an amazing cup of coffee. The mom-and-pop super couple behind the joint is chef Sarah Mouchot on food, and her partner Nico Alary on coffee. They recently added a larger space along Rue Lucien Sampaix—so patrons can drink more of their coffee in the two restaurants.

LA FONTAINE DE BELLEVILLE

31–33 Rue Juliette Dodu
10th Arrondissement
Paris 75010
France
www.lafontaine.cafesbelleville.com

Opening hours...Daily from 8 am
Credit cards...Visa and MasterCard
Style..Coffee and food

It seemed like the talented team behind Belleville Brûlerie was holding out from opening a traditional retail business. Many of the city's finest cafes already relied on their beans. But in 2016, owners Thomas Lehoux and American expat David Nigel Flynn proved to their fans in the 10th that their wait was not in vain: La Fontaine de Belleville became the first contemporary specialty cafe to open in Paris in the style of a traditional Parisian cafe. The classically styled corner spot is filled with the vintage charm (and delicious food) you'd expect from the city—replete with a smoker-filled patio—but with, in a new twist, brilliant coffee alongside. And there is wine.

TEN BELLES

10 Rue de la Grange aux Belles
10th Arrondissement
Paris 75010
France
+33 142409078
www.tenbelles.com

Opening hours......................................Mon–Fri from 8 am,
                                                                      Sat–Sun from 9 am
Credit cards...Visa and MasterCard
Style..Coffee and food

"It's the French interpretation of an American coffee bar. The best of both worlds."—Eileen Hassi Rinaldi

HEXAGONE CAFÉ

121 Rue du Château
14th Arrondissement
Paris 75014
France
www.hexagone-cafe.fr

Opening hours......................................Mon–Fri from 8 am,
                                                                      Sat–Sun from 10 am
Credit cards...Visa and MasterCard
Style..Coffee bar

When Brittany-based artisan roaster Stéphane Cataldi teamed up with a crew to build a chic and perhaps unlikely cafe in Paris's 14th arrondissement, the city's eyes, ears, and tongues perked up. The simple, sunny space is serious, quiet, and Parisian and very much a neighborhood place. It's not the kind of coffee shop where you sit and work on your laptop. But it's exactly the kind of place you'd be delighted to discover.

CAFÉ LOMI

3 ter Rue Marcadet
18th Arrondissement
Paris 75018
France
+33 980395624
www.cafelomi.com

Opening hours...Daily from 10 am
Credit cards...Visa and MasterCard
Style...Roastery cafe

"One of the original players on the Parisian specialty coffee scene, Café Lomi is an established favorite hub for Parisian coffee lovers. The roastery cafe also serves as a retail location for Café Lomi beans, offers workshops to get its customers acquainted with the world of coffee, and features a cafe menu full of particularly French renditions of specialty coffee offerings, like a shot of espresso served with blue cheese. With a full breakfast and lunch menu and an in-house team of chefs, the food is just as good as the coffee, and you're welcome to sit and stay awhile."
—Anna Brones

CREAM

50 Rue de Belleville
20th Arrondissement
Paris 75020
France
+33 983665843
www.facebook.com/cream.belleville

Opening hours...............................Mon–Fri from 7:30 am,
                                            Sat–Sun from 8:30 am
Credit cards..Visa and MasterCard
Style..Coffee bar

"With its tiled floor and vintage mirror at the back of the bar,
hailing from the building's previous days, CREAM combines
a Parisian aesthetic with a cosmopolitan sensibility. Opened
by two former Ten Belles baristas, attention is put into every
drink they make, whether it's for a coffee aficionado or a
local from the neighborhood who's just popping in for an
espresso before work."—Anna Brones

"BETTINA, NICCÒLO, FÁBRICA, AND GRÉMIO ALL HAVE A PASSION FOR QUALITY COFFEE AND ARE MORE THAN WILLING TO INVITE YOU INTO THIS WORLD OF THEIRS."

HELLE JACOBSEN P.138

PORTUGAL & SPAIN

"NO WI-FI, NO TROLLEYS, NO DECAF. MARCOS IS ONE OF THE BEST COFFEE PROFESSIONALS I'VE EVER KNOWN."

SANTIAGO RIGONI P.138

"ONE OF A FEW GREAT PLACES IN BARCELONA. THE PLACE IS NEAT AND THE COFFEE IS GREAT. A BIT OF GREAT COFFEE IN A HOT, CROWDED BARCELONA."

NICHOLAS CHISTYAKOV P.138

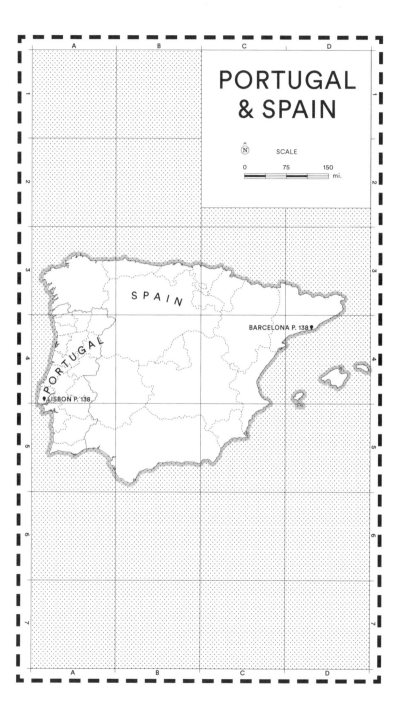

PORTUGAL & SPAIN

N   SCALE

0   75   150
mi.

SPAIN

PORTUGAL

BARCELONA P. 138

LISBON P. 138

BETTINA & NICCOLÒ CORALLO
Rua de Escola Politécnica 4
Rato
Lisbon 1200-280
Portugal
+351 213862158

Opening hours..Mon–Sat from 10 am
Credit cards...Visa and MasterCard
Style..Coffee and chocolate

"Bettina, Niccolò, Fábrica, and Grémio all have a passion for quality coffee and are more than willing to invite you into this world of theirs."—Helle Jacobsen

FÁBRICA COFFEE ROASTERS
Rua das Portas de Santo Antão 136
Rato
Lisbon 1150-265
Portugal
+351 211399261
www.fabricacoffeeroasters.com

Opening hours..Daily from 9 am
Credit cards..Visa
Style..Coffee bar

NOMAD
Pasaje de Sert 12
Ciutat Vella
Barcelona 8003
Spain
+34 628566235
www.nomadcoffee.es

Opening hours..Mon–Fri from 9 am
Credit cards...Cash only
Style..Roastery cafe

"One of a few great places in Barcelona. The place is neat and the coffee is great. A bit of great coffee in hot, crowded Barcelona."—Nicholas Chistyakov

SATAN'S COFFEE CORNER
Carrer de l'Arc de Sant Ramon del Call 11
Ciutat Vella, Gothic Quarter
Barcelona 8002
Spain
+34 666222599
www.satanscoffee.com

Opening hours.....................................Mon–Sat from 8 am,
Sun from 10 am
Credit cards...........................Visa, MasterCard, and Amex
Style..Coffee bar

"No Wi-Fi, no trolleys, no decaf. Marcos is one of the best coffee professionals I've ever known."—Santiago Rigoni

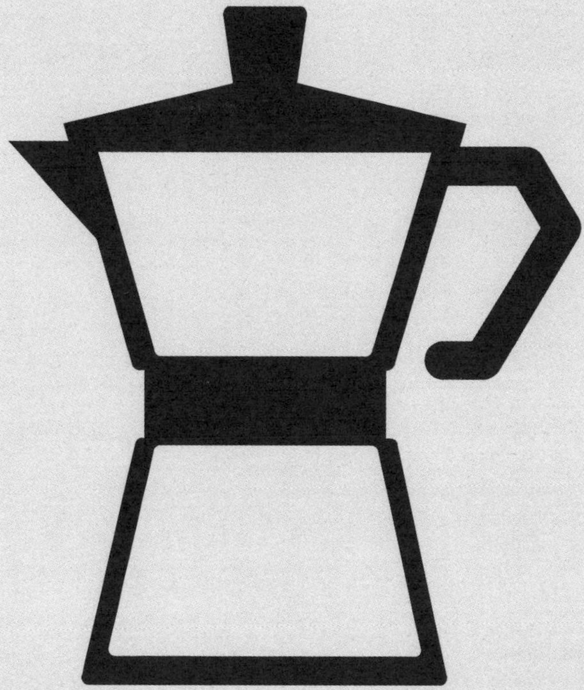

"THOMAS, THE OWNER, REALLY KNOWS HOW TO PULL A DECENT SHOT OUT OF HIS BEAUTIFUL RED SLAYER MACHINE." ANDRÉ KRÜGER P.142

"A SWEET, BALANCED, TASTY ESPRESSO WITH A GENTLE, SMOOTH FINISH."
GWILYM DAVIES P.142

GERMANY

"A HIDDEN GEM FOR COFFEE LOVERS, AND THE OWNER IS OLD-SCHOOL IN COFFEE—HIGHLY INTELLECTUAL WITH A COMPLETE UNDERSTANDING OF ITS HISTORY IN TERMS OF ROASTING, GRINDING, AND BREWING."
KHALID AL MULLA P.142

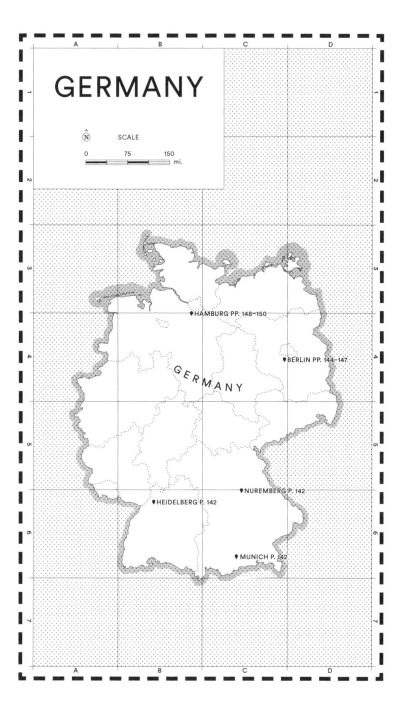

GERMANY

N SCALE

0   75   150
mi.

HAMBURG PP. 148–150

BERLIN PP. 144–147

GERMANY

NUREMBERG P. 142

HEIDELBERG P. 142

MUNICH P. 142

Berlin, see pages 144–147

Hamburg, see pages 148–150

COFFEE NERD
Rohrbacherstrasse 9
Heidelberg 69115
Germany
www.coffeenerd.de

Opening hours	Mon–Fri from 9 am,
	Sat from 10 am, Sun from noon
Credit cards	Cash only
Style	Coffee bar

"Thomas, the owner, really knows how to pull a decent shot out of his beautiful red Slayer machine. He's a real geek. My girlfriend's parents live near Heidelberg. We visit them from time to time, but to be honest, the main reason for me to travel to Heidelberg is to get a perfect shot at Coffee Nerd."—André Krüger

KAFFEE, ESPRESSO UND BARISTA
Schlörstrasse 11
Neuhausen-Nymphenburg
Munich 80634
Germany
+49 8916783878
www.kaffee-espresso-barista.com

Opening hours	Mon–Fri from 7 am,
	Sat from 8:30 am, Sun from 9 am
Credit cards	Visa and MasterCard
Style	Coffee and waffles

"Owned by Thomas Leep who has been in the coffee business for so many years. Situated in the heart of Munich, it's a hidden gem for coffee lovers and the owner is old school in coffee—highly intellectual with a complete understanding of its history all the way to modern technology in terms of roasting, grinding, and brewing."
—Khalid Al Mulla

MACHHÖRNDL KAFFEE
Obere Kieselbergstrasse 13
Gostenhof
Nuremberg 90429
Germany
+49 09112740664
www.machhoerndl-kaffee.de

Opening hours	Tue–Sat from 9:30 am
Credit cards	Cash only
Style	Coffee bar

"On a road trip to judge the German AeroPress Competition, we stopped at Machhörndl Kaffee, a small roastery in a backstreet of Nuremberg. The barista played with my concepts: being a gentle bloke who likes light-roast washed coffee extracted for a longer time. I had a sweet, balanced, tasty espresso with a gentle, smooth finish."
—Gwilym Davies

"THE MOST CONSISTENT COFFEE IN TOWN."

CORY ANDREEN P.147

"I'M STILL VERY IMPRESSED BY THE REALLY HIGH QUALITY OF THE BERLIN-BASED ROASTERIES."

ANDRÉ KRÜGER P.147

BERLIN

"THEY CAP A TEN-COURSE MEAL WITH A FILTER COFFEE IN A REALLY GREAT WAY."

KRIS SCHACKMAN P.147

"THIS QUAINT YET BUZZING CAFE, WITH TABLES SPILLING OUT ONTO PEACEFUL AUGUSTSTRASSE, OPENED IN 2010, WITH LITTLE SIGN THAT IT WOULD ONE DAY BECOME A FOODIE DESTINATION AND THE ORIGIN OF CENTRAL EUROPE'S NOW THRIVING COFFEE INDUSTRY." DEREK LAMBERTON P.147

BERLIN

$\widehat{N}$ SCALE

0   580   1165   1745
yd.

1. COFFEE PROFILERS (P. 146)
2. CHAPTER ONE (P. 146)
3. COMPANION COFFEE (P. 146)

4. FIVE ELEPHANT (P. 146)
5. NANO KAFFEE (P. 147)
6. NOBELHART & SCHMUTZIG (P. 147)

7. BONANZA (P. 147)
8. FATHER CARPENTER (P. 147)
9. THE BARN (P. 147)

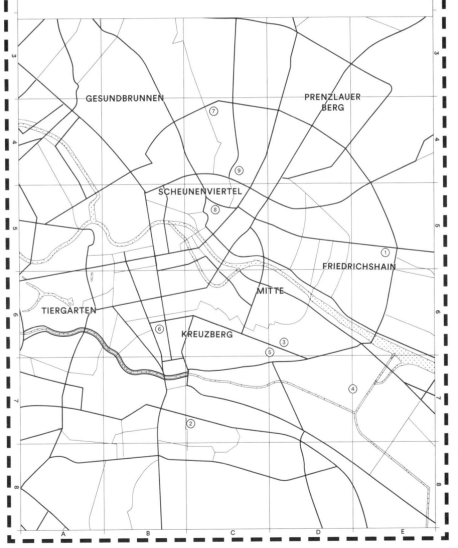

COFFEE PROFILERS

Karl-Marx Allee 136
Friedrichshain
Berlin 10243
Germany
+49 3029777178
www.coffeeprofilers.com

Opening hours.................................Mon–Fri from 8 am,
Sat from 9 am, Sun from 11 am
Credit cards............................Visa, MasterCard, and Amex
Style..Coffee bar

"Coffee Profilers has raised the standards in Friedrichshain. Run by one of Europe's most accomplished baristas, its level of quality is remarkably high. There is plenty of outdoor seating and a cozy, bright interior where you can enjoy your coffee in peace."—Derek Lamberton

CHAPTER ONE

Mittenwalderstrasse 30
Kreuzberg
Berlin 10961
Germany
+49 3025922799
www.chapter-one-coffee.com

Opening hours.................................Mon–Sat from 9 am,
Sun from 11 am
Credit cards..Cash only
Style..Coffee bar

"Great for filter."—André Krüger

"This Kreuzberg coffee bar offers a wide selection of beans from all over Europe available as filter along with a daily espresso. Top quality coffee in an unpretentious and relaxed setting."—Derek Lamberton

COMPANION COFFEE

Oranienstrasse 24
Kreuzberg
Berlin 10999
Germany
www.companioncoffee.com

Opening hours.................................Mon–Sat from 10 am
Credit cards..Cash only
Style..Coffee and barista training

"Great for espresso."—André Krüger

"Run by a pair of talented baristas from Perth and Vancouver, this sunny coffee bar overlooking a courtyard from inside Voo Store is one of Berlin's very best. The beans regularly rotate among the best roasts available across Europe. Their high-quality teas can also be found here and in leading cafes throughout Berlin."—Derek Lamberton

FIVE ELEPHANT

Reichenbergerstrasse 101
Kreuzberg
Berlin 10999
Germany
+49 3096081527
www.fiveelephant.com

Opening hours.................................Mon–Fri from 8:30 am,
Sat–Sun from 10 am
Credit cards..Cash only
Style..Coffee and food

"The 2014 crop of Biftu Gudina roasted by Five Elephant in Berlin is still my favorite filter of all time."—Cory Andreen

"Started as a bakery/cafe by an Austrian-American couple, this light, airy, and curiously named cafe has grown to become a leading coffee destination in Europe. The coffee, prepared by some of Berlin's best baristas, is excellent, rivaled in quality by the cafe's famous cheesecake."
—Derek Lamberton

If you are hanging out in Kreuzberg, you half expect the place to be packed with hip coffee shops. Five Elephant doesn't disappoint. While the coffee is the main attraction, it's worth making a special trip for the cheesecake alone.

NANO KAFFEE

Dresdenerstrasse 14
Kreuzberg
Berlin 10999
Germany
+49 3025209838
www.nano-kaffee.de

Opening hours	Mon–Fri from 8:30 am,
Credit cards	Sat from 9:30 am
	MasterCard
Style	Coffee bar

"A variety of beans from German roasters are pulled on a Strada or at the dedicated brew bar, and quality is paramount. Watch for regular 'Brew Up' events involving many of Europe's top roasteries."—Derek Lamberton

NOBELHART & SCHMUTZIG

Friedrichstrasse 218
Kreuzberg
Berlin 10969
Germany
+49 3025940610
www.nobelhartundschmutzig.com

Opening hours	Tue–Sat from 6 pm
Credit cards	Visa, MasterCard, and Amex
Style	Restaurant

"They cap a ten-course meal with a filter coffee in a really great way. I've not seen anything like it anywhere."
—Kris Schackman

BONANZA

Oderbergerstrasse 35
Mitte
Berlin 10435
Germany
www.bonanzacoffee.de

Opening hours	Mon–Fri from 8:30 am,
	Sat–Sun from 10 am
Credit cards	Visa, MasterCard, and Amex
Style	Coffee bar

"I'm still very impressed by the really high quality of the Berlin-based roasteries: Bonanza, The Barn, and Five Elephant. All of them are getting better all the time."
—André Krüger

FATHER CARPENTER

Münzstrasse 21
Mitte
Berlin 10178
Germany
+49 17625219805
www.fathercarpenter.com

Opening hours	Mon–Fri from 9 am,
	Sat from 10 am
Credit cards	Cash only
Style	Full service

"The most consistent in town."—Cory Andreen

THE BARN

Auguststrasse 58
Mitte
Berlin 10119
Germany
www.thebarn.de

Opening hours	Mon–Fri from 8 am,
	Sat–Sun from 10 am
Credit cards	Cash only
Style	Coffee bar

"This quaint yet buzzing cafe, with tables spilling out onto peaceful Auguststrasse, opened in 2010, with little sign that it would one day become a foodie destination and the origin of central Europe's now thriving coffee industry."
—Derek Lamberton

"BEST ESPRESSO."

KHALID AL MULLA P.150

"ROASTING AND BREWING ARE SEPARATED BY STATE-OF-THE-ART SILOS."

KHALID AL MULLA P.150

HAMBURG

"STOCKHOLM ESPRESSO CLUB MIGHT BE MY FAVORITE SPOT. DAVID AND BEN, THE OWNERS, BROUGHT THE SWEDISH COFFEE CULTURE TO HAMBURG. IT'S AN AMAZING PLACE."

ANDRÉ KRÜGER P.150

HAMBURG

EPPENDORF

HARVESTEHUDE

EIMSBÜTTEL

③

SCHANZE

NEUSTADT

MITTE
WEST

MITTE
EAST

ST PAULI

DE BAARSJES

②

①

HAFENCITY

N̂

SCALE

0   325   655   985
                          yd.

1. KAFFEEMUSEUM (P. 150)
2. SPEICHERSTANDT
    KAFFERÖSTEREI (P. 150)

3. ELBGOLD (P. 150)
4. STOCKHOLM ESPRESSO
    CLUB (P. 150)

KAFFEEMUSEUM

Strasse Annenufer 2
Speicherstadt
Hamburg 20457
Germany
+49 4055204258
www.kaffeemuseum-burg.de

Opening hours..............................Tue–Sun from 10 am
Credit cards.........................Visa, MasterCard, and Amex
Style..Coffee bar

"Best espresso."—Khalid Al Mulla

SPEICHERSTANDT KAFFERÖSTEREI

Kehrwieder 5
Speicherstadt
Hamburg 20457
Germany
+49 04037518683
www.speicherstadt-kaffee.de

Opening hours..Daily from 10 am
Credit cards...Visa and MasterCard
Style..Roastery cafe

ELBGOLD

Lagerstrasse 34c
Sternschanze
Hamburg 20357
Germany
+49 4023517520
www.elbgold.com

Opening hours................................Mon–Fri from 8 am,
Sat from 9 am, Sun from 10 am
Credit cards...Visa and MasterCard
Style..Roastery cafe

"This is a cafe and roastery in a warehouse close to the
exhibition center, a coffee-culture place where you can
experience live roasting. Roasting and brewing are
separated by state-of-the-art silos."—Khalid Al Mulla

STOCKHOLM ESPRESSO CLUB

Peter-Marquard Strasse 8
Winterhude
Hamburg 22303
Germany
+49 1604837361
www.stockholmespressoclub.de

Opening hours................................Mon–Fri from 8 am,
Sat–Sun from 10 am
Credit cards...Cash only
Style...Coffee and food

"Stockholm Espresso Club might be my favorite spot.
David and Ben, the owners, brought the Swedish coffee
culture to Hamburg. It's an amazing place that always serves
the freshest stuff roasted by the great Koppi roasters from
Helsingborg in southern Sweden. And it's a very friendly
space with great hospitality. They also have an awesome
selection of fine Swedish craft beers on their menu."
—André Krüger

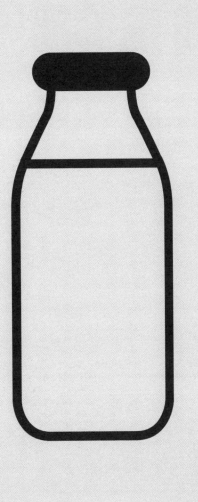

"UNUSUALLY COMFORTABLE, GREAT COFFEE, PROBABLY THE BEST TEA OF ANY THIRD-WAVE CAFE IN EUROPE, AND DELICIOUS FOOD." SCOTT RAO P.154

"SOMEHOW YOU LOVE THIS PLACE THE MOMENT YOU SEE IT."

NICHOLAS CHISTYAKOV P.154

THE CZECH REPUBLIC, HUNGARY & POLAND

"THEY ARE LIKE THE MOTHER OF SPECIALTY IN WARSAW."

GWILYM DAVIES P.155

"CATERING SPECIFICALLY TO COFFEE GEEKS, OWNERS ANNA AND PETER FOCUS FIRMLY ON FILTER COFFEES WITH A ROTATION OF BEANS FROM SCANDINAVIAN ROASTERS."

DEREK LAMBERTON P.154

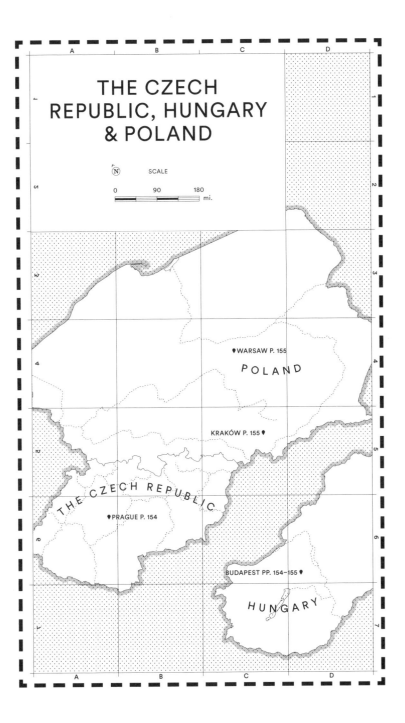

THE CZECH REPUBLIC, HUNGARY & POLAND

N

SCALE

0   90   180
mi.

A   B   C   D

WARSAW P. 155

POLAND

KRAKÓW P. 155

THE CZECH REPUBLIC

PRAGUE P. 154

BUDAPEST PP. 154–155

HUNGARY

EMA

Na Florenci 1420/3
Praha 1
Prague 11000
The Czech Republic
+420 730156933
www.emaespressobar.cz

Opening hours................................Mon–Fri from 8 am,
Sat–Sun from 9 am
Credit cards................................Visa and MasterCard
Style................................Coffee and food

"This cafe is pretty different from other Prague cafes: a simple, spacious, multiroasting concept with coffees from all over Europe that are frequently changing. Somehow you love this place the moment you see it."
—Nicholas Chistyakov

KAVARNA PRAZIRNA

Lublaňská 676/50
Praha 2 – Vinohrady
Prague 12000
The Czech Republic
+420 720385622
www.kavaprazirna.cz

Opening hours................................Mon–Fri from 8:30 am,
Sat from noon
Credit cards................................Cash only
Style................................Coffee and food

"It is a place where I can have multiple experiences: an espresso at the bar, a chance to focus on writing in the middle room with a pour-over, and my favorite seat in the back where I have quiet time eating cake with a cappuccino."—Gwilym Davies

MŮJŠÁLEK KÁVY

Křižíkova 386/105
Praha 8-Karlín
Prague 18600
The Czech Republic
+420 725556944
www.mujsalekkavy.cz

Opening hours................................Mon–Sat from 9 am,
Sun from 10 am
Credit cards................................Visa and MasterCard
Style................................Coffee and food

"One of my two favorite cafes in Europe. Unusually comfortable, great coffee, probably the best tea of any third-wave cafe in Europe, and delicious food. Beware that even though it's just a coffee shop, you have to make a reservation to get a table! There's nowhere like it."
—Scott Rao

KONTAKT

Károly krt. 22
Belváros
Budapest
1052
Hungary
+36 19521861
www.kontaktcoffee.com

Opening hours................................Mon–Fri from 8 am,
Sat from 10 am
Credit cards................................Visa and MasterCard
Style................................Coffee bar

"Tucked inside an unassuming courtyard, Kontakt is perhaps Budapest's foremost coffee shop. Catering specifically to coffee geeks, owners Anna and Peter focus firmly on filter coffees with a rotation of beans from Scandinavian roasters like Koppi, Drop, and La Cabra. Kontakt is also home to the popular Rocket nitro brew, which rears its head in cafes across continental Europe."—Derek Lamberton

MY LITTLE MELBOURNE

Madách Imre út 3 (Madách tér)
Erzsébetváros
Budapest 1075
Hungary
+36 703947002
www.mylittlemelbourne.hu

Opening hours............................Mon–Fri from 7 am,
                                        Sat–Sun from 9 am
Credit cards..Visa
Style..Coffee and food

ESPRESSO EMBASSY

Arany János ucta 15
Lipótváros
Budapest 1051
Hungary
+36 204450063
www.espressoembassy.hu

Opening hours............................Mon–Fri from 7:30 am,
                                        Sat–Sun from 9 am
Credit cards...........................Visa and MasterCard
Style..Coffee bar

"I was so delighted to see a coffee scene taking off in Budapest."—Tyler J. Wells

KARMA COFFEE ROASTERS

Krupnicza 12
Stare Miasto
Kraków
Lesser Poland 31-123
Poland
+48 662387281
www.karmaroasters.com

Opening hours............................Mon–Fri from 8 am,
                                        Sat–Sun from 10 am
Credit cards...........................Visa and MasterCard
Style..Coffee and food

"Kraków is a little town with a medieval look. It's pretty old-fashioned and everyone drinks vodka over beer there. I went there with my girl last year for a wedding and there was a guy in a place called Karma Coffee that saved me after a lot of vodka at that wedding. The machinery they had was completely up-to-date, way better than we have here in Spain."—Marcos Bartolomé

FILTRY DOBRA KAWA

Juliana Ursyna Niemcewicza 3
Filtry
Warsaw
Masovia 02-022
Poland
+48 508221432
www.filtrycafe.pl

Opening hours............................Mon–Fri from 8 am,
                                        Sat from 9 am, Sun from 10 am
Credit cards.....................Visa, MasterCard, and Amex
Style..Coffee bar

"Filtry was the first coffee shop to open in Warsaw, and people who have worked there use their knowledge when they move on, spreading the word in Poland. They are like the mother of specialty in Warsaw."—Gwilym Davies

RELAKS KAWIARNIA

Puławska 48
Old Mokotow
Warsaw
Masovia 00-999
Poland
www.relaksrelaks.pl

Opening hours.................................Mon–Fri from 7:30 am,
                                                        Sat–Sun from 9 am
Credit cards............................Visa, MasterCard, and Amex
Style...Coffee and food

KOFI BRAND

Minska 25
Praga
Warsaw
Masovia 03-808
Poland
+48 224658152
www.kofibrand.pl

Opening hours...Mon–Fri from 9 am
Credit cards............................Visa, MasterCard, and Amex
Style...Roastery cafe

"I love Kofi Brand. It was meant to be a roastery with a
training space but developed into a cafe as well, due to
locals coming in for a coffee. Ania and Konrad run a lovely
space that is welcoming and progressive."—Gwilym Davies

MINISTERSTWO KAVY

Marszałkowska St 27/35
Śródmieście
Warsaw
Masovia 00-639
Poland
+48 503080906
www.ministerstwokawy.pl

Opening hours.....................................Mon–Fri from 9 am,
                                                        Sat–Sun from 10 am
Credit cards............................Visa, MasterCard, and Amex
Style...Coffee and food

"I HAD AN UNFORGETTABLE COFFEE EXPERIENCE AT TAILOR MADE. I WAS FASCINATED BY THE HIGHEST LEVEL OF QUALITY."

NICHOLAS CHISTYAKOV P.160

CROATIA, GREECE, SERBIA & TURKEY

"THEY WERE THE FIRST ONES IN SERBIA WITH SPECIALTY COFFEE, IN-HOUSE ROASTING, PROPER LATTE ART, AND FILTER COFFEES ON THE MENU." NIK OROSI P.160

"THEY ALWAYS HAVE FANTASTIC COCKTAILS WITH STUNNING COFFEES AND THEIR UNIQUE ROASTING STYLE. THE CREW IS OBSESSED WITH QUALITY—JUST GO AND SEE THEM WORK."

NICHOLAS CHISTYAKOV P.160

CROATIA, GREECE, SERBIA & TURKEY

$\widehat{N}$ SCALE

0   60   125
mi.

ZAGREB PP. 162–164

BELGRADE P. 160

ISTANBUL PP. 166–169

CROATIA

SERBIA

TURKEY

GREECE

ATHENS P. 160

Zagreb, see pages 162–164

TAILOR MADE
Plateia Agias Eirinis 2
Monastiraki
Athens 10560
Greece
www.tailormade.gr

Opening hours	Mon–Sat from 8 am,
	Sun from 9 am
Credit cards	Visa and MasterCard
Style	Coffee bar

"I had an unforgettable coffee experience at Tailor Made. I was fascinated by the highest level of quality and speed of their work. It is beautifully designed, still it remains remarkable, almost shocking."—Nicholas Chistyakov

THE UNDERDOG
Iraklidon 8
Thiseio
Athens 118 51
Greece
+30 2130365393
www.underdog.gr

Opening hours	Daily from 9 am
Credit cards	Visa and MasterCard
Style	Coffee and food

"A coffeeplace by Tasos Delichristos, a superprofessional from Greece. Tasos and his crew members are the World Coffee in Good Spirits champions, so they always have fantastic cocktails with stunning coffees and their unique roasting style. The crew is obsessed with quality—just go and see them work."—Nicholas Chistyakov

PRŽIONICA D59B
Dobračina 59b
Dorćol
Belgrade 11000
Serbia
www.cafefoamy.ca

Opening hours	Mon–Fri from 7 am,
	Sat–Sun from 8 am
Credit cards	Cash only
Style	Coffee bar

"They were the first ones in Serbia with specialty coffee, in-house roasting, proper latte art, and filter coffees on the menu."—Nik Orosi

KOFEIN
Cara Dušana 65
Skadarlija
Belgrade 11000
Serbia
+381 113345105
www.koffein.rs

Opening hours	Mon–Fri from 7 am,
	Sat–Sun from 8 am
Credit cards	Visa and MasterCard
Style	Coffee bar

Istanbul, see pages 166–169

"ELISCAFFE WAS FOR A LONG TIME THE ONLY PLACE IN ZAGREB WHERE YOU COULD GET A NICE CUP OF COFFEE, AND EVEN AFTER WINNING NUMEROUS AWARDS AND BARISTA CHAMPIONSHIPS, NIK HAS NEVER STOPPED PUSHING THE QUALITY OF HIS COFFEE."

TIM WENDELBOE P.164

ZAGREB

"OWNED BY THE BEST PASTRY CHEF IN CROATIA."

NIK OROSI P.164

"THEY HAVE FAB SANDWICHES AND GREAT COFFEE. AND THE PEOPLE ARE GREAT."

NIK OROSI P.164

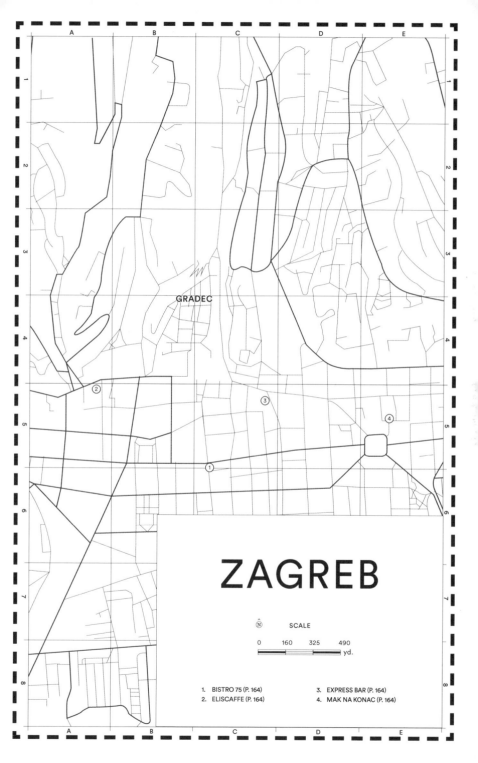

GRADEC

ZAGREB

$\hat{N}$ SCALE

0   160   325   490

yd.

1. BISTRO 75 (P. 164)   3. EXPRESS BAR (P. 164)

2. ELISCAFFE (P. 164)   4. MAK NA KONAC (P. 164)

BISTRO 75

Preradovićeva 34 i Zadarska 75
Zagreb 10000
Croatia
+385 912506022
www.bistro75.hr

Opening hours......................................Mon–Fri from 9 am,
Sat from 10 am
Credit cards...Cash only
Style..Coffee and food

"They have fab sandwiches (with a twist) and great coffee.
And the people are great."—Nik Orosi

ELISCAFFE

Ilica 63
Zagreb
Zagreb 10000
Croatia
+385 912506022
www.eliscaffe.com

Opening hours......................................Mon–Sat from 8 am,
Sun from 9 am
Credit cards...Cash only
Style..Roastery cafe

"Eliscaffe is run by Nik Orosi, who is the pioneer of
high-quality and modern coffee in Croatia. Eliscaffe was for
a long time the only place in Zagreb where you could get a
nice cup of coffee, and even after winning numerous awards
and barista championships, Nik has never stopped pushing
the quality of his coffee. Today Nik roasts his own beans and
is constantly developing his cafe with new design and
concepts. Nik never stops looking ahead, and that is why
he is still on top of the game even after ten years."
—Tim Wendelboe

EXPRESS BAR

Petrinjska 4
Zagreb 10000
Croatia
www.facebook.com/expresszg

Opening hours......................................Mon–Fri from 7 am,
Sat from 9 am, Sun from 11 am
Credit cards..........................Visa, MasterCard, and Amex
Style..Coffee bar

MAK NA KONAC

Ul. Popa Dukljanina 1
Zagreb 10000
Croatia
+385 14616654
www.maknakonac.com

Opening hours......................................Mon–Sat from 9 am
Credit cards...Visa and MasterCard
Style..Sweet shop

"Owned by the best pastry chef in Croatia, who has been
on *MasterChef* numerous times."—Nik Orosi

"I FAVOR NORM COFFEE AS THEY ARE NOT AFRAID OF BEING GEEKY AND METICULOUS IN THEIR APPROACH TO COFFEE AND ALWAYS TRY TO IMPROVE THEIR SKILLS."

CAGATAY GULABIOGLU P.168

"TRADITIONAL TURKISH COFFEE IS BREWED ON BURNING SAND."

GÖKÇE YILDIRIM P.169

ISTANBUL

"THE BEST VARIETY OF BEANS."

GÖKÇE YILDIRIM P.168

"THE TURKISH COFFEE IS MADE WITHOUT USING ANY MACHINES."

GÖKÇE YILDIRIM P.168

"A SPECIALTY CAFE THAT IMPORTS AND ROASTS ITS OWN BEANS, KRONOTROP HAS ITS OWN BLENDS FOR TRADITIONAL TURKISH COFFEE AND THEY PREPARE AND SERVE WITH THEIR OWN CUSTOM CEZVE POT."

GÖKÇE YILDIRIM P.168

ISTANBUL

SCALE

| 0 | 315 | 630 | 945 |

yd.

1. PETRA ROASTING CO. (P. 168)
2. KRONOTROP (P. 168)
3. MANDABATMAZ (P. 168)
4. NORM COFFEE (P. 168)
5. ŞARK KAHVESI (AT THE
   GRAND BAZAAR) (P. 169)

PETRA ROASTING CO.
Panorama Selenium Residence, Hoşsohbet Sokaği
Beşiktaş
Istanbul 34349
Turkey
+90 2123561053
www.petracoffee.com

Opening hours................................Tue–Fri from 9:30 am,
Sat–Sun from 10 am
Credit cards..........................Visa, MasterCard, and Amex
Style...Coffee bar

"The best variety of beans. Has a classic coffee menu."
—Gökçe Yildirim

KRONOTROP
Kuloğlu Mah, Firuzağa Cami Sokak 2/B
Beyoğlu
Istanbul 3340
Turkey
+90 2122499271
www.kronotrop.com

Opening hours................................Mon–Sat from 7:30 am,
Sun from 10:30 am
Credit cards.....................................Visa and MasterCard
Style...Roastery cafe

"A specialty cafe that imports and roasts its own beans,
Kronotrop has its own blends for traditional Turkish coffee
and they prepare and serve with their own custom Cezve
pot."—Gökçe Yildirim

MANDABATMAZ
İstiklal Caddesi Olivia Geçidi 1/A
Beyoğlu
Istanbul 34250
Turkey
+90 2122437737
www.mandabatmaz.com.tr/tr-TR/ana-sayfa

Opening hours...Daily from 9:30 am
Credit cards..Cash only
Style...Turkish coffee bar

"Located in the Beyoğlu district (a busy area with tourists),
Mandabatmaz is a small shop. The Turkish coffee is made
without using any machines, but the service is quite speedy.
There are only a couple of tables and it's always crowded."
—Gökçe Yildirim

NORM COFFEE
Güneşli Sokak 39/A
Beyoğlu
Istanbul 34410
Turkey
+90 5342014052
www.normcoffee.com

Opening hours.......................................Tue–Fri from 8 am,
Sat–Sun from 10:30 am
Credit cards.....................................Visa and MasterCard
Style...Coffee and food

"I favor Norm Coffee as they are not afraid of being geeky
and meticulous in their approach to coffee and always try to
improve their skills."—Cagatay Gulabioglu

ŞARK KAHVESI
(AT THE GRAND BAZAAR)

Yağlıkçılar Caddesi #134
Fatih
Istanbul 34126
Turkey
+90 2125121144
www.sarkkahvesi.com

Opening hours................................Mon–Sat from 8:30 am
Credit cards..Visa
Style..Turkish coffee bar

"Traditional Turkish coffee is brewed on burning sand. It's
one of the most historic cafes for Turkish coffee, here for
more than sixty years. It is located inside one of the oldest
and biggest bazaars in the world. A hot spot for tourists!"
—Gökçe Yildirim

"A SIMPLE CAFE NEAR A BIG OFFICE HEADQUARTERS BREWING VARIOUS ROASTERS' COFFEES."

NICHOLAS CHISTYAKOV P.174

THE RUSSIAN FEDERATION

"BEST ESPRESSO."

RAÚL RODAS P.175

"BEST FILTER COFFEE."

GWILYM DAVIES P.175

"I HAD THE BEST ESPRESSO AT COFFEEMANIA. IT WAS INCREDIBLY CRAFTED AND VERY WELL BREWED."

NICHOLAS CHISTYAKOV P.175

THE RUSSIAN
FEDERATION

♦MOSCOW PP. 172–175

SCALE

0   140   280
mi.

"THEY SELL AND BREW RAINBOW COFFEE ROASTERS BEANS AND ARE INFLUENCED BY OLGA MELIK-KARAKOZOVA AND HER TEAM OF BARISTA CHAMPIONS."

NICHOLAS CHISTYAKOV P.174

MOSCOW

"YOU CAN MEET THE OWNERS AT THE BAR AND TALK A LOT ABOUT COFFEE SUSTAINABILITY, ETHICS, ECOLOGY, AND MANY COFFEE TOPICS. THEY ROAST AND SOURCE AND BREW THEIR COFFEES."

NICHOLAS CHISTYAKOV P.174

MOSCOW

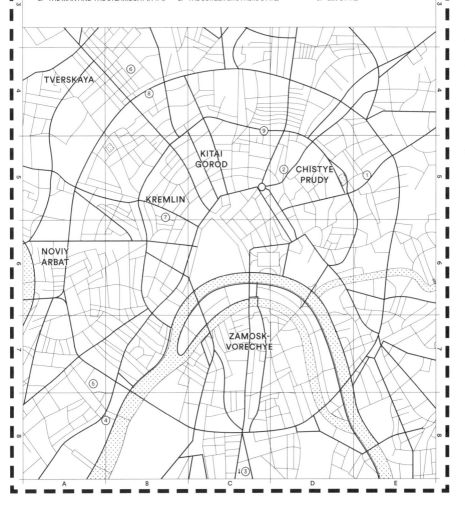

$\hat{N}$ SCALE

0   405   810   1220
yd.

1. CHERNYI COOPERATIVE (P. 174)
2. DOUBLE B (P. 174)
3. THE MAN AND THE STEAMBOAT (P. 174)
4. CAFÉ DEL PARCO (P. 174)
5. WAKEUP CAFÉ (P. 174)
6. THE BURGER BROTHERS (P. 175)
7. COFFEEMANIA (P. 175)
8. GOOD ENOUGH COFFEE (P. 175)
9. LES (P. 175)

TVERSKAYA

KITAI GOROD

CHISTYE PRUDY

KREMLIN

NOVIY ARBAT

ZAMOSK-VORECHYE

CHERNYI COOPERATIVE
Ul Pokrovka, 31
Basmanny District
Moscow 105064
The Russian Federation
www.chernyi.coffee

Opening hours...................................Mon–Fri from 8 am,
Sat–Sun from 10 am
Credit cards...Cash only
Style..Roastery cafe

"Chernyi Cooperative is a small coffee startup. They have
a famous subscription service that is well known in Moscow.
You can meet the owners at the bar and talk a lot about
coffee sustainability, ethics, ecology, and many coffee
topics. They roast and source and brew their coffees."
—Nicholas Chistyakov

DOUBLE B
Milyutinskiy Lane 3
Basmanny District
Moscow 101000
The Russian Federation
www.double-b.ru

Opening hours...................................Mon–Fri from 8 am,
Sat–Sun from 11 am
Credit cards...Visa and MasterCard
Style..Coffee bar

THE MAN AND THE STEAMBOAT
Mytnaya ul. 74 (Danilovsky Market)
Danilovsky District
Moscow 115191
The Russian Federation
+7 9853305847

Opening hours...................................Daily from 8 am
Credit cards...Cash only
Style..Coffee bar

CAFÉ DEL PARCO
Komsomolskiy pr., 7/3k1
Khamovniki District
Moscow 119146
The Russian Federation
+7 9031974995
www.cafedelparco.com

Opening hours...................................Daily from 8 am
Credit cards...Visa and MasterCard
Style..Coffee and food

"Nice food and well situated. They sell and brew Rainbow
Coffee Roasters beans and are influenced by Olga
Melik-Karakozova and her team of barista champions."
—Nicholas Chistyakov

WAKEUP CAFÉ
Timura Frunze 20
Khamovniki District
Moscow 119021
The Russian Federation
www.instagram.com/wakeupcafemoscow

Opening hours...................................Mon–Fri from 8 am,
Sat–Sun from 11 am
Credit cards...Visa and MasterCard
Style..Coffee bar

"A simple cafe near a big office headquarters brewing
various roasters' coffees."—Nicholas Chistyakov

THE BURGER BROTHERS
1-y Tverskoy-Yamskoy per. 11
Tverskoy District
Moscow 125047
The Russian Federation
+7 9263901320
www.theburgerbrothers.ru

Opening hours..Daily from noon
Credit cards.....................................Visa and MasterCard
Style...Coffee and food

LES
Rozhdestvenskiy bu'lvar 10/7
Tverskoy District
Moscow 107031
The Russian Federation
+7 9261775113

Opening hours.................................Mon–Fri from 9 am,
Sat–Sun from 11 am
Credit cards.....................................Visa and MasterCard
Style...Coffee and food

COFFEEMANIA
Mali Cherkasskiy Pereulok 2
Tverskoy District
Moscow 109012
The Russian Federation
+7 4959602295
www.coffeemania.ru

Opening hours.................................Mon–Fri from 8 am,
Sat–Sun from 10 am
Credit cards.........................Visa, MasterCard, and Amex
Style...Coffee bar

"I had the best espresso at Coffeemania. It was incredibly
crafted and very well brewed."—Nicholas Chistyakov

"Best espresso."—Raúl Rodas

TESLA COFFEE
Chernyshevskogo, 1
Sverdlovsk
Yekaterinburg 620014
The Russian Federation
+7 9221611411

Opening hours.................................Mon–Fri from 9 am,
Sat–Sun from 10 am
Credit cards.....................................Visa and MasterCard
Style...Coffee bar

"Best filter coffee."—Gwilym Davies

GOOD ENOUGH COFFEE
Sadovaya-Triumfalnaya Ul 4/1
Tverskoy District
Moscow 127006
The Russian Federation
+7 9636889616

Opening hours.............................Mon–Fri from 8:30 am,
Sat–Sun from 10 am
Credit cards.....................................Visa and MasterCard
Style...Coffee bar

"THE COFFEE BAR IS SMALL, AND TUCKED BETWEEN SOME OF THE WINDING STREETS OF THE CITY, AN EASY WALK FROM THE SANTA MARIA NOVELLA TRAIN STATION."

RYAN WILLBUR P.179

"YOU CAN GET A REALLY NICE BREAKFAST, GREAT COFFEES BREWED IN V60, OR PLAIN TRADITIONAL ESPRESSO DRINKS."

SONJA BJÖRK GRANT P.179

ITALY

"THE BEST COFFEE I HAVE FOUND IN ITALY. IT HAS AN AMAZING LOCATION AROUND THE CORNER FROM THE PANTHEON."

NATHAN MYHRVOLD P.178

"IT'S WHERE I FIRST FELL IN LOVE WITH COFFEE."

SEANNA FOREY P.178

"THE ESPRESSO WAS PULLED FROM A FULLY MANUAL ESPRESSO MACHINE AND SERVED BY A BARISTA NAMED MASSIMO." BRONWEN SERNA P.178

MILAN P. 178 ♥

VENICE P. 179 ♥

♥ TRIESTE P. 178

♥ BOLOGNA P. 178

LUCCA P. 179 ♥

♥ FLORENCE P. 179

ROME P. 178 ♥

ITALY

(N̂)   SCALE

0   80   160
                    mi.

CAFFÈ TERZI

Via Guglielmo Oberdan 10/d
Bologna
Emilia-Romagna 40126
Italy
+39 0510344819
www.caffeterzibologna.com

Opening hours...Mon–Sat from 8 am
Credit cards...Visa and MasterCard
Style...Coffee and food

"It's where I first fell in love with coffee. The feeling I had that first time I went there was an undeniable romance for a sophisticated yet simple European cafe. It was the first time I saw latte art, so maybe that's part of the reason I paid attention to the cafe, but the barista was proud and having fun and you could sense there was a community there."
—Seanna Forey

ESPRESSAMENTE ILLY

Via delle Torri 3
Trieste
Friuli-Venezia Giulia 34100
Italy
+39 40765251
www.illy.com

Opening hours................................Mon–Sat from 7:30 am
Credit cards...Cash only
Style...Coffee and bar

"The espresso was pulled from a fully manual espresso machine and served by a barista named Massimo. You cannot get more classic than that for an espresso."
—Bronwen Serna

SANT'EUSTACHIO IL CAFFÈ

Piazza Sant'Eustachio 82
Regola
Rome
Lazio 00186
Italy
+39 0668802048
www.santeustachioilcaffe.it

Opening hours.......................................Daily from 8:30 am
Credit cards...Cash only
Style...Coffee bar

"The best coffee I have found in Italy. It has an amazing location around the corner from the Pantheon. In my view it's by far the best in Rome and is a sentimental favorite of mine."—Nathan Myhrvold

TAZZA D'ORO

Via dei Pastini 11
Colonna
Rome
Lazio 00186
Italy
+39 066789792
www.tazzadorocoffeeshop.com

Opening hours.....................................Mon–Fri from 7 am,
Sat–Sun from 8 am
Credit cards...Visa and MasterCard
Style...Coffee bar

"For the romance, the best espresso is clearly at Tazza d'Oro."—Kris Schackman

TAGLIO

Via Vigevano 10
Milan
Lombardy 20144
Italy
+39 0236534294
www.taglio.me

Opening hours.......................................Mon–Fri from 8 am,
Sat–Sun from 8:30 am
Credit cards...Visa and MasterCard
Style...Coffee and food

"Yes, it is still surprising to find progressively oriented coffee (never mind filter) in Italy, but the real surprise is in how organic and obvious-feeling Taglio manages to make their combination of great coffee with the best parts of Italian food culture."—Alex Bernson

DITTA ARTIGIANALE
Via dei Neri 32/R
Santa Croce
Florence
Tuscany 50122
Italy
+39 0552741541
www.dittaartigianale.it

Opening hours..Daily from 8 am
Credit cards.............................Visa, MasterCard, and Amex
Style..Coffee and food

"The first third-wave cafe in Italy, owned by Francesco Sanapo, one of the most famous Italian baristas. The place is in downtown Florence in a beautiful house. You can get a really nice breakfast (Australian style), great coffees brewed in V60, or plain traditional espresso drinks. They also have alcoholic coffee drinks. The mixture of the design is Italian, Australian, and central European . . . cool but with old-fashioned hints. The LP player and books make a great spirit."—Sonja Björk Grant

"Ditta is famous for being Italy's first modern coffee bar, serving the best coffee in the country. But that's not why I love it. I love it for being one of the most energetic cafes I've ever been to, with people spilling out into the street all day and night outside the cafe, sipping their espresso or wine, having fun."—Scott Rao

"One of my favorite places to drink coffee. Part of the experience is being in Italy, where coffee is so traditional. You can visit hundreds of great cafes, but when you sit down at Ditta Artigianale, you get a more progressive coffee experience—coffee with bright, floral flavors. Plus, you have the opportunity to drink filter coffee, which is rare for that part of the world. The setting is also remarkable. The coffee bar is small, and tucked between some of the winding streets of the city, an easy walk from the Santa Maria Novella train station. Additionally, they offer a food menu of some very delicious and simple plates."—Ryan Willbur

BAR PASTICCERIA ELISA
Via Elisa 1
Lucca
Tuscany 55100
Italy
+39 0583493743

Opening hours...Tue–Sun from 7 am
Credit cards...Cash only
Style..Coffee and food

"The Bar Elisa sits across the parking lot from a church school, just outside the city walls of Lucca. Giovanni Bianchi and his wife are the proprietors, Giovanni tending to the coffee and his wife tending to the baked goods, all of which are made on-site. It was built in the mid-1960s and has all the elements of Italian mid-century design: stainless-steel minimalist bars, big glass panels everywhere, space-age touches. I went in one day in June, drank my espresso ristretto, quickly and went away. The next day I came back, and Giovanni remembered my order and gave me the same thing again without asking. That's the kind of place the Elisa is."—Peter Giuliano

CAFFÈ DEL DOGE
Venizia Rialto, Calle dei Cinque
San Polo
Venice
Veneto 609
Italy
+39 0415227787
www.caffedeldoge.com

Opening hours..Daily from 7 am
Credit cards...Cash only
Style..Coffee bar

"A strange little cafe tucked away and serving a host of single-origin coffees from different grinders. Still very Italian."—James Hoffmann

AFRICA

SCALE

0   350   700   mi.

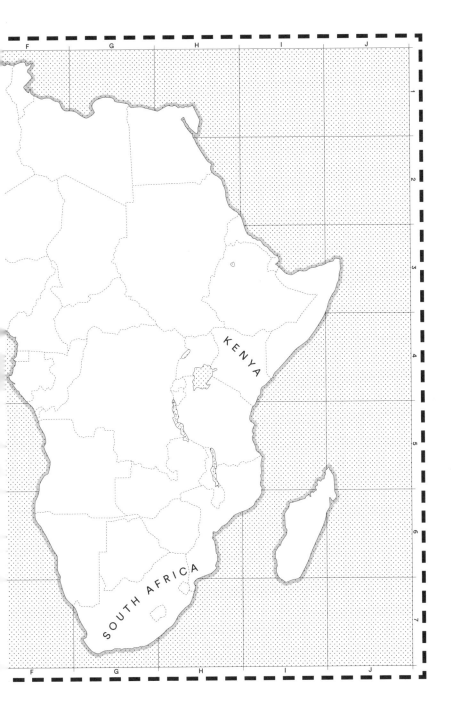

> "SO MUCH ATTENTION TO DETAIL, BOTH IN THE BREWING OF YOUR CUP AND IN THE SPACE AND ATMOSPHERE THE WHOLE EXPERIENCE IMPARTS."
>
> JOANNE BERRY P.184

KENYA & SOUTH AFRICA

> "EVERY ASPECT OF WHAT THEY DO IS EXECUTED WITH CLINICAL PRECISION, AND YOU ARE ALWAYS GREETED WITH THE WARMEST SMILES." JOANNE BERRY P.184

> "A FUN AND ADVENTUROUS CAFE AND ROASTERY THAT HAS CHALLENGED THE DURBAN COFFEE CULTURE INTO GROWTH."
>
> JOANNE BERRY P.184

> "I ALWAYS TRY TO STOP THERE, COMING BACK FROM TRIPS TO ANYWHERE IN RIFT VALLEY."
>
> METTE-MARIE HANSEN P.184

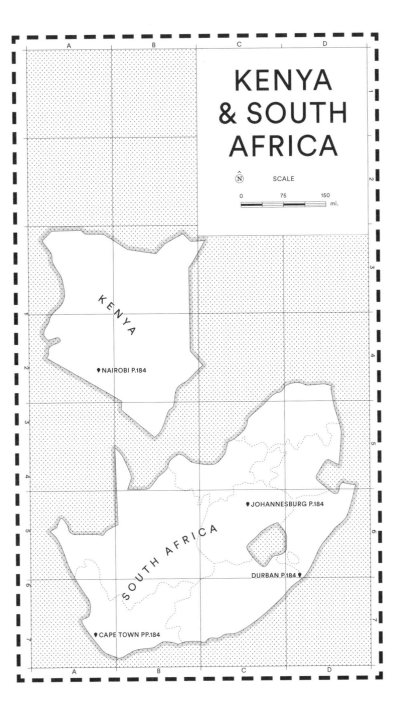

KENYA & SOUTH AFRICA

$\hat{N}$ SCALE

0   75   150
mi.

KENYA

● NAIROBI P.184

SOUTH AFRICA

● JOHANNESBURG P.184

DURBAN P.184 ●

● CAPE TOWN PP.184

CAFÉ UBUNTU

Off Old Naivasha Road
Maai Mahiu
Nairobi
Kenya
+254 715022162
www.cafeubuntublog.com

Opening hours............................Mon–Fri from 10 am,
Sat–Sun from 11 am
Credit cards...Cash only
Style...Coffee and food

"I always try to stop there, coming back from trips to
anywhere in Rift Valley."—Mette-Marie Hansen

FATHER COFFEE

73 Juta Street
Braamfontein
Johannesburg
Gauteng 2001
South Africa
+27 825134258
www.fathercoffee.co.za

Opening hours.........................Mon–Fri from 8:30 am,
Sat from 9 am
Credit cards............................Visa and MasterCard
Style...Roastery cafe

"A beautifully designed store, optimizing the space it
operates in and making you want to linger over every
delicious cup."—Joanne Berry

FACTORY CAFÉ

369 Magwaza Maphalala
Congela
Durban
KwaZulu-Natal 4001
South Africa
+27 312053283
www.factorycafe.co.za

Opening hours.........................Mon–Fri from 7:30 am,
Sat from 8:30 am
Credit cards............................Visa and MasterCard
Style...Roastery cafe

"A fun and adventurous cafe and roastery that has
challenged the Durban coffee culture into growth."
—Joanne Berry

ESPRESSO LAB MICROROASTERS

The Old Biscuit Mill, 373-375 Albert Road
Woodstock
Cape Town
Western Cape 7925
South Africa
+27 214470845
www.espressolabmicroroasters.com

Opening hours.......................................Mon–Sat from 8 am
Credit cards........................Visa, MasterCard, and Amex
Style...Roastery cafe

"Every aspect of what they do is executed with clinical
precision, and you are always greeted with the warmest
smiles."—Joanne Berry

ROSETTA ROASTERY

66 Albert Road
Woodstock
Cape Town
Western Cape 7925
South Africa
+27 214474099
www.rosettaroastery.com

Opening hours.........................Mon–Fri from 8 am,
Sat from 9 am
Credit cards............................Visa and MasterCard
Style...Roastery cafe

"So much attention to detail, both in the brewing of your
cup and in the space and atmosphere the whole experience
imparts."—Joanne Berry

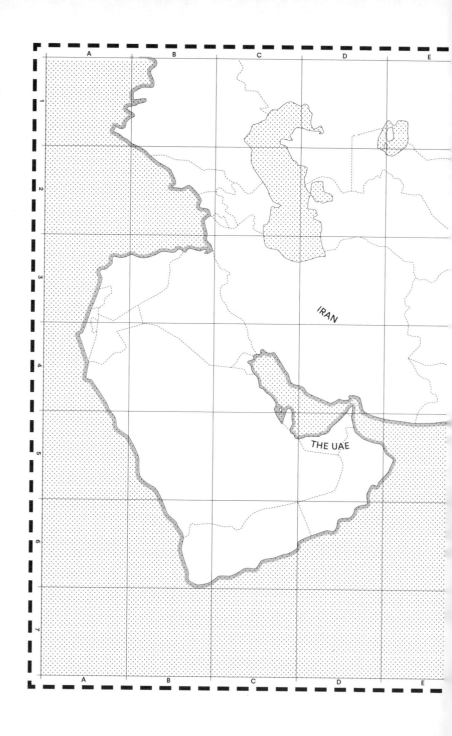

IRAN

THE UAE

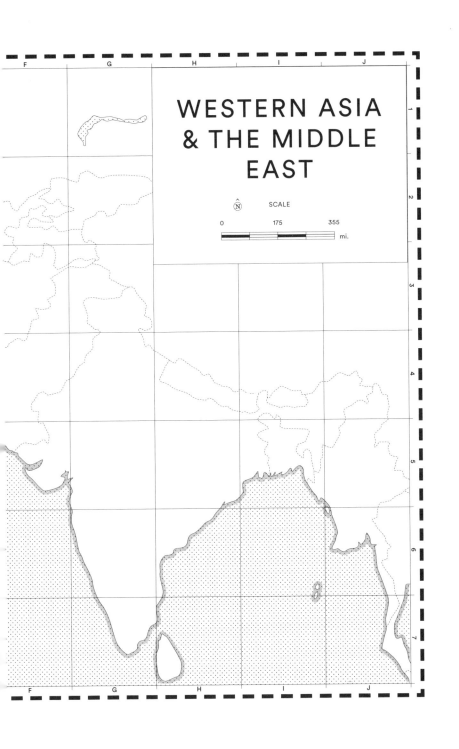

WESTERN ASIA
& THE MIDDLE
EAST

$\widehat{N}$

SCALE

0   175   355

mi.

"FULL IRANIAN TRADITIONAL MENU, BREWING BAR, POSTMODERN INTERIOR DESIGN, AND GREAT SERVICE."

MOHAMMAD KHANI P.190

"THE FIRST ROASTERY CAFE IN IRAN, WITH MORE THAN SIX OUTLETS IN TEHRAN AND OTHER CITIES, INCLUDING THE NORTHERN PART OF IRAN."

MOHAMMAD KHANI P.191

IRAN & THE UAE

"AWESOME EXECUTION OF COFFEE, FOOD, AND TEA."

LAILA GHAMBARI WILLBUR P.191

IRAN PP. 190-191

THE UAE P. 191

IRAN AND
THE UAE

(N̂)   SCALE

0   130   265
                    mi.

STREET LOUNGE CAFÉ
Almas Shashr Tower, Pezeshkan Street
Malli Abad
Shiraz
Fars
Iran
+98 9173047400
www.facebook.com/pg/street.lounge/
about/?ref=page_internal

Opening hours..Daily from 9 am
Credit cards...Cash only
Style...Coffee bar

"Full menu, Dalla Corte DC espresso machine, reasonable
menu prices, unique interior design, excellent service, and
specialty coffee."—Mohammad Khani

SARAYE AMERIHA BOUTIQUE CAFÉ
(inside Saraye Ameriha Boutique Hotel)
Kashan
Isfahan
Iran
+98 3155240220
www.sarayeameriha.com

Opening hours..Daily from 9 am
Credit cards...Cash only
Style..Coffee and food

"Full Iranian traditional menu, brewing bar, postmodern
interior design, and great service."—Mohammad Khani

MAHTAB CAFÉ
#60, ASP Residential Complex, 64th Street
(Kordestan Highway)
Amir Abad
Tehran
Iran
+98 2188054800
www.cafemahtab.ir

Opening hours..Daily from 9:30 am
Credit cards..Shetab
Style..Coffee and food

"Iranian menu, marvelous interiors, full menu, organic food
and beverages, and superb service."—Mohammad Khani

V CAFÉ
#336/2, Nayebi Street, Felestin Street
District 2 Tehran
Tehran
Iran
+98 2166976041
www.vcafetehran.ir

Opening hours..Daily from 9 am
Credit cards...Cash only
Style...Coffee bar

"Full menu, La Marzocco espresso machine, attractive
interior design, freshly baked bread, and excellent service."
—Mohammad Khani

ROBERTO CAFÉ
#4, 2nd Boustan, Pasdaran Avenue
District 4 Tehran
Tehran
Iran
+98 2126701830
www.robertocafe.ir

Opening hours.....................................Mon–Fri from 10 am,
Sat–Sun from 8:30 am
Credit cards..Shetab
Style...Coffee bar

"Brewing bar, Dalla Corte DC multiboiler espresso machine,
specialty coffee, pleasing ambience, grand interior design,
and full menu while maintaining service and quality
standards."—Mohammad Khani

SAM CAFÉ

Sam Center, 1st floor, Fereshteh Street
Elahiyeh
Tehran
Iran
+98 2122653842
www.samcafe.ir

Opening hours..Daily from 9 am
Credit cards..Cash only
Style..Roastery cafe

"Brewing bar, full menu, Slayer espresso machine,
coffee-roasting-process display using a Probat roasting
machine, and outstanding interior design."
—Mohammad Khani

"Interesting design and awesome execution of coffee,
food, and tea. It's really one of the only truly unique cafes
I've ever been to, meaning I have nothing to compare it
to. It's all open, no ordering counter. It almost feels more
like an open-concept kitchen restaurant, but it's very much
a cozy coffee shop."—Laila Ghambari Willbur

LAMIZ

#1435, Vali-e-Asr Street
Zafaraniyeh
Tehran
Iran
+98 2166462204
www.lamizcoffee.com

Opening hours..Daily from 7 am
Credit cards..Shetab
Style..Roastery cafe

"The first roastery cafe in Iran, with more than six outlets in
Tehran and other cities, including the northern part of Iran."
—Mohammad Khani

TOM & SERG

15A Street
Al Quoz Industrial 1
Dubai
United Arab Emirates
+971 564746812
www.tomandserg.com

Opening hours..Daily from 8 am
Credit cards..Visa and MasterCard
Style..Coffee and food

"Good food and good coffee."—Khalid Al Mulla

THE SUM OF US

6 Street
Trade Center 1
Dubai
United Arab Emirates
+971 564457526
www.thesumofusdubai.com

Opening hours..Daily from 8 am
Credit cards..Visa and MasterCard
Style..Coffee and food

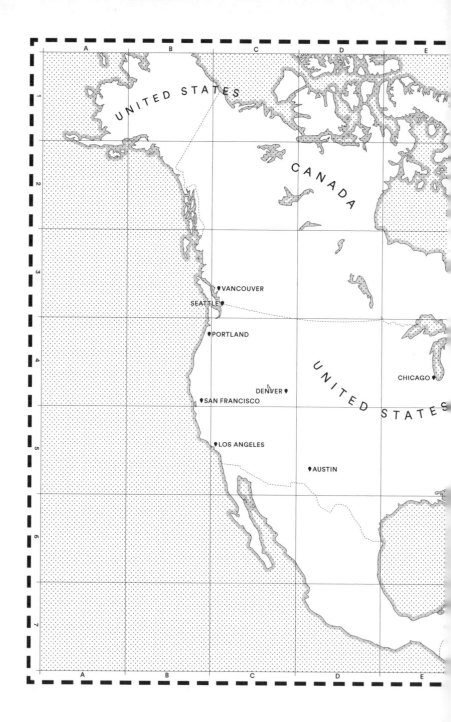

	A	B	C	D	E
1		UNITED STATES			
2			CANADA		
3			♥VANCOUVER		
		SEATTLE♥			
4		♥PORTLAND			CHICAGO♥
			DENVER♥	UNITED STATES	
	♥SAN FRANCISCO				
5		♥LOS ANGELES	♥AUSTIN		
6					
7					

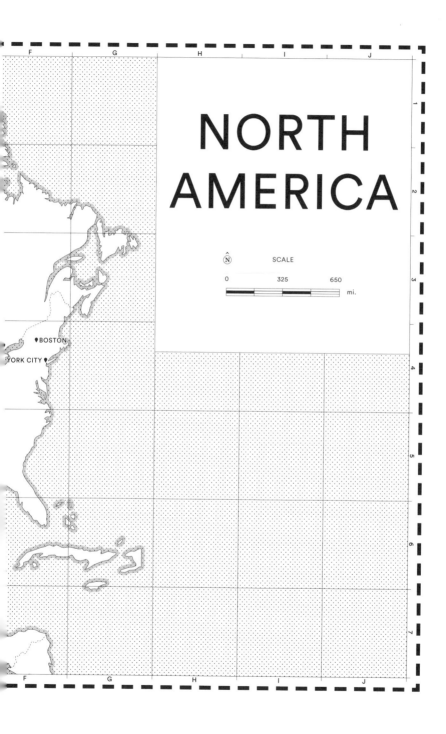

F G H I J

1

2

NORTH
AMERICA

N̂   SCALE

0   325   650
▬▬▬▬▬▬▬▬▬▬▬ mi.

3

♦BOSTON
YORK CITY ♦

4

5

6

7

F G H I J

"ENGAGED SERVICE, GOOD HUSTLE, AND AN INTENTIONAL MENU—EVERYTHING HAS BEEN CONSIDERED AND THOUGHT OUT."

DREW JOHNSON P.199

"THEY HAVE OUTSTANDING FILTER COFFEE AND THEIR ESPRESSO BLEND IS THE PERFECT BALANCE OF CHARACTER AND SWEETNESS."

SHANE DEVERAUX P.198

CANADA

"LIKE YOUR FAVORITE BAR WHERE YOU'RE GREETED WITH FRIENDLY FACES AFTER A HARD DAY AT WORK (OR IN THIS CASE, BEFORE ONE)—COMPLETE WITH A LIME-GREEN WALL TO MAKE YOU SMILE."

JESSICA JOHNSTON P.199

"THESE GUYS ARE COMMITTED TO QUALITY, CONSTANTLY STRIVING TO IMPROVE THEIR GREEN COFFEE BUYING AND ROASTING, AND TAKING THEIR COFFEE SERVICE TO THE NEXT LEVEL."

JESSICA JOHNSTON P.197

"A COFFEEHOUSE IN THE TRUE SENSE. A HUB FOR THE COMMUNITY." DREW JOHNSON P.198

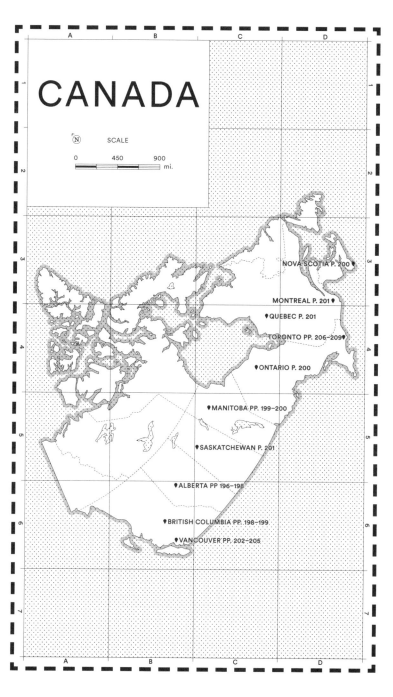

CANADA

SCALE

0   450   900 mi.

NOVA SCOTIA P. 200 ♥

MONTREAL P. 201 ♥

♥ QUEBEC P. 201

TORONTO PP. 206–209 ♥

♥ ONTARIO P. 200

♥ MANITOBA PP. 199–200

♥ SASKATCHEWAN P. 201

♥ ALBERTA PP 196–198

♥ BRITISH COLUMBIA PP. 198–199

♥ VANCOUVER PP. 202–205

MONOGRAM COFFEE

4814 16 Street Southwest
Altadore
Calgary
Alberta T2T 4J5
Canada
+1 4034733886
www.monogramcoffee.com

Opening hours........................Mon–Fri from 6:30 am,
Sat–Sun from 7:30 am
Credit cards...........................Visa, MasterCard, and Amex
Style..Coffee and small bites

"Barista champions create a friendly atmosphere and some world-class coffees."—Josh Hockin

"Monogram's location in Altadore is the closest thing Calgary has to a Melbourne-style hole-in-the-wall cafe in all the right ways: concrete floors, white walls, killer coffee, and effortless cool. They have a solid coffee menu for purists (espresso-based drinks, Espro and Kinto offerings) and an equally impressive list of high-quality alternatives (the London Fog is superpopular, and for good reason). This has also got to be the most dog-friendly cafe in the city." —Jessica Johnston

ANALOG COFFEE

740 17 Avenue Southwest
Beltline
Calgary
Alberta T2S 0B7
Canada
+1 4032652112
www.fratellocoffee.com/analog-coffee

Opening hours...Daily from 6:30 am
Credit cards...Visa and MasterCard
Style..Coffee and food

"Analog is a bustling, stylish blur of Calgarians gathering to enjoy coffee and conversation. This is one of my favorite spaces in the city—the right mix of trendy and classic, comforting and beautiful. They have a great pour-over bar and a dedicated clientele who love what the staff do. Situated on a busy corner, this is arguably some of the best people-watching this city has to offer. Order a coffee and sit by the window (if you can find a seat)—there's no better place to see Calgary do its thing."—Jessica Jonhston

PHIL & SEBASTIAN

Simmons Building, 618 Confluence Way Southeast
East Village
Calgary
Alberta T2G 0G1
Canada
+1 5873532268
www.philsebastian.com

Opening hours.............................Mon–Fri from 6:30 am,
Sat–Sun from 7:30 am
Credit cards..Visa and MasterCard
Style...Coffee bar

"Arguably the most progressive coffee roaster in Canada. An exacting approach to all aspects of coffee making." —Josh Hockin

"It's hard to overstate the impact Phil & Sebastian have had on specialty coffee in Calgary, and they continue to push the boundaries of what specialty coffee should be. They source green and roast with impeccable care and an unrelenting commitment to quality, and it shows in the cup. Their cafe in the historic Simmons Building, in the East Village of Calgary, is a gorgeous restored factory space with soaring ceilings and exposed brick that they share with a thriving local restaurant and a stunning bakery. You can't go wrong with their menu, but I love getting an AeroPress and settling in at Simmons to watch the parade as some of Calgary's hippest people mingle."—Jessica Johnston

"This was the place where my wife started to enjoy coffee and where I had my first naturally processed Ethiopian, my first really good espresso, and many other eye-opening coffee experiences. They have had such a profound impact on Calgary."—Benjamin Put

GRAVITY ESPRESSO & WINE BAR
909 10 Street Southeast
Inglewood
Calgary
Alberta T2G 0S7
Canada
+1 4034570697
www.cafegravity.com

Opening hours.................................Mon–Fri from 7 am,
Sat–Sun from 8 am
Credit cards.................................MasterCard and Visa
Style.................................Coffee and wine bar

"Specialty coffee by day, wine and craft beer by night. This is a true neighborhood cafe, dedicated to supporting other small businesses in the 'hood and offering a space for local musicians to play live gigs. Lots of reclaimed wood and art curated by a local gallery. A nice space to feel like you can sit and read a book without being rushed or crowded out, and also super family-friendly."—Josh Hockin

ROSSO COFFEE ROASTERS
803 24 Avenue Southeast #15
Ramsay
Calgary
Alberta T2G 4G5
Canada
+1 4039711800
www.rossocoffeeroasters.com

Opening hours.................................Mon–Fri from 7 am,
Sat–Sun from 8 am
Credit cards.................................Visa, MasterCard, and Amex
Style.................................Coffee and food

"In a short time, these guys have become a staple in the Calgary coffee scene. They're a young, energetic, and ambitious company determined to bring great coffee to their city. In the last few years, they've expanded to sourcing and roasting, and they continue to apply what they're learning to their product and service. They pop up at cool stores and markets all over the city. Rosso knows its customers well and offers a diverse selection of coffee, but I think their strong suit is their constantly evolving but always approachable house espresso—try it in a cappuccino. A classic."—Jessica Johnston

TRANSCEND
9869 62 Avenue Northwest
Argyll
Edmonton
Alberta T6E 0E4
Canada
+1 7804309198
www.transcendcoffee.ca

Opening hours.................................Mon–Fri from 7:30 am,
Sat from 9:30 am, closed Sundays
Credit cards.................................Visa, MasterCard, and Amex
Style.................................Coffee and food

"Three locations and a roasting facility. They do a good job."
—Shane Deveraux

"I recommend Transcend to anyone who so much as mumbles 'Edmonton' in a sentence. These guys are committed to quality, constantly striving to improve their green coffee buying and roasting, and taking their coffee service to the next level. They have extremely well trained, knowledgeable staff and a relaxed, stylish vibe in their cafes. You can't go wrong with anything on their menu, but I'm particularly partial to a Transcend cappuccino."
—Jessica Johnston

ELM CAFÉ
10140 117 Street Northwest
Oliver
Edmonton
Alberta
T5K 1X3
Canada
+1 7807563356
www.elmcafe.ca

Opening hours.................................Mon–Fri from 7:30 am,
Sat from 8 am, Sun from 9 am
Credit cards.................................Visa and MasterCard
Style.................................Coffee and food

"Good coffee and sandwiches made with fresh, local ingredients. They are rapidly expanding with a popular catering service and several other locations in Edmonton, including a mixed-use cafe/general store/event space. Superfriendly baristas."—Jessica Johnston

GRÉMIO
1919 West Caribou Street
Jasper
Alberta B0B 6G6
Canada
+351 920225478

Opening hours......................................Mon–Fri from noon
Credit cards..Cash only
Style...Coffee and food

DOSE
4912 50 Avenue
Downtown
Red Deer
Alberta T4N 4A8
Canada
+1 4033433722
www.dosecoffeeco.ca

Opening hours................................Mon–Fri from 7:30 am,
Sat from 10 am, Sun from noon
Credit cards.............................Visa, MasterCard, and Amex
Style...Coffee and food

Vancouver, see pages 202–205

RATIO COFFEE & PASTRY
3101 29th Street #4
Vernon
British Columbia V1T 5A8
Canada
+1 2505459800
www.ratiocoffee.ca

Opening hours......................................Mon–Fri from 7 am,
Sat from 8 am
Credit cards.............................Visa, MasterCard, and Amex
Style...Coffee and food

"Small-town killer."—Shane Deveraux

BOWS & ARROWS
483 Garbally Road
Burnside
Victoria
British Columbia V8T 2J9
Canada
+1 2505907792
www.bowsandarrowscoffee.com

Opening hours................................Mon–Fri from 7:30 am
Credit cards.............................Visa and MasterCard
Style...Roastery cafe

"Their coffees are the most consistent and interesting. They have outstanding filter coffee and their espresso blend, the Hathaway, is the perfect balance of character and sweetness while showing so well in milk or black."—Shane Deveraux

"It's hard not to sound like a groupie when it comes to Bows & Arrows. This place is a checklist of cool: a light-flooded warehouse roastery in an industrial area, superstylish walk-up coffee bar with a collection of unique teacups and ceramics to drink out of, mason jars filled with some of the finest coffee that exists, and an enviable vinyl collection to make your head spin. But it's also, more important, a collection of people who at once really care about what they're doing and acknowledge that specialty coffee is far more complex than just creating cool spaces to enjoy it. These guys are coffee professionals, but they're also, maybe more so, activists. Just go."—Jessica Johnston

HABIT COFFEE
808 Yates Street
Downtown
Victoria
British Columbia V8W 1L8
Canada
+1 2505905953
www.habitcoffee.com

Opening hours......................................Mon–Fri from 7 am,
Sat–Sun from 8 am
Credit cards.............................Visa, MasterCard, and Amex
Style...Coffee bar

"A coffeehouse in the true sense. A hub for the community. Good music in a comfortable space that isn't kitschy. And it isn't distracted by navel gazing."—Drew Johnson

"Habit's Atrium location offers a sleek, industrial-chic vibe with a wide-open, light-filled space and floor-to-ceiling windows to watch the happenings of downtown Victoria. This place is a community hub that makes Victoria feel like a small town (in a good way)."—Jessica Johnston

HEY HAPPY

560 Johnson Street
Downtown
Victoria
British Columbia V8W 1M2
Canada
+1 2505909680
www.heyhappycoffee.com

Opening hours...................................Mon–Fri from 7:30 am,
Sat–Sun from 9 am
Credit cards................................Visa and MasterCard
Style..Coffee bar

"There is engaged service, good hustle, and an intentional menu—as in, everything has been considered and thought out. No one on the face of the earth can sell whole-bean coffee better than Rob Kettner."—Drew Johnson

"Like your favorite bar where you're greeted with friendly faces after a hard day at work (or in this case, before one)—complete with a lime-green wall to make you smile. Hey Happy offers single-cup service, a menu that rotates daily, and Rob Kettner's wonderful imagination applied to interesting curated coffee cocktails, including an espresso mint julep."—Jessica Johnston

PARLOUR

468 Main Street
Exchange District
Winnipeg
Manitoba R2H 1E9
Canada
www.parlourcoffee.ca

Opening hours...Mon–Fri from 7 am,
Sat from 9 am
Credit cards...............................Visa and MasterCard
Style..Coffee bar

"A beautiful, light-filled space with a long wood bar, minimalist seating, and a gorgeous chandelier to give it a touch of old-world glamour. Owner Nils Vik is a former designer and it shows with his impeccable attention to detail and pared-down aesthetic. A great place to have ` a cappuccino and watch the world (or Winnipeg) go by."
—Shane Deveraux

"Clean, simple, and elegant design."—Benjamin Put

MAKE COFFEE + STUFF

751 Corydon Avenue
McMillan
Winnipeg
Manitoba R3M 0W5
Canada
+1 2044140101
http://stuffgroup.net/makecoffee/wp

Opening hours...................................Mon–Fri from 7:30 am
Credit cards..........................Visa, MasterCard, and Amex
Style..Coffee bar

"You'd be forgiven for thinking you were sitting in a hip young art gallery or well-curated design space instead of a cafe. In fact, you kind of are. MAKE is the intersection of design and coffee—these guys regularly showcase the work of emerging architects and fashion and design students and have a constantly changing and programmable, superminimalist space. I sat at one of their impressive long slabs of wood and sipped a coffee as I watched architecture students build models on another slab of wood nearby. A really peaceful and unique space."
—Jessica Johnson

LITTLE SISTER COFFEE MAKER

A-470 River Avenue
Osborne Village
Winnipeg
Manitoba R3L 0C8
Canada
www.littlesistercoffeemaker.ca

Opening hours...Mon–Fri from 7 am,
Sat–Sun from 8 am
Credit cards...............................Visa and MasterCard
Style..Coffee bar

"These guys are champions of Canadian roasters, offering a rotating selection of the best the country has to offer."
—Jessica Johnston

"Exceptional."—Benjamin Put

THOM BARGEN
64 Sherbrook Street
West Broadway
Winnipeg
Manitoba R3C 2B3
Canada
+1 2042345678
www.thombargen.com

Opening hours................................Mon–Fri from 7 am,
Sat–Sun from 8 am
Credit cards...........................Visa, MasterCard, and Amex
Style...Coffee bar

"A cozy, gorgeous space with the menu written on huge scrolls of brown butcher paper. They share it with a beautiful handcrafted leather goods boutique. It has less than a dozen seats, super friendly baristas, and a neighborhood feel. Pour-overs are their filter specialty. They are always on the hunt for new ways to improve their coffee game."—Jessica Johnston

"I was completely blown away by the quality, diversity, and maturity of the shops and the Winnipeg coffee scene!"
—Benjamin Put

TWO IF BY SEA
1869 Upper Water Street
Downtown
Halifax
Nova Scotia B3J 1S9
Canada
+1 9024924600
www.twoifbyseacafe.ca

Opening hours................................Mon–Fri from 7:30 am,
Sat from 8 am
Credit cards.......................................Visa and MasterCard
Style..Coffee and food

PINECONE
175 John Street South
Corktown
Hamilton
Ontario L8N 2C5
Canada
+1 2898538613
www.pineconecoffeeco.ca

Opening hours................................Mon–Sat from 8 am,
Sun from 9 am
Credit cards.......................................Visa and MasterCard
Style...Coffee bar

"While I was expecting serviceable coffee in this smaller city with very little specialty coffee, I instead got a near-perfect brew of an exceptionally tasty Ethiopian coffee."—Keaton Ritchie

BREAD & SONS BAKERY
195 Bank Street
Centretown
Ottawa
Ontario K2P 1W7
Canada
+1 6132305302
www.breadandsons.ca

Opening hours.................................Mon–Fri from 7:30 am
Credit cards...........................Visa, MasterCard, and Amex
Style..Coffee and food

"While offering probably the best croissants and bread in Canada, Bread & Sons also makes Ottawa's best coffee. The owner is one of the most quality-obsessed people I've ever met in my life, and it shows."—Scott Rao

Toronto, see pages 206–209

CAFÉ MYRIADE

1432 Rue Mackay
Downtown
Montreal
Quebec H3G 2H7
Canada
+1 5149391717
www.cafemyriade.com

Opening hours................................Mon–Fri from 7:30 am,
Sat–Sun from 9 am
Credit cards...........................Visa, MasterCard, and Amex
Style...Coffee bar

PIKOLO ESPRESSO BAR

3418B Avenue du Parc
Milton Park
Montreal
Quebec H2X 2H5
Canada
+1 5145086800
www.pikoloespresso.com

Opening hours................................Mon–Fri from 7:30 am,
Sat–Sun from 9 am
Credit cards...Visa and MasterCard
Style...Coffee bar

"Pikolo is a cozy space with friendly baristas who know their
regulars by name. It's a cafe that is popular with students
and freelancers and where regulars happily share tables
with strangers."—Keaton Ritchie

LE PISTA CAFÉ MONTRÉAL
(MOBILE CAFE; LOCATIONS VARY)

Montreal
Quebec H2S 1S5
Canada
+1 5144366329
www.cafepista.com

Opening hours...Vary
Credit cards...........................Visa, MasterCard, and Amex
Style...Mobile coffee bar

"A cart completely powered by a bike driveshaft. The
grinder even runs off a direct chain link to the pedals and
there's a lever espresso machine. I had an incredible shot
of an Ethiopian coffee from Dispatch Coffee Roasters."
—Josh Littlefield

MUSEO

730A Broadway Avenue
Nutana
Saskatoon
Saskatchewan S7N 1B4
Canada
+1 3069744880
www.museocoffee.com

Opening hours..Daily from 9 am
Credit cards........................Visa, MasterCard, and Amexr
Style...Coffee bar

COLLECTIVE COFFEE

220 20th Street West
Riversdale
Saskatoon
Saskatchewan S7M 0W9
Canada
www.collectivecoffee.com

Opening hours....................................Mon–Sat from 7 am,
Sun from 10 am
Credit cards.....................................Visa and MasterCard
Style...Coffee and food

"THE PLACE THAT MADE ME DETERMINED TO LEARN LATTE ART." ANDREW HETZEL P.204

"NO DETAILS ARE OVERLOOKED, FROM THE WALL BUILT WITH RECLAIMED BRICKS FROM HISTORIC GASTOWN TO THE GLASS-ENCASED PRODUCTION FACILITY FOR THEIR LUCKY'S DOUGHNUTS BRAND." ANTHONY BENDA P.205

VANCOUVER

"FANTASTIC STAFF AND PRODUCTION/CAFE SPACE." STEPHEN MORRISSEY P.204

"THE BEST ESPRESSO WAS AT 49TH PARALLEL— REALLY RICH, SWEET, AND CHOCOLATY." ROBERT DAN GRIFFIN P.205

"MY FAVORITE FILTER COFFEE ROUTINELY COMES FROM REVOLVER, A MULTI-ROASTER CAFE THAT CURATES COFFEES FROM ROASTERS AROUND THE WORLD." DAVID NIGEL FLYNN P.204

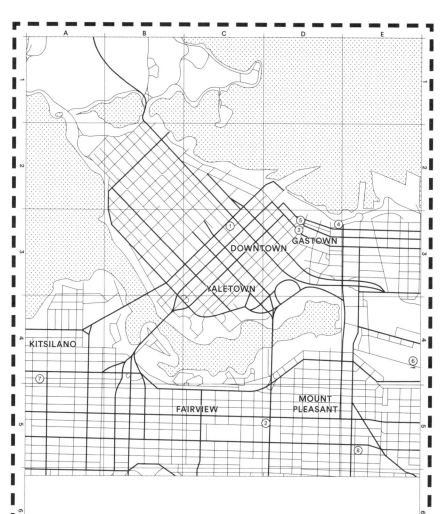

DOWNTOWN

GASTOWN

YALETOWN

KITSILANO

FAIRVIEW

MOUNT PLEASANT

VANCOUVER

N

SCALE

0   275   550   825

yd.

1. CAFFÈ ARTIGIANO (P. 204)
2. ELYSIAN COFFEE (P. 204)
3. REVOLVER COFFEE (P. 204)
4. THE BIRDS & THE BEETS (P. 204)

5. TIMBERTRAIN COFFEE ROASTERS (P. 205)
6. PRADO CAFÉ (P. 205)
7. 49TH PARALLEL
   COFFEE ROASTERS (P. 205)

8. 49TH PARALLEL
   COFFEE ROASTERS (P. 205)

CAFFÈ ARTIGIANO

763 Hornby Street
Downtown
Vancouver
British Columbia V6Z 1S2
Canada
+1 6046947737
www.caffeartigiano.com

Opening hours.................................Mon–Fri from 5:30 am,
Sat–Sun from 6:30 am
Credit cards............................Visa, MasterCard, and Amex
Style...Coffee bar

"This is the place that made me determined to learn latte art."—Andrew Hetzel

ELYSIAN COFFEE

590 West Broadway
Fairview
Vancouver
British Columbia V5Z 1E9
Canada
+1 6048745909
www.elysiancoffee.com

Opening hours...................................Daily from 7 am
Credit cards............................Visa, MasterCard, and Amex
Style...Coffee bar

"Best espresso."—Shane Deveraux

"Fantastic staff and production/cafe space."
—Stephen Morrissey

REVOLVER COFFEE

325 Cambie Street
Gastown
Vancouver
British Columbia V6B 1H7
Canada
+1 6045584444
www.revolvercoffee.ca

Opening hours................................Mon–Fri from 7:30 am,
Sat from 9 am
Credit cards..Visa and MasterCard
Style...Coffee bar

"My favorite filter coffee routinely comes from Revolver, a multiroaster cafe that curates coffees from roasters around the world. You know your favorite wine shop that only carries the coolest stuff from around the world? That's Revolver. The filter is always changing but always delicious."
—David Nigel Flynn

THE BIRDS & THE BEETS

55 Powell Street
Gastown
Vancouver
British Columbia V6A 1E9
Canada
+1 6048937832
www.birdsandbeets.ca

Opening hours..Mon–Fri from 7 am,
Sat–Sun from 9 am
Credit cards............................Visa, MasterCard, and Amex
Style..Coffee and food

"Finally, in Vancouver, you can eat something good and have excellent coffee in the same place. No more cardboard cookies and dry scones. It's what more shops will start doing all over North America, and they'll then surely point to Melbourne to say it's the one thing we haven't ripped off from Scandinavia. And they have the best barista in Vancouver."—Drew Johnson

TIMBERTRAIN COFFEE ROASTERS

311 West Cordova Street
Gastown
Vancouver
British Columbia V6B 2B2
Canada
+1 6049159188
www.timbertrain.ca

Opening hours................................Mon–Fri from 7 am,
Sat–Sun from 8 am
Credit cards...Visa and MasterCard
Style..Coffee bar

This is a stunning cafe. Beautiful booths, just the right amount of wood trim on everything, and each detail is perfect, down to the sparkling water on tap. If you are in the neighborhood, plan to get a coffee here and around the corner at Revolver on Cambie Street.

PRADO CAFÉ

1938 Commercial Drive
Grandview-Woodland
Vancouver
British Columbia V5N 4A7
Canada
+1 6042555537
www.pradocafevancouver.com

Opening hours..................................Mon–Sat from 7 am,
Sun from 8 am
Credit cards............................Visa, MasterCard, and Amex
Style..Coffee bar

49TH PARALLEL COFFEE ROASTERS

2198 West 4th Avenue
Kitsilano
Vancouver
British Columbia V6K 4S2
Canada
+1 6044204901
www.49thcoffee.com

Opening hours...Daily from 7 am
Credit cards............................Visa, MasterCard, and Amex
Style...Coffee and doughnuts

"This is a large space that is designed to feel cozy and small. No details are overlooked, from the wall built with reclaimed bricks from historic Gastown to the glass-encased production facility for their Lucky's Doughnuts brand. Despite the huge number of drink orders they fulfill every day, the line is smooth and wait times short, and the consistency in quality is second to none. They produce their own almond milk in-house, no small feat for a store doing the number of drinks they do, and offer their own roasted coffees sourced directly from producers with whom they have long-standing relationships."—Anthony Benda

"The best espresso was at 49th Parallel—really rich, sweet, and chocolaty. They know how to layer in flavors with their espresso; there seems to always be a nice floral note floating on top."—Robert Dan Griffin

"Best espresso."—Pete Licata

"I've been known to drink two cups of filter coffee in one sitting at 49th Parallel's cafes, which certainly places it high in the rankings."—Keaton Ritchie

"Best filter coffee."—Wille Yli-Luoma

49TH PARALLEL COFFEE ROASTERS

2902 Main Street
Mount Pleasant
Vancouver
British Columbia V5T 3G3
Canada
+1 6048724901
www.49thcoffee.com

Opening hours...Daily from 7 am
Credit cards............................Visa, MasterCard, and Amex
Style...Coffee and doughnuts

There are a few locations around Vancouver, but this 49th Parallel Cafe location is combined with affiliated business Lucky's Doughnuts. There is really nothing better than a cup of coffee and an old-school glazed doughnut.

"THIS IS WHERE THE COFFEE INDUSTRY CONVERGES—EXPERTS RUNNING A SHOP FOR EXPERTS."

ALEX TRAN P.208

TORONTO

"JASON'S IS A BEAUTIFUL CORNER UNIT WITH LOTS OF WINDOWS . . . IT IS BY FAR THE MOST UNIQUE CAFE IN ALL OF CANADA."

SAMUEL JAMES P.208

TORONTO

⌃N SCALE

0   345   690   1035
▬▬▬▬▬▬▬▬▬ yd.

1. JACKED UP (MOBILE CAFE;
   LOCATIONS VARY) (P. 208)
2. TOKYO SMOKE FOUND (P. 208)

3. JASON'S COFFEE SHOP (P. 208)
4. REUNION ISLAND COFFEE (P. 208)
5. MANIC COFFEE AND GELATO (P. 208)

6. SAM JAMES COFFEE BAR (P. 209)
7. BOXCAR SOCIAL (P. 209)
8. BUD'S COFFEE BAR (P. 209)

UNIVERSITY

PALMERSTON/
LITTLE ITALY

KENSINGTON
MARKET

COLLEGE
DUNDAS WEST

LITTLE PORTUGAL

ENTERTAINMENT
DISTRICT

LIBERTY
VILLAGE

TORONTO
ISLANDS

JACKED UP
(MOBILE CAFE; LOCATIONS VARY)
Toronto
Ontario
Canada
+1 9059240031
www.jackedupcoffee.com

Opening hours..Vary
Credit cards..........................Visa, MasterCard, and Amex
Style...Mobile coffee bar

"Good cafe in an old decommissioned Citröen truck."
—Samuel James

TOKYO SMOKE FOUND
850B Adelaide Street West
Niagara
Toronto
Ontario M6J 2S1
Canada
+1 6473486596
www.tokyosmoke.com

Opening hours.........................Daily from 7:30 am
Credit cards..........................Visa, MasterCard, and Amex
....Coffee and food

"Big ideas start in small spaces."—Alex Tran

JASON'S COFFEE SHOP
1498 Queen Street West
Parkdale
Toronto
Ontario M6R 1A4
Canada
+1 4165387978

Opening hours.........................Daily from 6 am
Credit cards...Cash only
Style..........................Old-fashioned coffee shop and food

"Jason's is in a beautiful corner unit with lots of windows . . .
Lots of gambling and floor sitting and old-school Parkdale
crowd. It is by far the most unique cafe in all of Canada."
—Samuel James

REUNION ISLAND COFFEE
385 Roncesvalles Avenue
Roncesvalles Village
Toronto
Ontario M6R 2N1
Canada
+1 9058298520
www.reunionislandcoffee.com

Opening hours.........................Mon–Fri from 8 am
Credit cards..........................Visa, MasterCard, and Amex
Style...Coffee bar

"For the eco-conscious consumer looking for a friendly
neighborhood shop."—Alex Tran

MANIC COFFEE AND GELATO
426 College Street
South Annex
Toronto
Ontario M5T 1T3
Canada
+4169663888
www.maniccoffee.com

Opening hours.........................Mon–Fri from 7 am,
Sat–Sun from 8 am
Credit cards..........................Visa and MasterCard
Style...Coffee and gelato

"This is where the coffee industry converges—experts
running a shop for experts."—Alex Tran

SAM JAMES COFFEE BAR
297 Harbord Street
South Annex
Toronto
Ontario M6G 1G7
www.samjamescoffeebar.com

Opening hours..Mon–Fri from 7 am,
Sat from 8 am, Sun from 9 am
Credit cards...Cash only
Style...Coffee bar

"The combination of sparse white and black and
back-to-basics offerings could easily make for a sterile
environment, but the minimalism of the shop instead makes
it a canvas for the neighborhood. The coffee is always
delicious (likely the best in the city), and service is friendly
and efficient. But it's the harder to quantify 'feel' of a
community space in a city that has few of them that
really makes it special."—Keaton Ritchie

"Great atmosphere and streamlined service."—Alex Tran

Before opening several shops across Toronto, James was
on the competition circuit, diving headfirst into what was then
a nascent local coffee consciousness. He's now well-known
not just for his popular eponymous cafes and roasting
operations, but for a no-nonsense presentation that feels
both punk rock and sophisticated, all in one cup.

BOXCAR SOCIAL
1208 Yonge Street
Summerhill
Toronto
Ontario M4T 1W1
Canada
+1 4167925873
www.boxcarsocial.ca

Opening hours...Daily from 8 am
Credit cards..................................Visa and MasterCard
Style.......................................Coffee, food, beer, and wine

"A curated selection of quality coffees, beers, and spirits."
—Josh Hockin

"Like a fancy wine bar for coffee, it turns into a great place
to get wine in the evening."—Alex Tran

BUD'S COFFEE BAR
1934 Queen Street East
The Beach
Toronto
Ontario M4L 1H6
Canada
+1 4168941956
www.facebook.com/pg/budscoffeebar/

Opening hours...Daily from 7 am
Credit cards...Visa and MasterCard
Style...Coffee bar

"They have a skylight and a nice view of the beach."
—Samuel James

USA

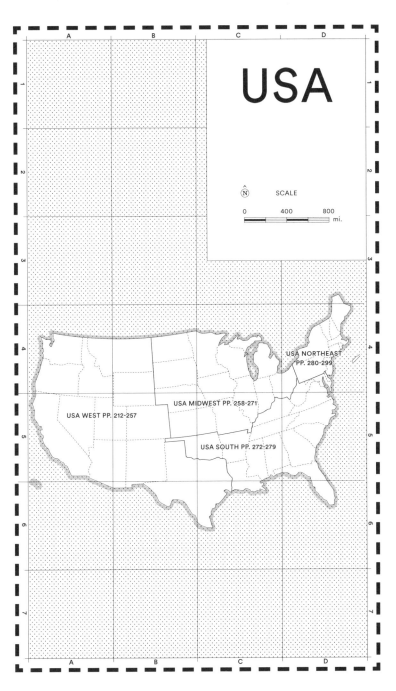

USA

SCALE

0   400   800
mi.

USA NORTHEAST
PP. 280-299

USA MIDWEST PP. 258-271

USA WEST PP. 212-257

USA SOUTH PP. 272-279

"I HAD AN AMAZING COFFEE EXPERIENCE BY VERY YOUNG AND QUALITY BARISTAS."

SANTIAGO RIGONI P.216

"WELL APPOINTED, GREAT FOOD, AND GREAT SERVICE. VERY PHOTOGENIC."

BRENT FORTUNE P.217

USA WEST

"IT'S THE BEST EXECUTION OF ALL OF THE HOPES AND DREAMS OF A THIRD-WAVE COFFEE EXPERIENCE: WORLD-CLASS COFFEE, SERVED SO UNPRETENTIOUSLY THAT IT BELIES ITS NEWNESS."

NICHOLAS CHO P.215

"NEVER BEFORE HAVE I HAD GOOD COFFEE IN A MOUNTAIN TOWN, AND I HAVE BEEN TO LOTS OF THEM."

JAY DEROSE P.217

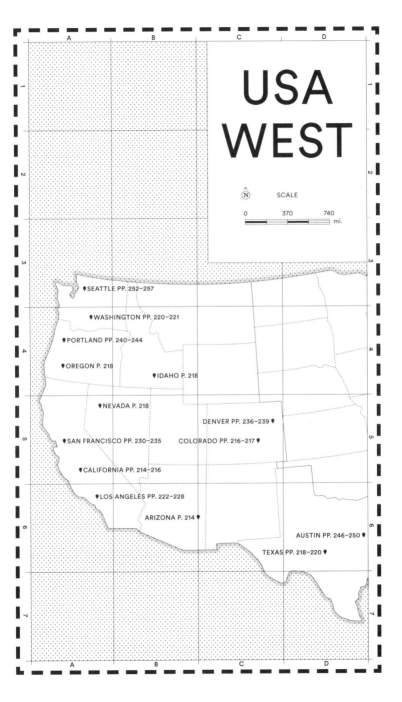

USA
WEST

N̂   SCALE

0   370   740
              mi.

♥SEATTLE PP. 252–257

♥WASHINGTON PP. 220–221

♥PORTLAND PP. 240–244

♥OREGON P. 218

♥IDAHO P. 218

♥NEVADA P. 218

DENVER PP. 236–239 ♥

♥SAN FRANCISCO PP. 230–235   COLORADO PP. 216–217 ♥

♥CALIFORNIA PP. 214–216

♥LOS ANGELES PP. 222–228

ARIZONA P. 214 ♥

AUSTIN PP. 246–250 ♥

TEXAS PP. 218–220 ♥

THE FLATIRON

416 Main Street
Jerome
Arizona 86331
United States
+1 9286342733
www.theflatironjerome.com

Opening hours..Mon from 8:30 am,
Thu–Sun from 8:30 am
Credit cards............................Visa, MasterCard, and Amex
Style...Coffee and food

CARTEL COFFEE LAB

1 North 1st Street
Downtown
Phoenix
Arizona 85004
United States
+1 4804328237
www.cartelcoffeelab.com

Opening hours..Mon–Sat from 7 am
Credit cards............................Visa, MasterCard, and Amex
Style...Coffee bar

This is where the book got started. We took a bag of coffee
from Michael Phillips of Handsome Coffee Roasters in Los
Angeles and asked him where to bring the bag in Arizona.
That's how we found ourselves at our first stop of a
cross-country road trip. But it was actually how the barista
reacted that created the book. Upon receiving this bag of
coffee, we were promptly handed two bags of his coffee,
and asked, "Where are you going next?" We said "Denver,"
and we walked out with a handwritten list of the best coffee
shops in Denver!

KUPPA JOY

518 Clovis Avenue
Old Town
Clovis
California 93612
United States
+1 5592987234
www.kuppajoy.com

Opening hours......................................Mon–Sat from 7 am
Credit cards............................Visa, MasterCard, and Amex
Style...Coffee and food

Los Angeles, see pages 222–228

ZOMBIE RUNNER

429 South California Avenue
Evergreen Park
Palo Alto
California 94306
United States
+1 6503252048
www.zombierunner.com

Opening hours..Mon–Fri from 7 am,
Sat–Sun from 8 am
Credit cards...Visa and MasterCard
Style...Running gear and coffee cart

"The best espresso in Silicon Valley (and maybe all of
California) is in the back of a place called Zombie Runner in
Palo Alto. It is mainly a store for running shoes, but there
is an espresso cart in the back that is just amazing. To make
it even stranger, the running store is in an old converted
movie theater, so it still has the marquee above it."
—Nathan Myhrvold

The roasts here might be a bit heavier than at some of the
more modern cafes, but Zombie gets a pass—because the
café is in a running shoe store!

San Francisco, see pages 230–235

BIRD ROCK COFFEE ROASTERS

5627 La Jolla Boulevard
Bird Rock
San Diego
California 92037
United States
+1 8585511707
www.birdrockcoffee.com

Opening hours...Mon–Fri from 6 am,
Sat–Sun from 6:30 am
Credit cards.............................Visa, MasterCard, and Amex
Style...Coffee bar

"When their in-shop roasted coffee is good, it is good.
The setting is this amazing indoor/outdoor combination,
where the front wall is also the seating that faces the
sidewalk and you watch surfers and a whole community
of barefooters walk by. The staff is as excited by coffee
and full of pride as I have seen in any coffee shop."
—Jonathan Rubinstein

SCOUT COFFEE

1130 Garden Street
Downtown
San Luis Obispo
California 93401
United States
+1 8054392175
www.scoutcoffeeco.com

Opening hours...Daily from 6:30 am
Credit cards.............................Visa, MasterCard, and Amex
Style..Coffee and food

"It's the best execution of all of the hopes and dreams of
a third-wave coffee experience: world-class coffee, served
so unpretentiously that it belies its newness, located in a
smallish American city."—Nicholas Cho

If you are driving between San Francisco and Los Angeles,
you should be stopping in San Luis Obispo anyway. While
there, treat yourself to an amazing coffee from some of the
friendliest people in coffee.

THE FRENCH PRESS

1101 North State Street
Downtown
Santa Barbara
California 93101
United States
+1 8059632721
www.thefrenchpress.com

Opening hours...Mon–Fri from 6 am,
Sat from 7 am, Sun from 8 am
Credit cards.............................Visa, MasterCard, and Amex
Style...Coffee bar

CHROMATIC COFFEE

5237 Stevens Creek Boulevard
Santa Clara
California 95051
United States
+1 4082484500
www.chromaticcoffee.com

Opening hours.................................Mon–Fri from 7 am,
Sat–Sun from 8 am
Credit cards...........................Visa, MasterCard, and Amex
Style...Coffee bar

"Superb drinks made with coffee."—Alex Bernson

CAT & CLOUD COFFEE CO.

3600 Portola Drive
Opal Cliffs
Santa Cruz
California 95062
United States
www.catandcloud.com

Opening hours..Daily from 6 am
Credit cards...........................Visa, MasterCard, and Amex
Style...Coffee bar

VERVE COFFEE ROASTERS

816 41st Avenue
Opal Cliffs
Santa Cruz
California 95060
United States
+1 8314757776
www.vervecoffee.com

Opening hours......................................Mon–Fri from 6 am,
Sat–Sun from 7 am
Credit cards...Visa and MasterCard
Style...Coffee bar

"Verve in Santa Cruz always has some really special coffees."—Phil Goodlaxson

"I had an amazing coffee experience served by very young and quality baristas."—Santiago Rigoni

BLACK OAK COFFEE ROASTERS

476 North State Street
Ukaiah
California 95482
United States
+1 8663901427
www.blackoakcoffee.com

Opening hours...............................Mon–Fri from 6:30 am,
Sat–Sun from 7 am
Credit cards...........................Visa, MasterCard, and Amex
Style...Coffee and food

"On a recent trip to the States, we were visiting some friends who make biodynamic wines in Mendocino, California, and happened to stumble upon great coffee when we least expected it!"—Felipe Croce

TWO RIVERS CRAFT COFFEE COMPANY

7745 Wadsworth Boulevard
Arvada
Colorado 80003
United States
+1 3034241313
www.tworiverscoffee.com

Opening hours...............................Mon–Fri from 6:30 am,
Sat from 7 am
Credit cards...........................Visa, MasterCard, and Amex
Style...Coffee bar

"In Arvada there is a wonderfully surprising place called Two Rivers. They roast their own and feature local roasters (chiefly Sweet Bloom). They exist among places that serve coffee that is 100 percent based on speed and convenience."
—Mark Smesrud

Denver, see pages 236–239

ALPINE MODERN CAFÉ
904 College Avenue
University Hill
Boulder
Colorado 80302
United States
+1 3032842052
www.alpinemodern.com

Opening hours..Daily from 7 am
Credit cards............................Visa, MasterCard, and Amex
Style..Coffee and food

"Well appointed, great food, and great service. Very photogenic."—Brent Fortune

HARBINGER COFFEE
505 South Mason Street
University North
Fort Collins
Colorado 80524
United States
+1 8472742253
www.harbingercoffee.com

Opening hours.......................................Mon–Sat from 7 am,
                                                                    Sun from 8 am
Credit cards............................Visa, MasterCard, and Amex
Style...Coffee bar

"Harbinger used to be hidden away in the underground court of the world's smallest mall in Fort Collins, Colorado."—Cory Andreen

THE RISTRETTO COFFEE LOUNGE
635 Lincoln Avenue
Steamboat Springs
Colorado 80487
United States
+1 9708793393
www.theristrettocoffeelounge.com

Opening hours..Daily from 7 am
Credit cards............................Visa, MasterCard, and Amex
Style...Coffee bar

"Never before have I had good coffee in a mountain town, and I have been to lots of them. They definitely do it right here. Great equipment, great baristas, a nice guest roaster lineup. I was pretty amazed."—Jay DeRose

DOMA

6240 East Seltice Way, Unit A
Post Falls
Idaho 83854
United States
+1 2086671267
www.domacoffee.com

Opening hours................................Mon–Fri from 7 am
Credit cards............................Visa, MasterCard, and Amex
Style..Roastery cafe

PUBLICUS

1126 Fremont Street
Downtown
Las Vegas
Nevada 89101
United States
+1 7023315500
www.publiclv.com

Opening hours..Daily from 7 am
Credit cards............................Visa, MasterCard, and Amex
Style..Coffee and food

TRIED & TRUE COFFEE

160 Southwest Madison Avenue
Corvallis
Oregon 97333
United States
+1 5035107010
www.triedandtruecoffee.co

Opening hours................................Mon–Fri from 7 am,
Sat–Sun from 8 am
Credit cards............................Visa, MasterCard, and Amex
Style..Coffee bar

Portland, see pages 240–244

PALACE COFFEE COMPANY

817 South Polk Street #102
Amarillo
Texas 79109
United States
+1 8064760111
www.palacecoffee.co

Opening hours................................Mon–Fri from 7 am,
Sat from 8 am
Credit cards............................Visa, MasterCard, and Amex
Style..Coffee bar

"Palace in Amarillo/Canyon has always been that place
where it is surprising and funny to find great coffee."
—Ryan Fisher

Austin, see pages 246–250

ZENZERO KITCHEN

171 North Denton Tap Road, Suite 600
Coppell
Texas 75019
United States
+1 4692933550
www.zenzerokitchen.com

Opening hours................................Mon–Fri from 6 am,
Sat from 7 am, Sun from 8 am
Credit cards............................Visa, MasterCard, and Amex
Style..Restaurant

DAVIS STREET ESPRESSO

819 West Davis Street
Kessler
Dallas
Texas 75208
United States
+1 2149410381
www.davisstreetespresso.com

Opening hours................................Mon–Fri from 6 am,
Sat from 7 am
Credit cards............................Visa, MasterCard, and Amex
Style..Coffee and breakfast

CULTIVAR COFFEE BAR
1155 Peavy Road
Reinhardt
Dallas
Texas 75218
United States
+1 9726777895
www.cultivarcoffee.com

Opening hours...Tue–Sun from 7 am
Credit cards...........................Visa, MasterCard, and Amex
Style...Coffee bar

AVOCA
1311 West Magnolia Avenue
Fairmount
Fort Worth
Texas 76104
United States
+1 6822330957
www.avocacoffee.com

Opening hours...Daily from 7 am
Credit cards...........................Visa, MasterCard, and Amex
Style...Roastery cafe

BREWED
801 West Magnolia Avenue
Fairmount
Fort Worth
Texas 76104
United States
+1 8179451545
www.brewedfw.com

Opening hours...Tue–Sun from 8 am,
Credit cards...........................Visa, MasterCard, and Amex
Style...Coffee and gastropub

BOOMTOWN COFFEE
242 West 19th Street
Greater Heights
Houston
Texas 77008
United States
+1 7138627018
www.boomtowncoffee.com

Opening hours...Daily from 7 am
Credit cards...........................Visa, MasterCard, and Amex
Style...Roastery cafe

BLACKSMITH
1018 Westheimer Road
Hyde Park
Houston
Texas 77006
United States
+1 8323607470
www.blacksmithhouston.com

Opening hours...Daily from 7 am
Credit cards...........................Visa, MasterCard, and Amex
Style...Coffee and food

SOUTHSIDE ESPRESSO
904 Westheimer Road
Montrose
Houston
Texas
77006
United States
+1 7139429990
www.southsideespresso.com

Opening hours................................Mon–Fri from 6:30 am,
                                      Sat–Sun from 7:30 am
Credit cards...........................Visa, MasterCard, and Amex
Style...Coffee bar

LOCAL COFFEE
5903 Broadway
San Antonio
Texas 78209
United States
+1 2102675494
www.localcoffeesa.com

Opening hours.................................Mon–Fri from 6:30 am,
                                                     Sat–Sun from 7 am
Credit cards.............................Visa, MasterCard, and Amex
Style..Coffee bar

DICHOTOMY COFFEE & SPIRITS
508 Austin Avenue
Waco
Texas 76701
United States
www.dichotomycs.com

Opening hours..Daily from 6 am
Credit cards.............................Visa, MasterCard, and Amex
Style..Coffee and cocktails

GARAGE AUTO HERO
720 132nd Southwest, Suite 205
Everett
Washington 98204
United States
+1 4259313121
www.garageautohero.com

Opening hours..Wed from 4:30 pm,
                                                          Sat from 8 am
Credit cards...Cash only
Style.......................Coffee and custom car modifications

"Run by a guy who does some pretty amazing work on cars
and who also loves coffee and collects and repairs espresso
machines. If I needed some custom work done to my car,
I'd go there."—Andrew Milstead

BAR FRANCIS
110 Franklin Street Northeast
Downtown
Olympia
Washington 98501
United States
+1 3602925446
www.barfrancis.com

Opening hours...Mon–Fri from 7 am,
                                                     Sat–Sun from 8 am
Credit cards.............................Visa, MasterCard, and Amex
Style..Coffee bar

"Superb drinks made with coffee."—Marcus Boni

OLYMPIA COFFEE ROASTERS
600 4th Avenue East
Downtown
Olympia
Washington 98501
United States
+1 3607530066
www.olympiacoffee.com

Opening hours................................Mon–Fri from 6:30 am,
                                          Sat from 7 am, Sun from 8 am
Credit cards.............................Visa, MasterCard, and Amex
Style...Roastery cafe

"Any day I'm drinking Olympia Coffee Roasters is a good
day."—Andrew Milstead

LAVA JAVA

2 South 56th Place, Suite 102
Ridgefield
Washington 98642
United States
+1 3608873980
www.lava-java.com

Opening hours.................................Mon–Fri from 6 am,
                            Sat from 7 am, Sun from 8 am
Credit cards............................Visa, MasterCard, and Amex
Style...Coffee bar

"I always think of Lava Java and their small shopping-center location off the freeway. I would tell people to check it out on their way to Portland and always had to convince them it was real."—Andrew Milstead

Seattle, see pages 252–257

CAFÉ MELA

17 North Wenatchee Avenue
Wenatchee
Washington 98101
United States
+1 5098880374
www.caffemela.com

Opening hours.................................Mon–Fri from 6 am,
                            Sat–Sun from 8 am
Credit cards............................Visa, MasterCard, and Amex
Style...Roastery cafe

"YOU CAN'T BEAT THE SERVICE AND KNOWLEDGE BEHIND THEIR IN-HOUSE PRODUCTS AND ALL THEIR BEVERAGES."

MATT LEE P.226

LOS ANGELES

"I LIKE THE FRIENDLY SERVICE AND THE WAY THAT THE SERVICE MODEL IS MORE AKIN TO A BAR THAN A COFFEE SHOP."

DOUG PALAS P.225

"FOR THE QUALITY OF THE DRINKS, BUT ALSO FOR ALL THE SYSTEMS THEY'VE PUT TOGETHER TO PROVIDE THE BEST SERVICE POSSIBLE AND THE BEST DRINKS."

NICOLAS CLERC P.225

"BLACKTOP HAS SIMPLICITY, SUPERB QUALITY, AND FRIENDLY SERVICE."

JOSH LITTLEFIELD P.224

"ONE OF MY FAVORITE SHOTS OF ESPRESSO WAS AT THE VERVE IN LA."

CAMILA RAMOS P.224

LOS ANGELES

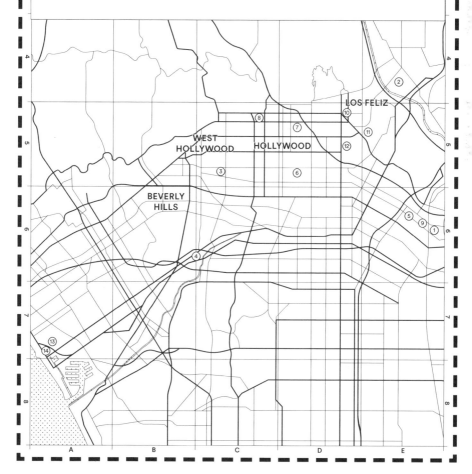

N̂   SCALE

0   1120   2240   3360
|___|___|___|___| yd.

1. BLACKTOP COFFEE (P. 224)
2. PROOF BAKERY (P. 224)
3. VERVE COFFEE ROASTERS (P. 224)
4. COGNOSCENTI COFFEE (P. 224)
5. G&B COFFEE (P. 225)

6. GO GET EM TIGER (P. 226)
7. COFFEE COMMISSARY (P. 226)
8. TIAGO COFFEE BAR
    + KITCHEN (P. 226)
9. CAFÉ DULCE (P. 227)

10. GO GET EM TIGER (P. 227)
11. INTELLIGENTSIA (P. 227)
12. SQIRL (P. 227)
13. INTELLIGENTSIA (P. 228)
14. MENOTTI'S COFFEE STOP (P. 228)

LOS FELIZ

WEST
HOLLYWOOD   HOLLYWOOD

BEVERLY
HILLS

BLACKTOP COFFEE

826 East 3rd Street
Arts District
Los Angeles
California 90013
United States
www.blacktop.la

Opening hours...Daily from 7 am
Credit cards............................Visa, MasterCard, and Amex
Style...Coffee bar

"The guys at Blacktop gave me some of the all-time best customer service I've ever had. Everyone went out of their way to make us feel welcome and cared for. Two of them even came and sat with us for a few minutes to talk."
—Ryan Fisher

"Blacktop has simplicity, superb quality, and friendly service."—Josh Littlefield

PROOF BAKERY

3156 Glendale Boulevard
Atwater Village
Los Angeles
California 90039
United States
+1 3236648633
www.proofbakeryla.com

Opening hours...Daily from 8 am
....Visa, MasterCard, and Amex
Style...Coffee and food

Proof has one of the greatest collaborations in coffee. Inside this tiny bakery you will find some of the best pastries in Los Angeles, and the original permanent pop-up of Cognoscenti Coffee (which now operates multiple locations and a roaster). If you were to order a croissant and coffee together anywhere in the world, pick here.

VERVE COFFEE ROASTERS

8051 West 3rd Street
Beverly Grove
Los Angeles
California 90048
United States
+1 3237465070
www.vervecoffee.com

Opening hours...Daily from 7 am
Credit cards..Visa and MasterCard
Style...Coffee bar

"One of my favorite shots of espresso was at the Verve in Los Angeles: I was at the end of a long coffee crawl, completely overcaffeinated. But I knew it was my only chance to stop at the store, so I had a shot of Streetlevel espresso anyway. It was immaculately dialed in: tasted sweet and juicy, red fruit, caramel, round. A clean finish."—Camila Ramos

COGNOSCENTI COFFEE

6114 Washington Boulevard
Culver City
Los Angeles
California 90232
United States
+1 3103637325
www.popupcoffee.com

Opening hours..Mon–Fri from 8 am,
Sat–Sun from 9 am
Credit cards............................Visa, MasterCard, and Amex
Style...Coffee bar

G&B COFFEE (GRAND CENTRAL MARKET)

317 South Broadway
Downtown
Los Angeles
California 90013
United States
+1 2136250747
www.gandbcoffee.com

Opening hours..Daily from 7 am
Credit cards............................Visa, MasterCard, and Amex
Style...Coffee bar

"For the quality of the drinks, but also for all the systems they've put together to provide the best service possible and the best drinks. They are able to deliver what the customers want but also lead them to more specialized cups."
—Nicolas Clerc

"My favorite place to have an espresso is at G&B. I prefer that my espresso taste like and be experienced more like a filter coffee. I prefer their larger extractions that are served in a Gibraltar glass that you sip on at a warm temperature, while saddled up at the bar chatting with friends."
—Laila Ghambari Willbur

"The Fizzy Hoppy Tea soda at G&B was startlingly delicious. I wasn't quite sure what it was when it was served to me with my espresso, but since it was bubbly, I assumed it was some type of soda water. It was such an amazing complement to the espresso (an Ethiopian coffee from Heart) and I was taken aback. They make it in-house and at the time I had it, it was a blend of two black teas, which they then infused with hops and carbonated it. A lot more gentle on the palate than straight-up soda water."—Ben Helfen

"G&B is lucky to exist, and at the same time, they're at the forefront of what's being done with coffee service, which I think you can say about any business doing anything innovative or new in food. They lucked into an amazing location at Grand Central Market, because for the first time someone saw them as Angelenos in a sea of coffee companies from elsewhere trying to infiltrate the LA coffee market (neither G nor B is from Los Angeles). The service is casual. You come as you are; they meet you halfway. They somehow manage this dance while maintaining really high quality in the cup, which no one else had really cracked the code to until G&B. They seem to want to rewrite the way everything has been done in coffee to this point, including how much a barista can produce, which has been an amazing thing to observe, but as a customer, all they ask is that you approach the bar instead of queuing in line—the rest is really seamless."—Ben Kaminsky

"I've never cared about coffee pairings. I like the idea of using coffee as an ingredient. The only notable way that I've really seen it work, though, is in the espresso milkshake at G&B."—Jay Lijewski

"I like the friendly service and the way that the service model is more akin to a bar than a coffee shop. I often find myself engaging the staff and other customers due to this layout, and that matches the social ideal that I appreciate in a coffeehouse. They consistently add new offerings and this evolution of their menu ensures that I can experience something different on a regular basis. Additionally, I have a lot of friends on the staff and it makes it that much more welcoming."—Doug Palas

GO GET EM TIGER

230 North Larchmont Boulevard
Hancock Park
Los Angeles
California 90004
United States
+1 3233805359
www.gandb.coffee/gget

Opening hours..Daily from 7 am
Credit cards...........................Visa, MasterCard, and Amex
Style..Coffee and food

"It's conveniently located several blocks from my house,
but I go there because there isn't a better or more consistent
place that I have been in all of North America. I really enjoy
their drink combinations, like the Business and Pleasure. You
get a shot of espresso and a sweet and tasty shaken iced
almond macadamia nut milk latte. It's a nice combo and it's
rare to get an iced drink of that caliber."—Robert Dan Griffin

"You can't beat the service and knowledge behind their
in-house products and all their beverages."—Matt Lee

"I love the concept of neighborhood cafe with exceptional
coffee and service. The open sight lines and counter seating
create a unique coffee experience for guests, and everything
is executed with a lot of care and intention."—Cora Lambert

"G&B and Go Get Em Tiger are both pushing the envelope
and adding new and interesting things to the cafe
experience."—Camila Ramos

"Best filter coffee."—Scott Rao

It's easy to pick out a coffee shop owned by two barista
champions, but it's really about how much fun the team
of Kyle Glanville and Charles Babinski have with their shops.
On holidays, this shop serves up Starbucks-styled holiday
drinks, but executed as only a barista champ would serve.
All the ingredients are made by hand, and the pumpkin spice
latte is a work of art. The other 364 days a year? It's just damn
good coffee.

COFFEE COMMISSARY

6087 West Sunset Boulevard
Hollywood
Los Angeles
California 90028
United States
+1 3234673559
www.coffeecommissary.com

Opening hours..Daily from 7 am
Credit cards...........................Visa, MasterCard, and Amex
Style..Coffee bar

"Coffee Commissary serves out of a hole-in-the-wall in
an artist's collective in Hollywood."—Donald Niemyer

TIAGO COFFEE BAR + KITCHEN

7080 Hollywood Boulevard
Hollywood
Los Angeles
California 90028
United States
+1 3234665600
www.tiagocoffee.com

Opening hours..Mon—Fri from 7 am,
                                                                   Sat—Sun from 8 am
Credit cards...........................Visa, MasterCard, and Amex
Style..Coffee and food

"Best espresso."—Josue Morales

In the depths of the most touristy part of Hollywood, Tiago is
an oasis to coffee lovers. The owner, Santiago Garfunkel, puts
his obsession with coffee front and center in this office lobby
cafe. The multi-roaster selection means there is always an
interesting option. The brunch is pretty solid, too.

CAFÉ DULCE

134 Japanese Village Plaza Mall
Little Tokyo
Los Angeles
California 90012
United States
+1 2133469910
www.cafedulce.co

Opening hours..Daily from 7 am
Credit cards............................Visa, MasterCard, and Amex
Style..Coffee and food

"I had an amazing pour-over of a washed Yirgacheffe from Four Barrel to go along with some amazing doughnuts. The service was really amazing as well. The staff is very nice and accommodating. I also enjoyed how it's kind of tucked away in Little Tokyo and away from the chaos of the city. It really felt like a little oasis. I will definitely want to go back there next time I'm in LA."—Ben Helfen

GO GET EM TIGER

4630 Hollywood Blvd
Los Feliz
Los Angeles
California 90027
United States
+1 3235434438
www.gandb.coffee/gget

Opening hours..Daily from 6 am
Credit cards............................Visa, MasterCard, and Amex
Style..Coffee and food

This third—and probably busiest—outpost of the thriving G&B Coffee/Go Get Em Tiger empire was founded by local coffee heroes Kyle Glanville and Charles Babinski. It continues to explore the pair's dedication to delivering great coffee at high customer volume with personal, exceptional customer service. Enjoy a coffee from one of their featured roasters while mingling at the standing bar, or try a healthy and hearty housemade dish from their chefs to savor on the spacious patio. Inventive pastries, baked in-house, are available as well.

INTELLIGENTSIA

3922 West Sunset Boulevard
Silver Lake
Los Angeles
California 90029
United States
+1 3236636173
www.intelligentsiacoffee.com

Opening hours..Daily from 6 am
Credit cards............................Visa, MasterCard, and Amex
Style..Coffee bar

"Best filter coffee."—Gabriel Boscana

"To date, the best espresso of my life was still at Intelligentsia Silver Lake."—Emily Oak

The first Intelligentsia located outside of Chicago blew the doors off the Los Angeles coffee scene. Ever since opening in 2007, there has been a line to the West Sunset Boulevard spot filled with local hipsters, writers, artists, and even tourists. Silver Lake was cool before this cafe opened, but it became the anchor of Sunset Junction for the newest generation of the neighborhood. Many of the best cafe owners in LA began their careers at this location.

SQIRL

720 North Virgil Avenue
Silver Lake
Los Angeles
California 90029
United States
+1 2133946526
www.sqirlla.com

Opening hours................................Mon–Fri from 6:30 am,
Sat–Sun from 8 am
Credit cards............................Visa, MasterCard, and Amex
Style..Coffee and food

"My favorite place that balances exceptional food with incredible coffee is Sqirl. Everything I've had there has always been delicious."—Jared Linzmeier

It's unbelievably rare to find a kitchen serving impeccable and creative dishes with a world-class coffee program. Coffee here started as a pop-up concept from the Go Get Em Tiger/G&B team and has continued strong, while the food menu gets better and better.

INTELLIGENTSIA

1331 Abbot Kinney Boulevard
Venice
Los Angeles
California 90291
United States
+1 3103991233
www.intelligentsiacoffee.com

Opening hours...Daily from 6 am
Credit cards............................Visa, MasterCard, and Amex
Style..Coffee bar

"I had a very memorable espresso experience at
Intelligentsia's Venice location. The shot was pulled by a
dear friend of mine, M'lissa Muckerman, and it was a coffee
called Finca La Tina from Honduras. It was very bright, with
lots of lemon and grapefruit, and at first I thought it was
almost too intense. But I found myself unable to stop sipping
it. I came back the next day and the day after to have that
shot again and again."—Ben Helfen

"While it remains a very controversial shop, I still love going
to the Intelligentsia in Venice. This shop was a game changer
of cafe design, and I still find it to be a very impressive
shop."—Cora Lambert

After the immense success of the original Intelligentsia in
Silver Lake, the team committed to building an entirely new
experience in Venice. The "pod" design of putting a cash
register at each espresso machine was definitely controversial,
but it seems the long lines simply attract more and more of the
Venice locals and tourists.

MENOTTI'S COFFEE STOP

56 Windward Avenue
Venice
Los Angeles
California 90291
United States
+1 3103927232
www.menottis.com

Opening hours...Daily from 8 am
Credit cards............................Visa, MasterCard, and Amex
Style..Coffee bar

"Menotti's Coffee Stop in Venice is currently my favorite
place to go for coffee. It's perfect. It's right on the Venice
Beach boardwalk, sporting an intimate setting with a true
neighborhood vibe. The baristas here care just as much
about people as they do about coffee, and it shows; you can
even grab a record off the shelf and one of the baristas will
throw it on for you! There's just something so authentic
about this place I can't get enough. If I had a shop, it would
be just like this. Oh, and the drinks are amazing also."
—Chris Baca

"When Nicely is working, his hospitality is next level. The
drinks are cared for, he puts together signature drinks on
the fly, and it's all in a small intimate setting. He fully treats
everyone like family."—Jared Truby

"I'VE HAD SOME REALLY GREAT FILTER AND ESPRESSO COFFEES AT RITUAL ROASTERS."
JASON SCHELTUS P.233

"IT WAS THE KIND OF COFFEE YOU JUST CAN'T STOP DRINKING." DAN STREETMAN P.233

SAN FRANCISCO

"THE KAFFETONIC AT SAINT FRANK IS WITHOUT QUESTION THE BEST COMBINATION OF ESPRESSO AND ANYTHING OUT THERE." BEN KAMINSKY P.234

"THE FLOW IS INCREDIBLE, THE ARCHITECTURE IS ELEGANT AND RUSTIC, AND THE COFFEE IS LOVELY."
FELIPE CROCE P.235

"ITS HUGE SPACE AND NATURAL MATERIALS AND MEZZANINE—PLUS THE ON-PREMISES ROASTING SPACE—MAKE IT A UNIQUE AND ENTERTAINING PLACE."
AARON ULTIMO P.235

SAN FRANCISCO

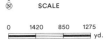

$\hat{N}$ SCALE

0   1420   850   1275
yd.

1. BARTAVELLE COFFEE
    & WINE BAR (P. 232)
2. ALGORITHM COFFEE CO. (P. 232)
3. MODERN COFFEE (P. 232)
4. TIMELESS COFFEE ROASTERS (P. 232)
5. ARBOR (P. 232)

6. WRECKING BALL COFFEE
    ROASTERS (P. 233)
7. FOUR BARREL COFFEE (P. 233)
8. LINEA CAFFE (P. 233)
9. RITUAL COFFEE ROASTERS (P. 233)
10. TROUBLE COFFEE CO. (P. 234)

11. SAINT FRANK (P. 234)
12. BLUE BOTTLE COFFEE (P. 234)
13. MAZARINE (P. 234)
14. SIGHTGLASS COFFEE (P. 235)
15. RITUAL COFFEE ROASTERS (P. 235)

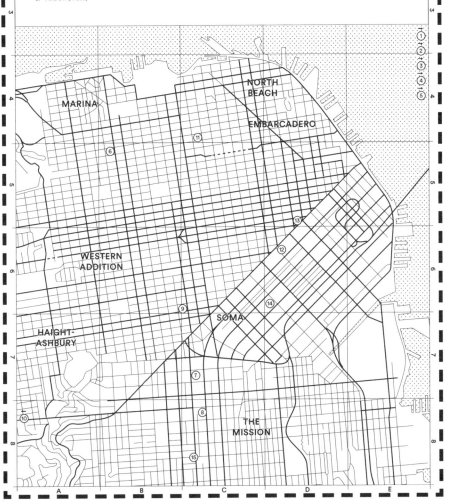

BARTAVELLE COFFEE & WINE BAR

1603 San Pablo Avenue
Northwest Berkeley
Berkeley
California 94702
United States
+1 5105242473
www.bartavellecafe.com

Opening hours......................................Mon–Sat from 7 am,
Sun from 8 am
Credit cards............................Visa, MasterCard, and Amex
Style...Coffee, food, and wine

"Great filter coffee."—Gabriel Boscana

ALGORITHM COFFEE CO.

1122 University Avenue
Poets Corner
Berkeley
California 94702
United States
+1 4102805153
www.algorithmcoffee.com

Opening hours.......................................Mon–Fri from 7 am,
Sat–Sun from 8 am
Credit cards............................Visa, MasterCard, and Amex
Style...Coffee bar

"Berkeley desperately needed a nice space like this."
—Gabriel Boscana

MODERN COFFEE

411 13th Street
Downtown
Oakland
California 94612
United States
+1 5108358000
www.moderncoffeeoakland.com

Opening hours...Daily from 7 am
Credit cards............................Visa, MasterCard, and Amex
Style...Coffee bar

"Go for the coffee."—Evan Gilman

TIMELESS COFFEE ROASTERS

4252 Piedmont Avenue
Piedmont Avenue
Oakland
California 94611
United States
+1 5109851360
www.timelesscoffee.com

Opening hours...Daily from 7 am
Credit cards............................Visa, MasterCard, and Amex
Style..Coffee and vegan food

"A neighborhood shop, nothing fancy. All vegan (and not really advertised anywhere, which rules). The owner is super nice and friendly; coffee is roasted in-house on a tiny roaster in a tiny space. They have great food, treats, and coffee, and people are always happy to be there."—Gabriel Boscana

"I loved Timeless. 100% vegan. No dairy, but making delicious and beautiful drinks with almond and soy milk. And they are also a chocolatier. Hello!"—Donald Niemyer

ARBOR

4210 Telegraph Avenue
Temescal
Oakland
California 94609
United States
+1 5109236117

Opening hours...Daily from 8 am
Credit cards..Cash only
Style..Coffee and food

"For that Oakland feeling."—Evan Gilman

WRECKING BALL COFFEE ROASTERS

2271 Union Street
Cow Hollow
San Francisco
California 94123
United States
www.wreckingballcoffee.com

Opening hours..Daily from 7 am
Credit cards............................Visa, MasterCard, and Amex
Style..Coffee bar

"I was there for Christmas 2014 and had Nicholas Cho make me a pour-over of Ethiopian Yirgacheffe. It was the kind of coffee you just can't stop drinking. I even thought, 'I shouldn't drink anymore of this because it is late afternoon and it will keep me awake . . . but I really want to.' The sweetness in that cup really set it apart."—Dan Streetman

FOUR BARREL COFFEE

375 Valencia Street
Mission District
San Francisco
California 94103
United States
+1 4152520800
www.fourbarrelcoffee.com

Opening hours..Daily from 7 am
Credit cards............................Visa, MasterCard, and Amex
Style..Coffee bar

"Fantastic coffees. It feels like a second home when I'm there."—Scott Lucey

One of the more rustic-feeling cafes in San Francisco, Four Barrel gives you full view of the roasting operations at all times. While the space always feels organic and relaxed, the roasting team keeps the output precise and controlled. The synergy of an unpolished environment with a perfectly balanced espresso is always memorable.

LINEA CAFFE

3417 18th Street
Mission District
San Francisco
California 94110
United States
+1 4155903011
www.lineacaffe.com

Opening hours..Daily from 7 am
Credit cards............................Visa, MasterCard, and Amex
Style..Coffee and waffles

"Simple, and there's no pretentiousness."
—JoEllen Depakakibo

RITUAL COFFEE ROASTERS

1026 Valencia Street
Mission District
San Francisco
California 94110
United States
+1 4156411011
www.ritualroasters.com

Opening hours......................................Mon–Fri from 6 am,
Sat–Sun from 7 am
Credit cards............................Visa, MasterCard, and Amex
Style..Coffee bar

"I've had some really great filter and espresso coffees at Ritual Roasters."—Jason Scheltus

While many in the neighborhood had a hard time during a year-long renovation that turned Ritual from a dark and stormy café to a light and bright modern space, the coffee only improves. Rotating seasonal espressos always hit the mark, and the long communal tables in the back offer a respite from shopping on Valencia.

TROUBLE COFFEE CO.

4033 Judah Street
Outer Sunset
San Francisco
California 94122
United States
www.troublecoffee.com

Opening hours..Daily from 7 am
Credit cards..Cash only
Style...Coffee bar

"This is right next to the beach, in the middle of a quiet neighborhood in San Francisco. The owner, Giulietta Carrelli, put everything into this little beach cafe. The place is adorned with toys, an old cassette deck, a single copy of Yoko Ono's *Grapefruit* displayed about the espresso machine. I always order Build Your Own Damn House, a combination of a young coconut cut at the top and served with a straw and spoon (for digging out the meat), a cup of dark roast coffee, and a thick slab of cinnamon toast. It's nothin' fancy, the coffee just okay—but with a little cream and sugar it's absolutely delicious and the whole experience is lovely."—Zachary Carlsen

SAINT FRANK

2340 Polk Street
Russian Hill
San Francisco
California 94109
United States
+1 4157751619
www.stfrank.com

Opening hours.......................................Mon–Fri from 7 am,
                                               Sat–Sun from 8 am
Credit cards............................Visa, MasterCard, and Amex
Style...Coffee bar

"Clean and pretty, with tasty coffee."—Kyle Glanville

"The KaffeTonic at Saint Frank is without question the best combination of espresso and anything out there."
—Ben Kaminsky

BLUE BOTTLE COFFEE

66 Mint Street
South of Market
San Francisco
California 94103
United States
+1 5106533394
www.bluebottlecoffee.com

Opening hours..Daily from 7 am
Credit cards............................Visa, MasterCard, and Amex
Style...Coffee and food

"It sounds so generic, and perhaps a little basic, but I can't get my first experience at Blue Bottle at the Mint in San Francisco out of my head. It was so incredibly San Franciscan an experience, and as a Texan it really tore me up inside. Do I love this? Do I hate this? The coffee was not to my preference, yet it was distinctive and adhered to the Blue Bottle aesthetic. It was served in a small, heavy stone demitasse without a handle, with a small glass decanter of the strongly brewed filter coffee by its side. The space has incredibly high ceilings, a giant shared table in the center at bar height—everything about that moment was ethereal, intentional, almost meditative. This was truly the most artful retail experience I've had in my life, as if I were standing in front of Picasso's *Les Demoiselles d'Avignon* in 1907 and my previous notions of art and space shattered as I try to make sense of what is going on inside my heart."
—Lorenzo Perkins

"Three Africans at Blue Bottle Mint back in 2008 was the first time I realized that coffee can taste good."—Will Pratt

MAZARINE

720 Market Street
South Of Market
San Francisco
California 94102
United States
+1 4153987700
www.mazarinecoffee.com

Opening hours.......................................Mon–Fri from 7 am,
                                          Sat from 8 am, Sun from 9 am
Credit cards............................Visa, MasterCard, and Amex
Style...Coffee and food

"Great espresso."—Gabriel Boscana

SIGHTGLASS COFFEE

270 7th Street
South Of Market
San Francisco
California 94103
United States
+1 4158611313
www.sightglasscoffee.com

Opening hours...Daily from 7 am
Credit cards............................Visa, MasterCard, and Amex
Style..Roastery cafe

"Although I have only been to Sightglass twice, I fell in love
with the place. It is my dream cafe. The flow is incredible,
the architecture is elegant and rustic, and the coffee is
lovely. This is the best combination of cafe, roastery, office,
quality-control lab, and concept store that I have seen."
—Felipe Croce

"Its huge space and natural materials and mezzanine,
plus the on-premises roasting space, make it a unique and
entertaining place."—Aaron Ultimo

RITUAL COFFEE ROASTERS

432B Octavia Street
Western Addition
San Francisco
California 94102
United States
+1 4158650989
www.ritualroasters.com

Opening hours...Daily from 7 am
Credit cards............................Visa, MasterCard, and Amex
Style..Coffee and waffles

"Great espresso."—Gabriel Boscana

"I had a great filter coffee from Honduras at the Ritual
container location."—Jenni Bryant

"WHAT KEEPS ME COMING BACK IS THE FACT THAT I CAN GET REALLY WELL-MADE COFFEE WITH MY MEAL."

ZAC CADWALADER P.238

DENVER

"BOXCAR IS A COMMUNAL SPACE WITH GREAT RESTAURANTS, A BREWERY, AND A BIG SCREEN THAT WAS STREAMING THE WESTERN REGIONAL BARISTA COMPETITION WHEN I VISITED."

PETER LICATA P.239

"THE MOST MEMORABLE ESPRESSO I HAD WAS AT CREMA COFFEE HOUSE. IT WAS A SINGLE ORIGIN FROM COUNTER CULTURE."

JAY DEROSE P.238

"A CONSISTENT TONE OF QUIET INNOVATION WHEN IT COMES TO WHAT A SPECIALTY COFFEE BAR SERVES."

MARK SMESRUD P.239

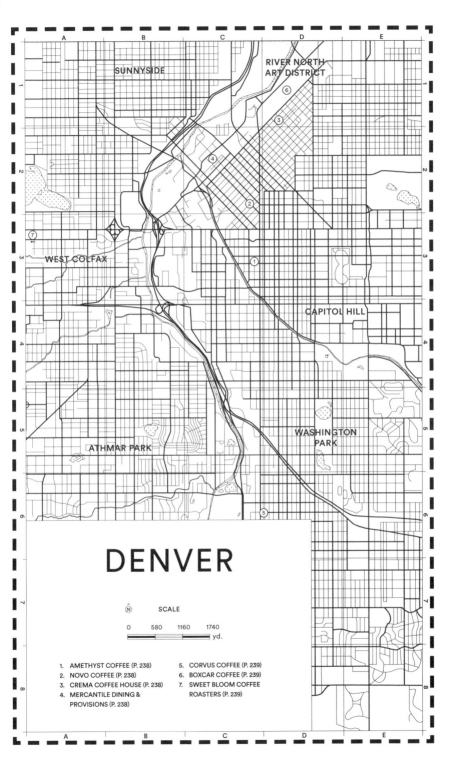

DENVER

N SCALE

0   580   1160   1740
yd.

1. AMETHYST COFFEE (P. 238)
2. NOVO COFFEE (P. 238)
3. CREMA COFFEE HOUSE (P. 238)
4. MERCANTILE DINING & PROVISIONS (P. 238)
5. CORVUS COFFEE (P. 239)
6. BOXCAR COFFEE (P. 239)
7. SWEET BLOOM COFFEE ROASTERS (P. 239)

SUNNYSIDE

RIVER NORTH ART DISTRICT

WEST COLFAX

CAPITOL HILL

ATHMAR PARK

WASHINGTON PARK

AMETHYST COFFEE

1111 Broadway #101
Capitol Hill
Denver
Colorado 80203
United States
www.amethystcoffee.co

Opening hours..Daily from 7 am
Credit cards...........................Visa, MasterCard, and Amex
Style...Coffee bar

"Amethyst is always the first place I stop when I'm in Denver. The coffee program is progressive but very approachable, the build-out is gorgeous, and the owner, Elle Taylor, is one of the nicest people I've met in the coffee world. It is without question one of my favorite cafes in the States."
—Zac Cadwalader

NOVO COFFEE

1600 Glenarm Place
Central Business District
Denver
Colorado 80202
United States
+1 3039990077
www.novocoffee.com

Opening hours...................................Mon–Fri from 6:30 am,
                                                              Sat–Sun from 7:30 am
Credit cards...........................Visa, MasterCard, and Amex
Style...Coffee bar

CREMA COFFEE HOUSE

2862 Larimer Street
Curtis Park
Denver
Colorado 80205
United States
+1 7202849648
www.cremacoffeehouse.net

Opening hours..Daily from 7 am
Credit cards...........................Visa, MasterCard, and Amex
Style...Coffee and vegetarian food

"The most memorable espresso I had was at Crema Coffee House. It was a single origin from Counter Culture. I'm pretty sure it was Apollo 7 from Ecuador. It tasted like mango purée."—Jay DeRose

MERCANTILE DINING & PROVISIONS

1701 Wynkoop Street #155
Denver
Colorado 80202
United States
+1 7204603733
www.mercantiledenver.com

Opening hours..Daily from 7 am
Credit cards...........................Visa, MasterCard, and Amex
Style...................................Coffee bar, restaurant, and cafe

"Mercantile is so many things—a restaurant, a market, a bar, and a cafe—and it's very good at all of them. Run by renowned chef Alex Seidel, you'd expect the food to be top-notch, which it is, but what keeps me coming back is the fact that I can get really well-made coffee with my meal."—Zac Cadwalader

CORVUS COFFEE

1740 South Broadway
Platt Park
Denver
Colorado 80210
United States
+1 3037151740
www.corvuscoffee.com

Opening hours......................................Daily from 6:30 am
Credit cards...........................Visa, MasterCard, and Amex
Style..Coffee bar

"I love Corvus, as there is a consistent tone of quiet
innovation when it comes to what a specialty coffee bar
serves."—Mark Smesrud

BOXCAR COFFEE

3350 Brighton Blvd #110
River North Art District
Denver
Colorado 80216
United States
www.boxcarcoffee.com

Opening hours..Mon–Fri from 7 am,
Sat from 7:30 am, Sun from 8 am
Credit cards...........................Visa, MasterCard, and Amex
Style..Coffee and waffles

"Boxcar is a communal space with many other businesses,
great restaurants, a brewery, and a big screen that was
streaming the Western Regional Barista Competition when
I visited."—Pete Licata

SWEET BLOOM COFFEE ROASTERS

1619 Reed Street
Edgewood
Lakewood
Colorado 80214
United States
+1 3032615954
www.sweetbloomcoffee.com

Opening hours.......................................Mon–Sat from 7 am
Credit cards...Visa and MasterCard
Style..Coffee bar

"I got the best filter coffee at Sweet Bloom Coffee Roasters
made by Andy Sprenger and Caleb Sprenger."—Dawn Chan

"I love going to Sweet Bloom Coffee Roasters because of
the knowledge and skill that is present when it comes to the
craft, as well as the atmosphere being devoid of pretense."
—Mark Smesrud

"THEY OPERATE ABOVE THE TRENDS AND ARE TRULY FOCUSED ON MAKING DELICIOUS COFFEE AND SERVING IT UP WITH SMILES."

CHRIS BACA P.242

PORTLAND

"SWEETNESS TENDS TO BE THE NAME OF THE GAME FOR HEART, AND I'VE HAD SOME REALLY DELICIOUS ESPRESSOS FROM THAT TEAM."

RYAN WILLBUR P.243

"ON THE BLEEDING EDGE OF LIGHT ROASTS, ESPECIALLY IN AMERICA, AND THEY'RE SERVING THESE ENORMOUS LONG ESPRESSO SHOTS IN A CAPPUCCINO CUP."

JORDAN MICHELMAN P.243

"I LOVE THE NOSTALGIA OF DRINKING A MUG OF COFFEE ON A GRAY RAINY DAY WHILE HOLED UP IN A COZY COFFEE SHOP."

LAILA GHAMBARI WILLBUR P.243

PORTLAND

N̂   SCALE

0   730   1460   2185
yd.

1. BARISTA (P. 242)
2. COAVA COFFEE ROASTERS (P. 242)
3. WATER AVENUE COFFEE (P. 242)

4. HEART COFFEE ROASTERS (P. 243)
5. GOOD COFFEE (P. 243)
6. EITHER/OR (P. 243)

7. STUMPTOWN COFFEE
   ROASTERS (P. 244)
8. BARISTA (P. 244)

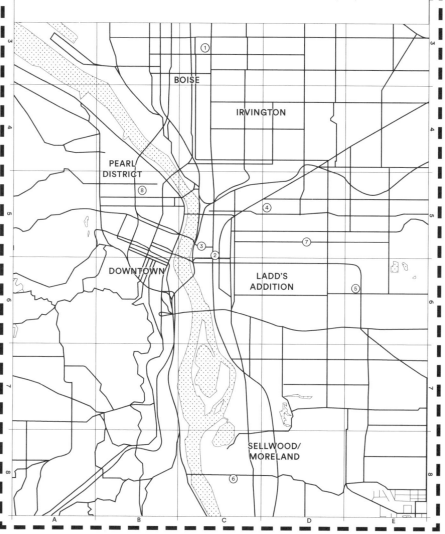

BARISTA

175 Northeast Alberta Street
Alberta
Portland
Oregon 97211
United States
+1 5032082568
www.baristapdx.com

Opening hours............................Mon–Fri from 6 am,
Sat–Sun from 7 am
Credit cards............................Visa, MasterCard, and Amex
Style...Coffee bar

"My favorite espresso beverages have always come from any one of the Barista locations in Portland (their Alberta store is secretly my favorite). I feel like Billy Wilson and his team have views similar to mine when it comes to espresso drink preparation, and that shines through in every drink I have from any of his stores. They operate above the trends and are truly focused on making delicious coffee and serving it up with smiles."—Chris Baca

"The best espresso I can remember being served came from the Barista location on Alberta. I don't remember what the coffee was, but I remember it being good enough that it made me feel as though there were some secret involved—that the barista who served it knew some things about espresso preparation to which I wasn't privy. I took a sip and thought, 'Shit. I'm not trying hard enough.'" —Samuel Lewontin

"I just think it's the perfect coffee bar for the location, the 'hood, the time, and the place."—Tyler J. Wells

COAVA COFFEE ROASTERS

1300 Southeast Grand Avenue
Buckman
Portland
Oregon 97214
United States
+1 5038948134
www.coavacoffee.com

Opening hours............................Mon–Fri from 6 am,
Sat–Sun from 7 am
Credit cards............................Visa, MasterCard, and Amex
Style...Roastery cafe

"Having a personal experience with Coava in the early days and watching them grow and help solidify the Portland coffee scene's identity has been cool."—Anna Brones

"I had a memorable espresso experience at Coava."
—Aaron Ultimo

In a space shared with an amazing bamboo furniture designer, Coava oozes beauty and design. Their coffee is some of the best in the Pacific Northwest.

WATER AVENUE COFFEE

1028 Southeast Water Avenue #145
Buckman
Portland
Oregon 97214
United States
+1 5038087083
www.wateravenuecoffee.com

Opening hours...Daily from 7 am
Credit cards...Visa and MasterCard
Style...Coffee bar

"I love Water Avenue Coffee, as I attended the business and barista training program there."—Mark Smesrud

HEART COFFEE ROASTERS

2211 East Burnside Street
Kerns
Portland
Oregon 97214
United States
+1 5032066602
www.heartroasters.com

Opening hours..Daily from 7 am
Credit cards............................Visa, MasterCard, and Amex
Style..Coffee bar

"The single-origin espresso program at Heart Coffee
Roasters is among the most innovative and chance taking
I've found. They're out there on the bleeding edge of light
roasts, especially in America, and they're serving these
enormous long espresso shots in a cappuccino cup. It is just
delicious. You can be innovative and take chances as long
as you work really hard and make smart choices along the
way."—Jordan Michelman

"I always have a great espresso experience at Heart Coffee
Roasters."—Andrew Milstead

"The best espresso has come from Heart Coffee Roasters.
Wille's perfectionist nature means the coffee is not
necessarily consistent but that it continually improves
from the first roast batch of the season to the last. He's not
afraid to make changes, and when he nails a certain coffee,
it shows. Sweetness tends to be the name of the game for
Heart, and I've had some really delicious espressos from
that team."—Ryan Willbur

GOOD COFFEE

4725 Southeast Division Street
Richmond
Portland
Oregon 97206
United States
+1 9712546599
www.goodcoffeepdx.com

Opening hours..Daily from 7 am
Credit cards............................Visa, MasterCard, and Amex
Style...Coffee and waffles

"I had some great filter coffee at Good Coffee."
—Jared Linzmeier

"My favorite place to enjoy filter coffee is Good Coffee.
They batch-brew on a Fetco using coffee from four
different roasters. Coffee is served in a mug (handmade
ceramic) with a sidecar. Growing up in the Pacific
Northwest, I love the nostalgia of drinking a mug of coffee
on a gray rainy day while holed up in a cozy coffee shop.
The modern craft aesthetic and gentle demeanor of Good
Coffee is a welcome exception to the rule in the Northwest."
—Laila Ghambari Willbur

EITHER/OR

8235 Southeast 13th Avenue #2
Sellwood-Moreland
Portland
Oregon 97202
United States
+1 5032353474
www.tanglewoodbevco.com

Opening hours..Mon–Fri from 7 am,
Sat–Sun from 8 am
Credit cards............................Visa, MasterCard, and Amex
Style..Coffee bar

I think Either/Or is doing some really fun stuff with flights
and simple, thoughtful pairings."—Jared Linzmeier

STUMPTOWN COFFEE ROASTERS
3356 Southeast Belmont Street
Sunnyside
Portland
Oregon 97214
United States
+1 5032328889
www.stumptowncoffee.com

Opening hours	Mon–Fri from 6 am, Sat–Sun from 7 am
Credit cards	Visa, MasterCard, and Amex
Style	Coffee bar

"Best filter coffee."—Gabriel Boscana

BARISTA
539 Northwest 13th Avenue
The Pearl
Portland
Oregon 97217
United States
+1 5032741211
www.baristapdx.com

Opening hours	Mon–Fri from 6 am, Sat–Sun from 7 am
Credit cards	Visa, MasterCard, and Amex
Style	Coffee bar

"The first time I set foot in the (then) new Barista in Portland, I immediately thought, 'This is my perfect coffee shop.' It's small, it's efficient, the coffee is very tasty, the baristas are kind and professional, and there is a sense of movement in a beautifully designed space."—Ellie Hudson

"ON A TWO-GROUP GB5 ESPRESSO, THE BARISTA WILL PREPARE YOU SOME FANTASTIC COFFEE."
LORENZO PERKINS P.249

"THE BEST SHOT THAT I'VE EVER HAD WAS PULLED AT CUVEE COFFEE BAR." LORENZO PERKINS P.249

AUSTIN

"THE MOST MEMORABLE EXPERIENCES I'VE HAD WITH FILTER COFFEE HAVE HAPPENED AT THIS ORIGINAL HOUNDSTOOTH COFFEE." LORENZO PERKINS P.250

"THEY REALLY DROVE THE AUSTIN SCENE FROM THE EARLY DAYS."
DAN STREETMAN P.250

"PATRICK AND LORENZO ARE TWO AMAZING INDIVIDUALS WITH MANY YEARS OF EXPERIENCE IN COFFEE AND CUSTOMER SERVICE."
MICHAEL VACLAV P.249

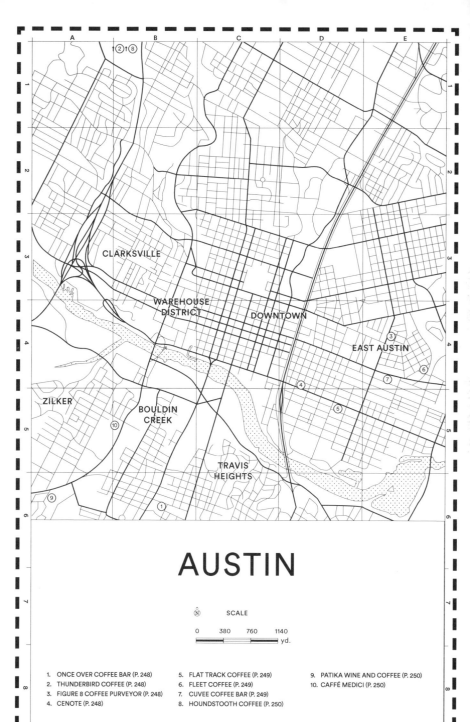

A B C D E

CLARKSVILLE

WAREHOUSE
DISTRICT
DOWNTOWN

EAST AUSTIN

ZILKER

BOULDIN
CREEK

TRAVIS
HEIGHTS

AUSTIN

N̂   SCALE

0   380   760   1140
                        yd.

1. ONCE OVER COFFEE BAR (P. 248)   5. FLAT TRACK COFFEE (P. 249)   9. PATIKA WINE AND COFFEE (P. 250)
2. THUNDERBIRD COFFEE (P. 248)   6. FLEET COFFEE (P. 249)   10. CAFFÉ MEDICI (P. 250)
3. FIGURE 8 COFFEE PURVEYOR (P. 248)   7. CUVEE COFFEE BAR (P. 249)
4. CENOTE (P. 248)   8. HOUNDSTOOTH COFFEE (P. 250)

ONCE OVER COFFEE BAR
2009 South 1st Street
Bouldin
Austin
Texas 78704
United States
+1 5123269575
www.onceovercoffeebar.com

Opening hours..................................Mon–Sat from 7 am,
Sun from 8 am
Credit cards...Visa and MasterCard
Style..Coffee bar

FIGURE 8 COFFEE PURVEYOR
1111 Chicon Street
East Austin
Austin
Texas 78702
United States
+1 5125183230
United States
www.figure8coffeepurveyors.com

Opening hours...Daily from 7 am
Credit cards...........................Visa, MasterCard, and Amex
Style..Coffee bar

THUNDERBIRD COFFEE
1401 West Koenig Lane
Brentwood
Austin
Texas 78756
United States
+1 5124208660
www.thunderbirdcoffee.com

Opening hours................................Mon–Fri from 6:30 am,
Sat–Sun from 7:30 am
Credit cards...........................Visa, MasterCard, and Amex
Style..Coffee bar

CENOTE
1010 East Cesar Chavez Street
East Cesar Chavez
Austin
Texas 78702
United States
+1 5125241311
www.cenoteaustin.com

Opening hours..Mon–Fri from 7 am,
Sat–Sun from 8 am
Credit cards...........................Visa, MasterCard, and Amex
Style..Restaurant

FLAT TRACK COFFEE
1619 East Cesar Chavez Street
East Cesar Chavez
Austin
Texas 78702
United States
+1 5128146010
www.flattrackcoffee.com

Opening hours..Mon–Fri from 8 am,
                                                                    Sat–Sun from 9 am
Credit cards............................Visa, MasterCard, and Amex
Style...Coffee bar

"In the back of what amounts to an indoor hipster flea
market (it's an indie bookstore, vinyl record store, and
custom tailor) there is a tiny shop of about a hundred square
feet called Flat Track Coffee. On a two-group GB5 espresso
machine, the barista will prepare you some fantastic coffee,
again with little pretense, for you to drink as you peruse
the rest of the space. Out back is a vegan food truck, and
more often than not the owner sits there, sipping an
espresso and chatting it up with some of his fellow Cafe
Racer motorcycle enthusiast friends."—Lorenzo Perkins

FLEET COFFEE
2427 Webberville Road
Govalle
Austin
Texas 78702
United States
www.fleetcoffee.com

Opening hours...Daily from 7 am
Credit cards............................Visa, MasterCard, and Amex
Style...Coffee bar

"Patrick and Lorenzo are two amazing individuals with many
years of experience in coffee and customer service. Fleet is
the result of that dedication and love."—Michael Vaclav

CUVEE COFFEE BAR
2000 East 6th Street
Holly
Austin
Texas 78702
United States
+1 5123685636
www.cuveecoffee.com

Opening hours..................................Mon–Fri from 6:30 am,
                                                                  Sat–Sun from 7:30 am
Credit cards............................Visa, MasterCard, and Amex
Style...Coffee bar

"The best shot that I've ever had was pulled at Cuvee Coffee
Bar. Some magic balancing act of a pressure-profiling
Modbar espresso machine, the delicate hands of a skilled
roaster, and the intentionality of a caring barista coalesced
into a fantastically sweet, creamy single-origin espresso
from Colombia."—Lorenzo Perkins

HOUNDSTOOTH COFFEE

4200 North Lamar Boulevard
Rosedale
Austin
Texas 78756
United States
+1 5125319417
www.houndstoothcoffee.com

Opening hours.................................Mon–Fri from 6:30 am,
Sat–Sun from 7 am
Credit cards...Visa and MasterCard
Style...Coffee bar

"The most memorable experiences I've had with filter
coffee have happened at this original Houndstooth Coffee.
The pour-over bar is not on the front counter; the theater
of it all is hidden on the back service counter. The coffee
itself is served without much fanfare in a branded diner mug
filled to the brim, as if to challenge the guest to consume a
little before adding cream or sugar. A rotating roster of
various roasters from around the country ensures a selection
of a fine Kenya, a delicately sweet Costa Rica, or a brazen
and punchy El Salvador at almost any time of the year."
—Lorenzo Perkins

PATIKA WINE AND COFFEE

2159 South Lamar Boulevard
South Lamar
Austin
Texas 78704
United States
+1 5125353955
www.patikacoffee.com

Opening hours..Daily from 7 am
Credit cards.............................Visa, MasterCard, and Amex
Style...Coffee and wine

CAFFÉ MEDICI

1100 South Lamar Boulevard
Zilker
Austin
Texas 78704
United States
+1 5124457212
www.caffemedici.com

Opening hours..Daily from 7 am
Credit cards.............................Visa, MasterCard, and Amex
Style...Coffee bar

"They really drove the Austin scene from the early days."
—Dan Streetman

"ANALOG COFFEE IN SEATTLE IS THE QUINTESSENTIAL SEATTLE COFFEE BAR TO ME."

EILEEN HASSI RINALDI P.254

"I HAVE TRIED A LOT OF ESPRESSO AND THERE IS NO BETTER COFFEE ON EARTH."

NATHAN MYHRVOLD P.254

SEATTLE

"THE COFFEE THEY SERVE IS TASTY, THE SPACE IS WELL DESIGNED, AND THE HOSPITALITY IS ALWAYS ON POINT."

SAMUEL LEWONTIN P.256

"CLEAR, CLEAN EXTRACTIONS OF DISTINCTIVE COFFEES ARE A GREAT WAY TO START A CONVERSATION ABOUT THE INTERPLAY BETWEEN FLAVORS IN COFFEE AND FLAVORS IN A MEAL."

SAMUEL LEWONTIN P.255

"A CLASSIC, STRAIGHT-FORWARD CAFE."

SHANE DEVERAUX P.257

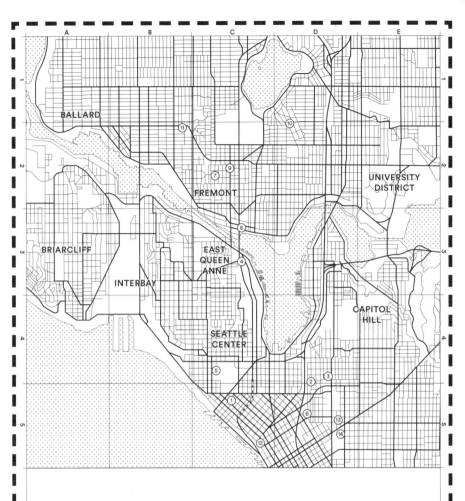

SEATTLE

SCALE

0   640   1280   1925
yd.

1. STREET BEAN (P. 254)
2. ANALOG COFFEE (P. 254)
3. ESPRESSO VIVACE (P. 254)
4. CANLIS (P. 255)
5. LA MARZOCCO CAFE AND
   SHOWROOM AT KEXP (P. 255)

6. VICTROLA COFFEE ROASTERS (P. 255)
7. LIGHTHOUSE ROASTERS (P. 255)
8. MILSTEAD & CO. (P. 256)
9. VIF (P. 256)
10. ZOKA COFFEE (P. 256)
11. SLATE COFFEE BAR (P. 256)

12. ZIG ZAG CAFÉ (P. 257)
13. CAFFE VITA (P. 257)
14. STUMPTOWN (P. 257)

STREET BEAN

2711 3rd Avenue
Belltown
Seattle
Washington 98121
United States
+1 2067086803
United States
www.streetbeanespresso.com

Opening hours...Mon–Fri from 6 am,
Sat–Sun from 8 am
Credit cards...Visa and MasterCard
Style..Coffee bar

"I usually don't really enjoy drinking espresso. However, every time I have espresso at Street Bean I love it. They have a way of pulling out sweetness while muting sourness almost every time. They are great at turning something that I usually have to chase with water into a refreshing li'l sip!"
—Jay Lijewski

ANALOG COFFEE

235 Summit Avenue East
Capitol Hill
Seattle
Washington 98102
United States
www.analogcoffee.com

Opening hours..Daily from 7 am
Credit cards...........................Visa, MasterCard, and Amex
Style..Coffee bar

"Analog Coffee in Seattle is the quintessential Seattle coffee bar to me. It's neighborhoody and charming, with carefully chosen furniture and fixtures, without being precious. I always run into someone I know there or meet a new friend. The quality is great, but there isn't a scene about it. I love it."—Eileen Hassi Rinaldi

ESPRESSO VIVACE

321 Broadway Avenue East
Capitol Hill
Seattle
Washington 98102
United States
+1 2068605869
www.espressovivace.com

Opening hours..Daily from 6 am
Credit cards...........................Visa, MasterCard, and Amex
Style..Coffee stand

"Ideal walk-up sidewalk cafe. Typically staffed with some of the most veteran baristas you can find in the United States. To me, the research, techniques, and flavor profile developed at Vivace helped define one valuable end of the specialty coffee industry's spectrum. The drinks are classic. No bullshit, just a quaint little spot to have a bevi while immersed in Capitol Hill, one of Seattle's most eclectic neighborhoods."—Christopher Alameda

"Before I opened my cafe, I was inspired by the espresso at Vivace in Seattle."—Caroline Bell

"Vivace has been at the forefront of the modern espresso movement from its beginning, and the technical details, like brewing temperature, are listed on the menu. I have tried a lot of espresso and there is no better coffee on earth."
—Nathan Myhrvold

"I will forever associate Seattle with Espresso Vivace. It was my introduction to coffee and strong memories were forged there."—Sebastian Sztabzyb

CANLIS

2576 Aurora Avenue North
East Queen Anne
Seattle
Washington 98109
United States
+1 2062833313
www.canlis.com

Opening hours.................................Mon–Fri from 5:30 pm,
Sat from 5 pm
Credit cards............................Visa, MasterCard, and Amex
Style...Fine dining

"Probably the most memorable coffee service I've yet
experienced with a meal happened at Canlis in Seattle,
where the barista came to our table and talked us through
each of the options on the coffee menu, much as the
sommelier would've done with the wine list, had we been
drinking wine. That menu focused strongly on filter coffee,
which is, I think, underappreciated in conjunction with food.
Clear, clean extractions of distinctive coffees are a great
way to start a conversation about the interplay between
flavors in coffee and flavors in a meal. It would be great to
see them used this way more often."—Samuel Lewontin

"The food is obscenely delicious, innovative, and refreshing.
It shouldn't come as a surprise that their coffee program is
the best I've seen at restaurant. It is a must-visit for all."
—Andrew Milstead

LA MARZOCCO CAFE AND SHOWROOM AT KEXP

472 1st Ave North
East Queen Anne
Seattle
Washington 98109
United States
+1 2063883500
www.lamarzoccousa.com/locations

Opening hours...Mon–Fri from 7 am,
Sat–Sun from 8 am
Credit cards............................Visa, MasterCard, and Amex
Style..Coffee and food

VICTROLA COFFEE ROASTERS

310 Pike Street
First Hill
Seattle
Washington 98122
United States
+1 2066241725
www.victrolacoffee.com

Opening hours.................................Mon–Fri from 6:30 am,
Sat–Sun from 7 am
Credit cards...................................Visa and MasterCard
Style..Roastery cafe

"My favorite, or most memorable, espresso was Victrola's
Streamline, around 2006, at the 15th Avenue location, when
Tonx was roasting, Kyle Glanville was the trainer, and David
Latourell was the manager. It was a very 2006-style shot,
but it was the first time I had a coffee of any kind that
tasted more like melted chocolate than it did coffee, and
it completely blew me away."—Zak Rye

LIGHTHOUSE ROASTERS

400 North 43rd Street
Fremont
Seattle
Washington 98103
United States
+1 2066334775
www.lighthouseroasters.com

Opening hours.......................................Mon–Fri from 6 am,
Sat–Sun from 6:30 am
Credit cards...................................Visa and MasterCard
Style..Roastery cafe

"I like reminiscing at Lighthouse."—Vince Piccolo

MILSTEAD & CO.

900 North 34th Street
Fremont
Seattle
Washington 98103
United States
+1 2066594814
www.milsteadandco.com

Opening hours..Mon–Fri from 6 am,
                                                        Sat–Sun from 7 am
Credit cards..Visa, and MasterCard
Style...Coffee bar

"The coffee they serve is tasty, the space is well designed, and the hospitality is always on point, but more than any of that, this is where I get coffee with my dad every morning when I'm visiting home. Between that, all of the wonderful, welcoming folks behind the counter, and the high likelihood that I'll run into an old friend from the Seattle coffee scene, the place has a sense of family to it that no other shop has yet matched for me."—Samuel Lewontin

"I've had a lot of great espressos from Milstead & Co. Andrew and his crew do a great job brewing unique coffees while maintaining balance and an emphasis on sweetness."
—Jared Linzmeier

VIF

4401 Fremont Avenue North
Fremont
Seattle
Washington 98103
United States
+1 2065577357
www.vifseattle.com

Opening hours..Tue–Fri from 7 am,
                                                        Sat–Sun from 8 am
Credit cards..Visa and MasterCard
Style..Coffee, wine, and food

"It's cozy yet open with gentle, friendly, and knowledgeable staff. Its walls are mostly windows, and are a delight, be it rainy and gray or bright and blue."—Andrew Milstead

"Amazing food, pastries, and wine in a bright and inviting space."—Bronwen Serna

"My favorite place to enjoy coffee is at Vif. Owners Shawn and Lauren are two women I look up to greatly for their bravery and beautiful execution. They have managed to create a space that expresses their experience and talent in every single detail, from the pastries to the selection of natural wines. Coffee comes from Olympia Coffee Roasters brewed on a Strada EP or Kalita Wave. All the pastries are made in-house and are generally gluten-free or vegan in the most unassuming way. There is lots of natural light from large wraparound windows and clean wood and white walls. It's not often you find a cafe in Seattle that feels feminine."—Laila Ghambari Willbur

ZOKA COFFEE

2200 North 56th Street
Meridian
Seattle
Washington 98103
United States
+1 2065454277
www.zokacoffee.com

Opening hours..Mon–Fri from 7 am,
                                                        Sat–Sun from 8 am
Credit cards..Visa and MasterCard
Style...Coffee bar

"Zoka Coffee is where I had my first traditional cappuccino and my first Chemex."—Mark Smesrud

SLATE COFFEE BAR

5413 6th Avenue Northwest
Phinney Ridge
Seattle
Washington 98107
United States
www.slatecoffee.com

Opening hours..Mon–Fri from 7 am,
                                                        Sat–Sun from 8 am
Credit cards..Visa, MasterCard, and Amex
Style...Coffee bar

"I had a memorable Kenya pour-over at Slate."—Ryan Fisher

CAFFE VITA

1005 East Pike Street
Pike/Pine
Seattle
Washington 98122
United States
+1 2067094440
www.caffevita.com

Opening hours...Mon–Fri from 6 am,
                                                Sat–Sun from 7 am
Credit cards............................Visa, MasterCard, and Amex
Style..Coffee bar

"Seattle is still my favorite. It's there that I truly fell in love
with preparing and serving coffee, and I'll always feel some
mystical bond with the coffee scene there. There's a specific
and unique kind of pride I get from the baristas at some of
the older cafes in the city that make me feel, more than
anywhere else, that I'm experiencing something very
special. It would be hard to nail down a favorite shop there,
but if I was forced to, and this has nothing to do with the
actual coffee, I would have to say the loft area at the Caffe
Vita on Pike . . . so get a mocha and enjoy the space."
—Zak Rye

STUMPTOWN

1115 12th Avenue
Pike/Pine
Seattle
Washington 98122
United States
+1 2063231544
www.stumptowncoffee.com

Opening hours...Mon–Fri from 6 am,
                                                Sat–Sun from 7 am
Credit cards............................Visa, MasterCard, and Amex
Style..Coffee bar

"A classic, straightforward cafe. I can't think of ever missing
a cup when I'm in Seattle. Which is a lot."—Shane Deveraux

ZIG ZAG CAFE

1501 Western Avenue #202
Pike Place Market
Seattle
Washington 98101
United States
+1 2066251146
www.zigzagseattle.com

Opening hours...Daily from 5 pm
Credit cards............................Visa, MasterCard, and Amex
Style...Cocktail bar

"The best drink made with coffee that I have ever had
outside of a coffee bar exists at Zig Zag Cafe in Seattle.
Their Spanish coffee is made up of a French-pressed coffee,
rum, some spices, fresh cream, and fire show—basically
an Irish coffee but with rum. I want one right now."
—Christopher Alameda

"IT'S A BEAUTIFUL CAFE AND A BEAUTIFUL SPOT IN THE NEIGHBORHOOD. GREAT BUILDING, GREAT COFFEES, GREAT MENU, GREAT PEOPLE."

SCOTT LUCEY P.261

"A COFFEE SHOP THAT HAS MY HEART."

JOE MARROCCO P.263

USA MIDWEST

"A COMFORTABLE NEIGHBORHOOD CAFE WITH AN INTENSE FOCUS ON QUALITY."

SCOTT RAO P.263

"FIRST TRUE THIRD-WAVE SHOP THAT IS STILL CONSISTENTLY PUTTING OUT COFFEE IN ITS INTENDED DELICIOUS FORM."

ERIC MULLINS P.260

"THEY SERVE CAREFULLY SELECTED COFFEES FROM GREAT ROASTERS, WELL-CRAFTED ESPRESSO, AND DELICIOUS COMFORT FOOD IN A BEAUTIFUL SPACE IN THE SHADOW OF THE FAMOUS MICHIGAN CENTRAL STATION."

JAY CUNNINGHAM P.260

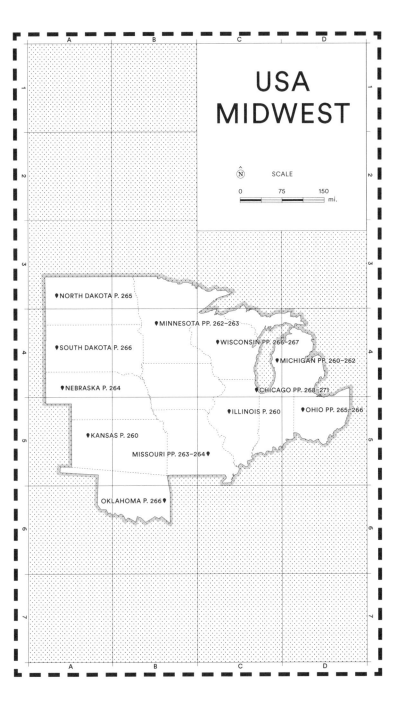

USA
MIDWEST

SCALE

0   75   150
mi.

♦ NORTH DAKOTA P. 265

♦ MINNESOTA PP. 262–263

♦ SOUTH DAKOTA P. 266

♦ WISCONSIN PP. 266–267

♦ MICHIGAN PP. 260–262

♦ NEBRASKA P. 264

♦ CHICAGO PP. 268–271

♦ ILLINOIS P. 260

♦ OHIO PP. 265–266

♦ KANSAS P. 260

MISSOURI PP. 263–264 ♦

OKLAHOMA P. 266 ♦

Chicago, see pages 268–271

BLACKBERRY MARKET

401 North Main Street
Glen Ellyn
Illinois 60137
United States
+1 6304749149
www.blackberry.is

Opening hours..Daily from 7 am
Credit cards....................................Visa, MasterCard, Amex,
Style..Coffee and food

"A very solid Intelligentsia-brewing cafe in my hometown with a bakery attached. It's one of the first random, small-town coffee experiences I've had."—Cora Lambert

PT'S COFFEE

1635 Southwest Washburn Avenue, Suite A
College Hill
Topeka
Kansas 66604
United States
+1 7854085675
www.ptscoffee.com

Opening hours...Mon–Fri from 7 am,
                                               Sat–Sun from 8 am
Credit cards............................Visa, MasterCard, and Amex
Style...Coffee bar

COMET COFFEE

16 Nickels Arcade
Burns Park
Ann Arbor
Michigan 48104
United States
+1 7342220579
www.squareup.com/store/comet-coffee

Opening hours...Mon–Fri from 7 am,
                                   Sat from 8 am, Sun from 8:30 am
Credit cards............................Visa, MasterCard, and Amex
Style...Coffee bar

"In a sea of old-fashioned coffee shops pretending to be third wave, Comet stands out as the first true third-wave shop that is still consistently putting out coffee in its intended delicious form."—Eric Mullins

ASTRO COFFEE

2124 Michigan Avenue
Detroit
Michigan 48216
United States
+1 3136382989
www.astrodetroit.com

Opening hours....................................Tue–Fri from 7:30 am,
                                 Sat from 8:30 am, Sun from 9 am
Credit cards............................Visa, MasterCard, and Amex
Style..Coffee and food

"Astro Coffee was one of the first progressive shops in Detroit. They serve carefully selected coffees from great roasters, well-crafted espresso, and delicious comfort food in a beautiful space in the shadow of the famous Michigan Central Station. Every time I'm in town I stop in and chat up the staff and regulars, and I usually learn something new about what's happening in the city."—Jay Cunningham

MADCAP COFFEE

98 Monroe Center Street Northwest
Downtown
Grand Rapids
Michigan 49503
United States
+1 8888669091
www.madcapcoffee.com

Opening hours	Mon–Fri from 7 am, Sat from 8 am, Sun from 10 am
Credit cards	Visa, MasterCard, and Amex
Style	Coffee bar

"I had that 'this place is perfect' feeling the first time I set foot in Madcap in downtown Grand Rapids. Madcap manages to strike that precise balance of approachability and uncompromising quality. It also has the best consistent customer service I have experienced (I've been back maybe twenty times since then). Their merchandising is so magnetic that literally every time I bring people into Madcap with me they leave with a pound of coffee, or a T-shirt, or a brewing device they've purchased. You almost can't help it. The space feels intimate and airy all at once."
—Ellie Hudson

"I have a soft spot for the Madcap in Grand Rapids. It's a beautiful cafe and a beautiful spot in the neighborhood. Great building, great coffees, great menu, great people."
—Scott Lucey

Grand Rapids was perhaps, not the most likely location to start an artisan coffee-roasting business in 2008, but that's exactly why it's become such a force of nature. The cafe space—sunny and welcoming—contributed greatly to a revitalized downtown streetscape. The company's larger movements, from barista competitions to direct sourcing of excellent coffees, to finding a roasting niche in an increasingly divided light-versus-dark landscape, set them apart. Madcap Coffee is in the top tier of the country's best big little roasters.

ROWSTER

632 Wealthy Street Southeast
Madison Area
Grand Rapids
Michigan 49503
United States
+1 6167807777
www.rowstercoffee.com

Opening hours	Mon–Fri from 7 am, Sat from 8 am, Sun from 9 am
Credit cards	Visa, MasterCard, and Amex
Style	Coffee bar

DEAD RIVER COFFEE

119 West Baraga Avenue
Marquette
Michigan 49855
United States
+1 9062262112
www.deadrivercoffee.com

Opening hours	Mon–Fri from 7 am, Sat from 9 am
Credit cards	Visa, MasterCard, and Amex
Style	Coffee bar

"Dead River Coffee, in Michigan's Upper Peninsula, is in a town of fewer than thirty thousand people. They were roasting their own, brewing everything by the cup, and making traditional-sized espresso drinks even back in 2002. A great shop."—Michael Phillips

BLK MRKT
144 Hall Street
Traverse City
Michigan 49684
United States
+1 2317145038
www.blkmrkt.coffee

Opening hours..................................Mon–Sat from 7 am,
Sun from 9 am
Credit cards...........................Visa, MasterCard, and Amex
Style..Coffee bar

"It is hard for me to explain how impressive it is to see an
owner willing to take a leap of faith on incredible equipment
and stunning coffees from all over, in a town where being
open on Sundays is a radical departure from the status quo.
The staff is always working on something new—it's the
epitome of modern in a town where Keens and a technical
vest are appropriate dress for a nice dinner or church. I am
not at all surprised that my fellow citizens here are flocking
to BLK MRKT, but it's still important to acknowledge the
risks Chuck is taking in pioneering a truly modern coffee
space. And the coffee is delicious."—Ellie Hudson

CULTIVATE COFFEE AND TAP HOUSE
307 North River Street
Depot Town
Ypsilanti
Michigan 48198
United States
+1 7342498993
www.cultivateypsi.com

Opening hours..Mon–Sat from 7 am
Credit cards...........................Visa, MasterCard, and Amex
Style..Coffee and beer

"Cultivate is gorgeous; it's the first business in Ypsi that
I think could survive in pretty much any city. From the
concept, build-out, and curation, they've done good work.
The passion is there and they're easily going to become a
coffee mecca in the area."—Zak Rye

HYPERION COFFEE
306 North River Street
Depot Town
Ypsilanti
Michigan 48198
United States
+1 7345475329
www.hyperioncoffee.com

Opening hours..Daily from 9 am
Credit cards...........................Visa, MasterCard, and Amex
Style..Roastery cafe

"Hyperion is a roaster and tasting room in Depot Town.
The partnership is well divided and, I suppose, logically
curated. Eric Mullins is the visionary, building off of and
evolving relationships and concepts he formed at the
Ugly Mug. They're producing some really fantastic coffee.
They also have a mad-scientist wonder of a Synesso that
Todd Osborne made for them."—Zak Rye

FIKA
5327 Highway 61
Lutsen
Minnesota 55612
United States
+1 2183874040
www.fikacoffee.com

Opening hours..Mon–Sat from 7 am
Credit cards...........................Visa, MasterCard, and Amex
Style..Coffee roastery

DOGWOOD COFFEE
4021 East Lake Street
Cooper
Minneapolis
Minnesota 55406
United States
+1 6128861585
www.dogwoodcoffee.com

Opening hours................................Mon–Fri from 6:30 am,
Sat–Sun from 8 am
....Visa, MasterCard, and Amex
Style..Coffee bar

"My favorite in the Minneapolis–St. Paul area."
—Mark Smesrud

FIVE WATT

3745 Nicollet Avenue South
Kingfield
Minneapolis
Minnesota 55409
United States
+1 6122597519
www.fivewattcoffee.com

Opening hours..Daily from 6 am
Credit cards...........................Visa, MasterCard, and Amex
Style..Coffee bar

"Superb drinks made with coffee."—Scott Lucey

KOPPLIN'S COFFEE

2038 Marshall Avenue
Union Park
St. Paul
Minnesota 55104
United States
+1 6516980457
www.kopplinscoffee.com

Opening hours......................................Mon–Fri from 6 am,
Sat–Sun from 7 am
Credit cards...Visa and MasterCard
Style..Coffee bar

"A comfortable neighborhood cafe with an intense focus
on quality."—Scott Rao

KALDI'S COFFEE

700 DeMun Avenue
DeMun
Clayton
Missouri 63105
United States
+1 3147279955
www.kaldiscoffee.com

Opening hours......................................Mon–Sat from 6 am,
Sun from 7 am
Credit cards...........................Visa, MasterCard, and Amex
Style..Coffee bar

"The feeling of pride and kinship I get from these companies
has to color my palate. Coffee never tastes as good as when
you are home."—Joe Marrocco

SECOND BEST COFFEE

328 West 85th Street
Waldo Homes
Kansas City
Missouri 64114
+1 8163770354
www.secondbestcoffee.com

Opening hours................................Mon–Fri from 6:30 am,
Sat from 7:30 am
Credit cards...........................Visa, MasterCard, and Amex
Style...Coffee and breakfast

"Best espresso."—Marcus Boni

PARISI ARTISAN COFFEE

710 W 24th Street
Westside South
Kansas City
Missouri 64108
United States
+1 8168425282
www.parisicoffee.com

Opening hours..Daily from 7 am
Credit cards...........................Visa, MasterCard, and Amex
Style..Coffee bar

"For the best drinks made with coffee, I have to give credit
to Kate Blackman at Parisi Coffee (my former employer).
She is in charge of drink recipe creation and has astounded
me with ingredients and the resulting flavors time and time
again."—Pete Licata

THE COFFEE ETHIC

124 Park Central Square
Downtown
Springfield
Missouri 65806
United States
+1 4178666645
www.thecoffeeethic.com

Opening hours......................................Mon–Fri from 7 am,
Sat–Sun from 8 am
Credit cards...Visa and MasterCard
Style..Coffee bar

"A coffee shop that has my heart. The owner, Tom Billionis,
brought incredibly high-end coffee to a rural market with no
pretense and tons of finesse. This is a shop that reminds me
of the shop where I started."—Joe Marrocco

BRICK & MORTAR COFFEE

1666 East St. Louis Street
Springfield
Missouri 65802
United States
+1 4178126539
www.brickandmortarcoffee.com

Opening hours..Daily from 7 am
Credit cards...........................Visa, MasterCard, and Amex
Style...Roastery cafe

OLIO

1634 Tower Grove Avenue
Botanical Heights
St. Louis
Missouri 63110
United States
+1 3149321088
www.oliostl.com

Opening hours..Daily from 7 am
Credit cards...........................Visa, MasterCard, and Amex
Style..Wine bar

SUMP COFFEE

3700 South Jefferson Avenue
Gravois Park
St. Louis
Missouri 63118
United States
+1 9174125670
www.sumpcoffee.com

Opening hours..Daily from 9 am
Credit cards...........................Visa, MasterCard, and Amex
Style..Coffee bar

BLUEPRINT COFFEE

6225 Delmar Boulevard
Skinker DeBaliviere
St. Louis
Missouri 63130
United States
+1 3142666808
www.blueprintcoffee.com

Opening hours..Daily from 7 am
Credit cards...........................Visa, MasterCard, and Amex
Style..Coffee bar

ARCHETYPE COFFEE

3926 Farnam Street
Midtown
Omaha
Nebraska 68131
United States
+1 4028583399
www.archetype.coffee

Opening hours...Mon–Fri from 7 am,
Sat–Sun from 8 am
Credit cards...........................Visa, MasterCard, and Amex
Style..Coffee bar

"Archetype Coffee was a treat in the small city of
Omaha."—Mark Smesrud

"Archetype Coffee is at the head of the pack, with amazing
attention to detail and impossibly high standards of quality.
They have the best coffee and the best service. A simple
menu has allowed them to focus on what they do well,
which is to roast and brew perfect coffee."—Tamara Vigil

FIREFLOUR PIZZA

111 North 5th Street
Bismarck
North Dakota 58501
United States
+1 7013239000
www.fireflourpizza.com

Opening hours...Mon–Fri from 7 am,
Sat from 8 am
Credit cards............................Visa, MasterCard, and Amex
Style...Coffee and food

"The most surprising place I've found great coffee might
be in Bismarck, North Dakota, at Fireflour Pizza. They're
also a coffee bar with all the right tools and training. A great
surprise for this North Dakota native."—Mark Smesrud

COLLECTIVE ESPRESSO

207 Woodward Street
Over-the-Rhine
Cincinnati
Ohio 45202
United States
+1 5133997207
www.collectiveespresso.com

Opening hours...Mon–Fri from 7 am,
Sat–Sun from 8 am
Credit Cards...........................Visa, MasterCard, and Amex
Style..Coffee bar

"A tiny shop that does a really nice job with the coffees
they've got on bar. They have a great mix of roasters at any
given time and serve really tasty drinks."—Charlie Eisenstat

POUR CLEVELAND

530 Euclid Avenue
Downtown
Cleveland
Ohio
44115
United States
+1 2164790395
www.pourcleveland.com

Opening hours...Mon–Fri from 7 am,
Sat from 8 am, Sun from 9 am
Credit cards............................Visa, MasterCard, and Amex
Style..Coffee bar

"As perfect a specialty shop as I have ever seen in a major
urban city: exquisite coffee, knowledgeable staff, and a
beautiful environment."—Jonathan Rubinstein

FOX IN THE SNOW

1031 North 4th Street
Italian Village
Columbus
Ohio 43201
United States
www.foxinthesnow.com

Opening hours...Mon–Fri from 7 am,
Sat–Sun from 8 am
Credit cards............................Visa, MasterCard, and Amex
Style..Coffee bar

"Bright and inviting, Fox in the Snow serves Tandem
Coffee and offers amazing pastries made in-house."
—Charlie Eisenstat

MISSION

11 Price Avenue
Short North
Columbus
Ohio 43201
United States
+1 6143000648
www.missioncoffeeco.com

Opening hours...Mon–Fri from 7 am,
Sat–Sun from 8 am
Credit cards............................Visa, MasterCard, and Amex
Style...Coffee bar

"A good mix of rustic, warm, and cozy, with a good rotation
of roasters on bar. The staff is knowledgeable about what
they're serving and drinks are always well prepared."
—Charlie Eisenstat

CAFÉ EVOKE

103 South Broadway
Edmond
Oklahoma 73034
United States
+1 4052851522
www.cafeevoke.com

Opening hours...Daily from 7 am
Credit cards............................Visa, MasterCard, and Amex
Style..Coffee and food

"Not only are they holding it down with a great cafe in
Oklahoma, they bring the coffee to wherever the people are,
in the form of an adorable cart, introducing the people of
Oklahoma to great coffees from across the United States."
—Eileen Hassi Rinaldi

COFFEA ROASTERIE

200 South Phillips Avenue
Downtown
Sioux Falls
South Dakota 57104
United States
+1 6059770888
www.coffearoasterie.com

Opening hours...Mon–Fri from 6 am,
Sat from 7 am, Sun from noon
Credit cards............................Visa, MasterCard, and Amex
Style...Coffee bar

BRADBURY'S

127 North Hamilton Street
Madison
Wisconsin 53703
United States
+1 6082040474
www.bradburyscoffee.com

Opening hours...Daily from 6:30 am
Credit cards............................Visa, MasterCard, and Amex
Style..Coffee and food

"What's remarkable are its tiny size, awkward shape
(a triangle), and quality offerings. They do coffee and
crepes. They're only a block away from what's possibly the
best farmers' market in Wisconsin and when possible use
100 percent of their ingredients from that market. Two of the
three walls in the place are glass, which let in a huge amount
of natural light."—Scott Lucey

Though Madison's food community in this university
town has shown great leaps in quality in past years,
the coffee scene has been a bit slower to follow in
its progress. Bradbury's is one of the first to have
changed that, with its wedged-shape downtown
cafe and fine selection of coffee and artisan crepes.

KICKAPOO COFFEE

232 East Erie Street
Historic Third Ward
Milwaukee
Wisconsin 53202
United States
+1 4142698546
www.kickapoocoffee.com

Opening hours...Mon–Fri from 7 am,
                                                Sat–Sun from 8 am
Credit cards.............................Visa, MasterCard, and Amex
Style...Coffee bar

COLECTIVO COFFEE

2999 North Humboldt
Riverwest
Milwaukee
Wisconsin 53212
United States
+1 4142923320
www.colectivocoffee.com

Opening hours..................................Mon–Fri from 6:30 am,
                                                Sat–Sun from 7 am
Credit cards.............................Visa, MasterCard, and Amex
Style...Coffee and food

"I'll always enjoy going into the Colectivo Coffee Roasters
headquarters, which is on Humboldt and Locust. The
roasting and headquarters are a cafe within a roasting
warehouse."—Scott Lucey

STONE CREEK COFFEE ROASTERS

422 North 5th Street
Westown
Milwaukee
Wisconsin 53203
United States
+1 4144312157
United States
www.stonecreekcoffee.com

Opening hours.................................Mon–Fri from 5:30 am,
                                                Sat–Sun from 7 am
Credit cards...Visa and MasterCard
Style...Coffee and food

"Among my favorite espressos."—Donald Niemyer

RUBY COFFEE ROASTERS

9515 Water Street
Nelsonville
Wisconsin 54458
United States
+1 7152541592
www.rubycoffeeroasters.com

Opening hours...Saturday from 8 am
Credit cards.............................Visa, MasterCard, and Amex
Style...Coffee tasting room

"Seeing a more in-depth view of who is roasting what and
where has opened my eyes to the reality that big cities
are not where coffee culture, or any culture, is stored."
—Joe Marrocco

"THE COFFEE THEY'RE ROASTING IS CONSISTENTLY IMPRESSIVE."

ZAK RYE P.270

CHICAGO

"WORMHOLE DOES A REALLY NICE JOB WITH SIGNATURE DRINKS. THEY TYPICALLY ROLL OUT A NEW ONE FOUR TIMES A YEAR, COORDINATING WITH THE SEASON, AND THE DRINKS ARE ALWAYS VERY THOUGHTFUL AND REFINED."

ZAK RYE P.271

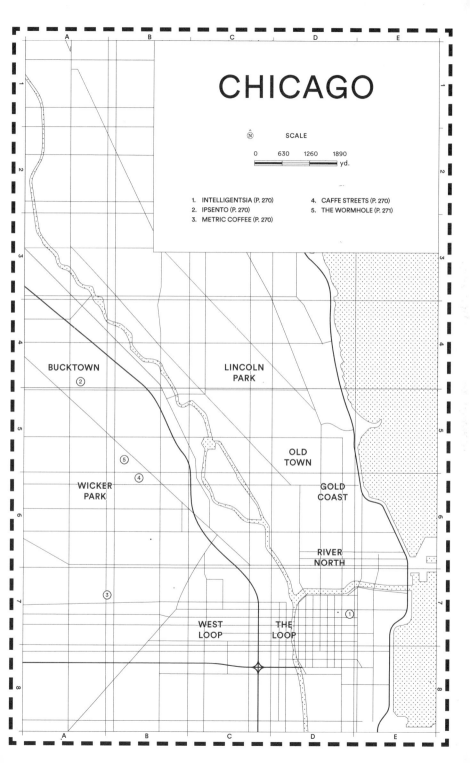

CHICAGO

N̂   SCALE

0   630   1260   1890
                            yd.

1.   INTELLIGENTSIA (P. 270)   4.   CAFFE STREETS (P. 270)
2.   IPSENTO (P. 270)   5.   THE WORMHOLE (P. 271)
3.   METRIC COFFEE (P. 270)

BUCKTOWN
②

LINCOLN
PARK

OLD
TOWN

⑤

④   GOLD
                                          COAST
WICKER
PARK

                                        RIVER
                                        NORTH

③

                                               ①
WEST   THE
LOOP   LOOP

IPSENTO

2035 North Western Avenue
Bucktown
Chicago
Illinois 60647
United States
+1 7739048177
www.ipsento.com

Opening hours..Mon–Fri from 6 am,
Sat–Sun from 7 am
Credit cards............................Visa, MasterCard, and Amex
Style..Coffee bar

"My most memorable filter-coffee experience was at
Ipsento, around the time that Jonathan Jarrow was the
head roaster. I unfortunately don't remember much about
the coffee other than that it was Brazilian from Sul de Minas.
I typically don't dig Brazils, but I thought about that cup
for days after."—Zak Rye

INTELLIGENTSIA

53 East Randolph Street
Millennium Park
Chicago
Illinois 60601
United States
+1 3129209332
www.intelligentsiacoffee.com

Opening hours...................................Mon–Fri from 6:30 am,
Sat–Sun from 7 am
Credit cards............................Visa, MasterCard, and Amex
Style..Coffee bar

"Best espresso."—Esther Shaw

METRIC COFFEE

2021 West Fulton Street
Near West Side
Chicago
Illinois 60612
United States
+1 3129822196
www.metriccoffee.com

Opening hours...Daily from 7 am
Credit cards............................Visa, MasterCard, and Amex
Style..Roastery cafe

"The coffee they're roasting is consistently impressive as
hell."—Zak Rye

CAFFE STREETS

1750 West Division Street
Wicker Park
Chicago
Illinois 60622
United States
+1 7732782739
www.caffestreets.com

Opening hours...Daily from 7 am
Credit cards............................Visa, MasterCard, and Amex
Style..Coffee bar

"I don't drink a tremendous amount of espresso, but I
enjoyed a shot of a single-origin Metric coffee (Ethiopian)
at Caffe Streets."—Doug Palas

"The design is breathtaking, the staff is knowledgeable
and incredibly approachable, and the offerings are widely
varied."—Zak Rye

THE WORMHOLE
1462 North Milwaukee Avenue
Wicker Park
Chicago
Illinois 60622
United States
+1 7736612468
www.thewormholecoffee.com

Opening hours..Daily from 7 am
Credit cards............................Visa, MasterCard, and Amex
Style..Coffee bar

"Wormhole does a really nice job with signature drinks.
They typically roll out a new one four times a year,
coordinating with the season, and the drinks are always
very thoughtful and refined."—Zak Rye

"ORDER SOME COFFEE AND BEIGNETS, FRESHLY MADE FRENCH DOUGHNUTS OVERFLOWING WITH POWDERED SUGAR."

JORDAN MICHELMAN P.277

"A QUIRKY, ALTERNATIVE VIDEO SHOP WITH ESPRESSO SERVICE."

JORDAN MICHELMAN P.275

USA SOUTH

"AN EXTREMELY SPECIAL AND SOULFUL SHOP, TUCKED AWAY IN THE BASEMENT OF A HOME IN THE 9TH WARD OF NEW ORLEANS."

CAMILA RAMOS P.276

"THEY ARE ABSOLUTELY ONE OF MY FAVORITES, AND NO KIDDING, THEIR COFFEE STANDS OUT AMONG THE REST."

DONALD NIEMYER P.274

"OUTSIDE OF OUR OWN CAFES, THE BEST FILTER COFFEE I'VE HAD WAS AT PANTHER COFFEE IN MIAMI BEACH."

DOUG ZELL P.275

USA
SOUTH

$\hat{N}$ SCALE

0   75   150
━━━━━━━━━━━━━━━━ mi.

MARYLAND P. 277 ♥
KENTUCKY P. 276 ♥
♥ VIRGINIA P. 279
TENNESSEE PP. 278–279 ♥
NORTH CAROLINA PP. 277–278 ♥
ARKANSAS P. 274 ♥
SOUTH CAROLINA P. 278 ♥
ALABAMA P. 274 ♥
♥ GEORGIA PP. 275–276
LOUISIANA PP. 276–277 ♥
♥ FLORIDA PP. 274–275

SEEDS COFFEE CO.

174 Oxmoor Road
Birmingham
Alabama 35209
United States
+1 2052596405
www.seedscoffee.com

Opening hours	Mon–Fri from 6:30 am,
	Sat from 7:30 am
Credit cards	Visa, MasterCard, and Amex
Style	Coffee bar

ONYX COFFEE LAB

100 2nd Street, Suite 106
Bentonville
Arkansas 72712
United States
+1 4797156492
www.onyxcoffeelab.com

Opening hours	Mon–Fri from 6:30 am,
	Sat–Sun from 7 am
Credit cards	Visa, MasterCard, and Amex
Style	Coffee bar

"They are absolutely one of my favorites, and no kidding, their coffee stands out among the rest."—Donald Niemyer

THE SEED

199 West Palmetto Park Road, Suite E
Boca Raton
Florida 33432
United States
+1 5614305640
www.theseedboca.com

Opening hours	Mon–Fri from 7 am,
	Sat–Sun from 8 am
Credit cards	Visa, MasterCard, and Amex
Style	Coffee and fresh juice

"The Seed has a simple but elegant design, functioning both as a juice bar and a coffee bar. Two women own the business, and each brings her own interest and expertise to the space in that way—one woman who loves juice and another who loves coffee. Additionally, The Seed is home to Wells Coffee Company. Owner Brendan roasts small batches on his little roaster in the front of the shop. His espresso blend is on tap at the bar."—Ryan Willbur

VOLTA COFFEE, TEA & CHOCOLATE

48 Southwest 2nd Street
Gainesville
Florida 32601
United States
+1 3522714361
www.voltacoffee.com

Opening hours	Mon–Fri from 8 am,
	Sat–Sun from 9 am
	Visa, MasterCard, and Amex
Style	Coffee bar

"Anthony Rue and his team at Volta in Gainesville are doing some amazing stuff across the board, using coffee as an ingredient in all kinds of dishes (meats, pastries, muffins, etc.). In general, I think Anthony's approach is really awesome."—Jared Linzmeier

BOLD BEAN COFFEE ROASTERS

869 Stockton Street, Suite 1
Five Points
Jacksonville
Florida 32204
www.boldbeancoffee.com

Opening hours	Mon–Fri from 6:30 am,
	Sat–Sun from 7 am
Credit cards	Visa and MasterCard
Style	Coffee bar

BREW FIVE POINTS

1024 Park Street
Five Points
Jacksonville
Florida 32204
United States
+1 9043745789
www.brewfivepoints.com

Opening hours	Mon–Fri from 7:30 am,
	Sat from 9 am, Sun from 10 am
Credit cards	Visa, MasterCard, and Amex
Style	Coffee, beer, and food

"A low-key shop with an amazing baker and a craft beer menu."—Anthony Rue

ALL DAY
1035 North Miami Avenue
Downtown
Miami
Florida 33136
United States
+1 305699EGGS

Opening hours...Daily from 7 am
Credit cards...........................Visa, MasterCard, and Amex
Style...Coffee and food

"Owner Camila Ramos is nothing if not driven."
—Anthony Rue

PANTHER COFFEE
1875 Purdy Avenue
Bayshore
Miami Beach
Florida 33139
United States
+1 3056773952
www.panthercoffee.com

Opening hours......................................Mon–Sat from 7 am,
                                                              Sun from 8 am
Credit cards...................................Visa and MasterCard
Style...Coffee bar

"Outside of our own cafes, the best filter coffee I've had was
at Panther Coffee in Miami Beach."—Doug Zell

STARDUST VIDEO & COFFEE
1842 East Winter Park Road
Audubon Park
Orlando
Florida 32803
United States
+1 4076233393
www.stardustvideoandcoffee.wordpress.com

Opening hours......................................Mon–Fri from 7 am,
                                                              Sat–Sun from 8 am
Credit cards...........................Visa, MasterCard, and Amex
Style...Coffee and video store

"I have a bunch of family in central Florida and this place
fits the bill: a quirky, alternative video shop with espresso
service."—Jordan Michelman

CHATTAHOOCHEE COFFEE
6640 Akers Mill Road Southeast
Cumberland
Atlanta
Georgia 30339
United States
+1 7709550788
www.chattahoocheecoffee.com

Opening hours......................................Mon–Fri from 7 am
Credit cards...........................Visa, MasterCard, and Amex
Style...Coffee bar

"There's this coffee shop in an apartment complex at
the corner of Interstates 285 and 75 here in Atlanta.
The apartment complex is gated and when you pull up to
the gate there's a call box. On tape on the call box it says,
'Dial 101 for Coffee Shop.' You hit 101 and someone picks
up and says 'Coffee Shop.' You say, 'I would like to come to
the coffee shop' or 'I would like to get coffee' or something
along those lines, and the gate opens for you. You drive
to the back of the apartment complex and park. The coffee
shop is called Chattahoochee Coffee, and in addition
to having supersolid coffee, the shop is right on the
Chattahoochee River and has one of the most beautiful
views for a coffee shop ever. It's peaceful and relaxing.
You can grab a pour-over, bring it down to the riverside,
chill out in a comfy seat, and do work on your laptop
because there's Wi-Fi. It's a combination of an oasis and
a speakeasy."—Ben Helfen

EMPIRE STATE SOUTH
999 Peachtree Street Northeast
Midtown
Atlanta
Georgia 30339
United States
+1 4045411105
www.empirestatesouth.com

Opening hours......................................Mon–Fri from 7 am,
                                    Sat from 4 pm, Sun from 10:30 am
Credit cards...........................Visa, MasterCard, and Amex
Style...Coffee and food

"Empire State South and the Florence have excellent
espresso and pour-over bars that stand alone as destinations
in Atlanta and Savannah, and both are integrated into the
meals served in the restaurants. The best coffees served
in both towns are in Hugh Acheson's restaurants."
—Anthony Rue

SPILLER PARK

675 Ponce de Leon Avenue Northeast
Ponce City Market
Atlanta
Georgia 30308
United States
+1 4049192978
www.spillerpark.com

Opening hours..Mon–Sat from 7 am,
                                                  Sun from 8 am
Credit cards...........................Visa, MasterCard, and Amex
Style..Coffee bar

Atlanta's food revolution has seen no shortage of high-end,
high-budget projects filling out the landscape, but the opening
of Ponce City Market's elite food court really drove the point
home. Within the center you'll find Spiller Park, a round,
bar-style cafe modeled after Los Angeles's wildly successful
G&B Coffee. Spiller Park serves a variety of national roasters
in a bustling setting amid gourmet hamburgers and boutique
shops. Like many of the South's more headline-garnering
food spots, Spiller Park also boasts the Georgia-based
celebrity chef (and coffee lover) Hugh Acheson as a partner
with Chris Wilkins.

THE FLORENCE

1 West Victory Drive #B
Bingville
Savannah
Georgia 31405
United States
+1 9122345522
www.theflorencesavannah.com

Opening hours..Tue–Sun from 9 am
Credit cards...........................Visa, MasterCard, and Amex
Style..Coffee and food

PERC

1802 East Broad Street
Thomas Square
Savannah
Georgia 31401
United States
+1 9122090025
www.perccoffee.com

Opening hours..Mon–Fri from 10 am,
                                                  Sat from 9 am
Credit cards...........................Visa, MasterCard, and Amex
Style...Roastery cafe

GRALEHAUS

1001 Baxter Avenue
Highlands
Louisville
Kentucky 40204
United States
+1 5024547075
www.gralehaus.com

Opening hours...Daily from 8 am
Credit cards...........................Visa, MasterCard, and Amex
Style...Coffee and beer

SÓLO ESPRESSO

1301 Poland Avenue
Bywater
New Orleans
Louisiana 70117
United States
+1 5044081377
www.soloespressobar.com

Opening hours..Mon–Sat from 8 am
Credit cards...........................Visa, MasterCard, and Amex
Style..Coffee bar

"An extremely special and soulful shop, tucked away in
the basement of a home in the 9th Ward of New Orleans.
Lauren Morlock, the owner, is a badass, incredibly
passionate and dedicated to delicious coffee."
—Camila Ramos

CAFÉ DU MONDE

800 Decatur Street
French Quarter
New Orleans
Louisiana 70116
United States
+1 5045254544
www.cafedumonde.com

Opening hours..Daily, 24 hours
Credit cards...Cash only
Style...Coffee and food

"Café du Monde opened its location on Decatur Street, adjacent to the French Market, in 1862, making it by all accounts the oldest coffeehouse in America. Coffee here is batch brewed, of course, in the high-volume, low-fuss style characteristic of America's coffee roots, served laced with chicory out of enormous urns and mixed with piping hot milk for a café au lait. Order some coffee and beignets, freshly made French doughnuts overflowing with powdered sugar. Dunk those little pastries into your coffee again and again, until the bottom of the cup is a mass of sugar sludge and milky sweetness, begging for a refill or more doughnuts or maybe both. Dear God, is it good. Best of all, this place is open twenty-four hours a day, 364 days a week (closed for Christmas), making Café du Monde perhaps the world's greatest coffee and doughnut nightcap after an evening of New Orleanian joie de vivre."—Jordan Michelman

CHERRY ESPRESSO BAR

4877 Laurel Street
West Riverside
New Orleans
Louisiana 70115
United States
+1 5048753699

Opening hours..Tue–Fri from 7 am,
Sat–Sun from 9 am
Credit cards...........................Visa, MasterCard, and Amex
Style...Coffee bar

"Cherry began as a permanent pop-up inside Stein's Market & Deli in the Garden District but has since opened up in its own space. The new space is great, but eating a Fernando sandwich at Stein's and grabbing an espresso from Cherry is such a big part of my New Orleans experience. It's my Bourbon Street."—Zac Cadwalader

CEREMONY COFFEE ROASTERS

90 Russell Street #500
The Warehouse
Annapolis
Maryland 21401
United States
+1 4106260011
United States
www.ceremonycoffee.com/coffeehouse

Opening hours..Mon–Fri from 7 am,
Sat–Sun from 8 am
Credit cards...........................Visa, MasterCard, and Amex
Style...Roastery cafe

"Some of my favorite filter coffee."—Andy Sprenger

NOT JUST COFFEE

224 East 7th Street
First Ward
Charlotte
North Carolina 28202
United States
+1 7048173868
www.notjust.coffee

Opening hours..Mon–Fri from 7 am,
Sat–Sun from 8:30 am
Credit cards...........................Visa, MasterCard, and Amex
Style...Coffee bar

THE DAILY PRESS

3227 North Davidson Street
Noda
Charlotte
North Carolina 28205
United States
+1 7043763737

Opening hours..Tue–Sat from 7 am,
Sun from 8 am
Credit cards...........................Visa, MasterCard, and Amex
Style...Coffee bar

"Killer signature beverages."—Jess Steffy

JUBALA

8450 Honeycutt Road #104
Raleigh
North Carolina 27615
United States
+1 9197588330
www.jubalacoffee.com

Opening hours..Mon–Fri from 7 am,
Sat–Sun from 8 am
Credit cards............................Visa, MasterCard, and Amex
Style...Coffee and food

"I love Jubala in Raleigh. Their waffle and biscuit options paired with carefully brewed coffee and espresso creates a delicious and memorable experience. I look forward to my visits in part for the chance to go here. And they have a free single-origin espresso on Friday. So good."—Aaron Ultimo

CITY LIGHTS COFFEE

141 Market Street
Charleston
South Carolina 29401
United States
+1 8438537067
www.citylightscoffee.com

Opening hours..Mon–Fri from 7 am,
Sat–Sun from 8 am
Credit cards............................Visa, MasterCard, and Amex
Style...Coffee and food

TRAVELERS REST

10 Road of Vines
Travelers Rest
South Carolina 29690
United States
+1 8645161254
United States
www.restaurant17.com

Opening hours..Daily from 7:30 am
Credit cards............................Visa, MasterCard, and Amex
Style..Coffee bar

BRASH COFFEE

1110 Market Street
Chattanooga
Tennessee 37402
United States
www.brashcoffee.com

Opening hours..Mon–Fri from 8 am,
Sat–Sun from 9 am
Credit cards............................Visa, MasterCard, and Amex
Style...Coffee and food

"I had a great surprise with Brash. They have an innovative presentation approach based on the idea of gathering around a table (the bar is a table set in the middle of the room). Then they identify the coffees by the name of the farmer, whom they are personally friends with—'Would you like the Miguel or the Leonel today?'"—Donald Niemyer

CITY AND STATE

2625 Broad Avenue
Binghampton
Memphis
Tennessee 38112
United States
+1 9012492406
www.cityandstate.us

Opening hours..Mon–Fri from 7 am,
Sat–Sun from 8 am
Credit cards............................Visa, MasterCard, and Amex
Style..Coffee bar

"They have really changed people's perceptions of quality coffee."—Jordan Chambers

CREMA COFFEE

15 Hermitage Avenue
Rolling Mill Hill
Nashville
Tennessee 37210
United States
+1 6152558311
www.crema-coffee.com

Opening hours...Mon–Fri from 7 am,
Sat from 8 am, Sun from 9 am
Credit cards............................Visa, MasterCard, and Amex
Style..Coffee and bar

"Definitely one of my favorite shops in the Southeast."
—Ben Helfen

SWINGS

501 East Monroe Avenue
Del Ray
Alexandria
Virginia
22301
United States
+1 7033705050
www.swingscoffee.com

Opening hours...Mon–Fri from 7 am,
Sat from 8 am
Credit cards............................Visa, MasterCard, and Amex
Style...Roastery cafe

"Beautiful build-out, friendly staff, and good balance of their
past and present."—Josh Littlefield

BLACK WATER LOFT

117 South Locust Street
Floyd
Virginia 24091
United States
+1 5407455638
www.floydbooksandcoffee.com

Opening hours...Mon–Fri from 7 am,
Sat from 8 am
Credit cards............................Visa, MasterCard, and Amex
Style...Coffee bar

THE LAB BY ALCHEMY COFFEE

814 West Broad Street
Carver
Richmond
Virginia 23220
United States
+1 8046089873
www.alchemycoffeerva.com

Opening hours...Mon–Fri from 7 am,
Sat–Sun from 8 am
Credit cards............................Visa, MasterCard, and Amex
Style...Coffee bar

"We really loved Alchemy."—Donald Niemyer

"FROM THEIR BOTTLED NITRO COLD BREW TO SKILLFUL LATTE ART POURED WITH SINGLE-ORIGIN ESPRESSO; THIS IS ONE TO PUT ON YOUR TRAVEL LIST IN A BEAUTIFUL PART OF THE WORLD."

SCOTT CONARY P.282

"A SERIOUS COFFEE PROGRAM WITH WELL-TRAINED STAFF."

JOSH LITTLEFIELD P.284

USA NORTHEAST

"SOME SHOPS ARE DIFFICULT TO FAULT: FOR EXAMPLE, THE SPECTACULAR FLAGSHIP LA COLOMBE IN FISHTOWN."

ANDREW HETZEL P.283

"AN ELEGANT, THOUGHTFUL SPACE WITH ENTHUSIASTIC AND KNOWLEDGEABLE BARISTAS."

DONALD NIEMYER P.284

"WHEN PEOPLE ASK WHICH SHOP WAS MY FAVORITE IN PITTSBURGH, I NEVER HESITATE TO TELL THEM ABOUT CONSTELLATION."

DONALD NIEMYER P.283

USA
NORTHEAST

N

SCALE

0   75   150 mi.

MAINE P. 282

VERMONT P. 285

NEW HAMPSHIRE P. 282

MASSACHUSETTS P. 282

BOSTON PP. 286–289

RHODE ISLAND P. 284

PENNSYLVANIA PP. 283–284

NEW YORK CITY PP. 290–298

BARD COFFEE

185 Middle Street
Portland
Maine 04101
United States
+1 2078994788
www.bardcoffee.com

Opening hours...Mon–Fri from 6 am,
Sat–Sun from 8 am
Credit cards............................Visa, MasterCard, and Amex
Style...Coffee bar

"Portland, Maine, has come into its own, with so many
culinary delights. Leading that charge in specialty coffee
was Bard, a brainchild of Bob Garver and his wife, who own
the Roastery Wicked Joe in Brunswick, north of Portland.
While there are other cafes popping up, Bard was the first
to spread the word of carefully crafted coffee and selective
sourcing. They constantly update both the space and
their offerings to match the cutting edge that Bob, a
World Barista Championship and United States Barista
Championship head judge, experienced firsthand. From
their bottled nitro cold brew to skillful latte art poured
with single-origin espresso; this is one to put on your
travel list in a beautiful part of the world."—Scott Conary

TANDEM COFFEE ROASTERS

742 Congress Street
Portland
Maine 04102
United States
+1 2078051887
www.tandemcoffee.com

Opening hours...Mon–Fri from 7 am,
Sat–Sun from 8 am
Credit cards............................Visa, MasterCard, and Amex
Style..Coffee and food

"One of my favorites."—Donald Niemyer

Blue Bottle Coffee alums Will and Kathleen Pratt cut their
coffee chops in San Francisco and New York before "retiring"
to idyllic Portland, Maine—a city with an explosive food
community, but without, until Tandem's arrival, great coffee
options. Their West End shop opened in 2014, and pastry
genius Briana Holt's, sweet and savory accompaniments to
Tandem's fine roasts make this one of the most pleasurable
destinations on the eastern seaboard.

Boston and Cambridge, see pages 286–289

SHAKER DAM COFFEEHOUSE

2 Main Street
West Stockbridge
Massachusetts 01266
United States
+1 4132327707
www.shakerdamcoffeehouse.com

Opening hours...Daily from 8 am
Credit cards............................Visa, MasterCard, and Amex
Style..Coffee and art gallery

"A charming haven. They use Counter Culture and it's
good."—Scott Rao

PRESSED CAFE

108 Spit Brook Road
Nashua
New Hampshire 03062
United States
+1 6037181250
www.pressedcafe.com

Opening hours...Daily from 6 am
Credit cards............................Visa, MasterCard, and Amex
Style...Coffee and smoothies

GIMME! COFFEE

430 North Cayuga Street
Ithaca
New York 14850
United States
+1 6072778393
www.buy.gimmecoffee.com

Opening hours...Daily from 7 am
Credit cards............................Visa, MasterCard, and Amex
Style...Coffee bar

New York City, see pages 290–298

ELIXR COFFEE ROASTERS
207 South Sydenham Street
Center City
Philadelphia
Pennsylvania 19102
United States
+1 2394041730
United States
www.elixrcoffee.com

Opening hours...................................Mon–Fri from 7 am,
Sat–Sun from 8 am
Credit cards...........................Visa, MasterCard, and Amex
Style..Coffee bar

"The best filtered coffee."—Josue Morales

LA COLOMBE
1335 Frankford Avenue
Fishtown
Philadelphia
Pennsylvania 19125
United States
+1 2674791600
www.lacolombe.com

Opening hours...Daily from 7 am
Credit cards...........................Visa, MasterCard, and Amex
Style...Coffee and food

"Some shops are difficult to fault: for example, the
spectacular flagship La Colombe in Fishtown."
—Andrew Hetzel

ULTIMO COFFEE
1900 South 15th Street
Point Breeze
Philadelphia
Pennsylvania 19145
United States
+1 2153395177
www.ultimocoffee.com

Opening hours...................................Mon–Fri from 7 am,
Sat–Sun from 8 am
Credit cards...........................Visa, MasterCard, and Amex
Style..Coffee bar

"Aaron Ultimo is a great coffee person, and the coffee at his
cafes is pretty much consistently the best coffee I've had."
—Katie Carguilo

CONSTELLATION COFFEE
4059 Penn Avenue
Lawrenceville
Pittsburgh
Pennsylvania 15224
United States
+1 8144199775
www.constellationcoffeepgh.com

Opening hours...................................Mon–Fri from 7 am,
Sat from 8 am, Sun from 9 am
Credit cards...........................Visa, MasterCard, and Amex
Style..Coffee bar

"When people ask which shop was my favorite in Pittsburgh,
I never hesitate to tell them about Constellation. When I
visited, it was a pretty new operation, with the owner
running the place alone with a somewhat sparsely outfitted
arsenal of equipment. But the simple Linea and Mazzer
espresso machine and grinder combo was all she needed
alongside her clear passion for great coffee and excellent
hospitality to leave a lasting impression. The drink was
perfectly balanced and delicious, and as I sat near the
counter and listened, I could hear in her conversations with
each customer a reverence for the craft and a tip of the hat
to the producers of those coffees."—Donald Niemyer

THE COMMONPLACE COFFEE CO.
5827 Forbes Avenue
Squirrel Hill North
Pittsburgh
Pennsylvania 15217
United States
+1 4124220404
www.commonplacecoffee.com

Opening hours...................................Mon–Fri from 9 am,
Sat from noon
Credit cards...........................Visa, MasterCard, and Amex
Style..Coffee bar

"I visited their newest location during what I later learned
was a challenging shift. The small yet smartly designed
space was packed, with only one barista running the
gorgeous red-and-black Synesso as well as everything
else in the shop. Even so, every drink was carefully
crafted—not rushed—and presented with the utmost
care and hospitality. Our cappuccino was delicious, and
of course I made my way back up to the tip jar and threw
in a little extra love for this frontline warrior who was
leaving everything he had on the battlefield, and doing so
with grace and excellence."—Donald Niemyer

21ST STREET COFFEE & TEA

2002 Smallman Street
Strip District
Pittsburgh
Pennsylvania 15222
United States
+1 4122810809
www.21streetcoffee.com

Opening hours...Mon–Fri from 7 am,
                                                     Sat–Sun from 8 am
Credit cards............................Visa, MasterCard, and Amex
Style..Coffee bar

"An elegant, thoughtful space with enthusiastic and
knowledgeable baristas. The space I visited, in what
Pittsburgh calls the Strip District because of its orientation
of businesses along a strip of the city, was clearly a mature
evolution of an operation that had been around awhile.
The drinks were well executed, the conversations insightful,
and the overall vibe of the space comfortable, spacious,
and inviting."—Donald Niemyer

ANGELINA'S

301 Hope Street
Bristol
Rhode Island 02809
United States
+1 4013965592

Opening hours...Mon–Fri from 6 am,
                                                     Sat–Sun from 7 am
Credit cards............................Visa, MasterCard, and Amex
Style..Coffee bar

"A serious coffee program with well-trained staff".
—Josh Littlefield

BOLT COFFEE (AT THE DEAN HOTEL)

122 Fountain Street
Downtown
Providence
Rhode Island 02903
United States
+1 4015336506
www.boltcoffeecompany.com

Opening hours...Daily from 7 am
Credit cards............................Visa, MasterCard, and Amex
Style..Coffee bar

"The best staff in Providence who are excited to brew
everything. They truly value the customer experience."
—Josh Littlefield

THE SHOP

460 Wickenden Street
Fox Point
Providence
Rhode Island 02903
United States
+1 4016841140
www.theshopfoxpoint.com

Opening hours...Mon–Fri from 7 am,
                                                     Sat–Sun from 7:30 am
Credit cards............................Visa, MasterCard, and Amex
Style...Coffee and food

"Beautiful shop, friendly folk."—Josh Littlefield

SEVEN STARS BAKERY

820 Hope Street
Hope
Providence
Rhode Island 02906
United States
+1 4015212200
www.sevenstarsbakery.com

Opening hours...................................Mon–Fri from 6:30 am,
                                                     Sat–Sun from 7 am
Credit cards............................Visa, MasterCard, and Amex
Style..Coffee and sandwiches

"Good coffee paired with phenomenal pastries."
—Josh Littlefield

SCOUT & CO.
237 North Avenue
Old North End
Burlington
Vermont 05401
United States
+1 8023431218
www.scoutandcompanyvt.com

Opening hours	Mon–Fri from 7 am, Sat–Sun from 8 am
Credit cards	Visa, MasterCard, and Amex
Style	Coffee and ice cream

"A cute place with homemade ice cream. They use good roasters. A little oasis of tastiness."—Scott Rao

BRIO COFFEEWORKS
696 Pine Street
South End
Burlington
Vermont 05401
United States
+1 8027776641
www.briocoffeeworks.com

Opening hours	Mon–Fri from 9 am, Sat from 11 am
Credit cards	Visa, MasterCard, and Amex
Style	Coffee bar

MAGLIANERO
47 Maple Street
South End
Burlington
Vermont 05401
United States
+1 8028613155
www.maglianero.com

Opening hours	Mon–Fri from 7 am, Sat–Sun from 8 am
Credit cards	Visa, MasterCard, and Amex
Style	Coffee bar

"LEGEND GEORGE HOWELL DOES HIGH VOLUME."

BOSTON

"I HAD A GREAT VISIT AT RENDER."

BOSTON

SCALE

0   340   680   1020
yd.

1. PAVEMENT COFFEEHOUSE (P. 288)
2. GEORGE HOWELL COFFEE (P. 288)
3. GEORGE HOWELL COFFEE (P. 288)

4. RENDER (P. 288)
5. 1369 COFFEE HOUSE (P. 289)
6. BARISMO (P. 289)

7. CREMA CAFE (P. 289)
8. SIMON'S COFFEE SHOP (P. 289)

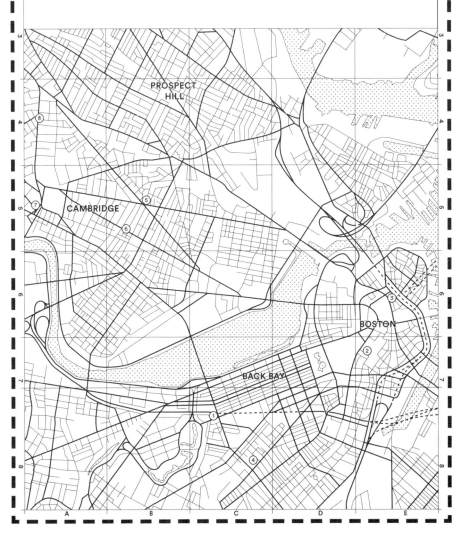

PAVEMENT COFFEEHOUSE

1096 Boylston Street
Back Bay
Boston
Massachusetts 02215
United States
+1 6172361500
www.pavementcoffeehouse.com

Opening hours	Daily from 7 am
Credit cards	Visa, MasterCard, and Amex
Style	Coffee bar

GEORGE HOWELL COFFEE

505 Washington Street
Downtown Crossing
Boston
Massachusetts 02111
United States
+1 8579570217
www.georgehowellcoffee.com

Opening hours	Daily from 6 am
Credit cards	Visa, MasterCard, and Amex
Style	Coffee and food

When Massachusetts coffee legend George Howell (the founder of the once-thriving 24-shop Coffee Connection) returned to Boston retail with Boston Public Market, the city took notice. But it was this spacious, elegant cafe within the Godfrey Hotel renovation that changed the city's cafe game. Every choice here is well considered; from brewing parameters to food offerings to the Huichol native art works that Howell has spent his life championing. Sit in the traditional cafe, or linger in the side room to talk coffee in-depth with staff, meet visiting farmers and producers, and partake in the shop's regular open cuppings. You'll probably see George holding court here as well. This is one of the nation's finest expressions of a serious and welcoming cafe.

GEORGE HOWELL COFFEE

100 Hanover Street at Boston Public Market
North End
Boston
Massachusetts 02108
United States
+1 6177772217
www.georgehowellcoffee.com

Opening hours	Wed–Sun from 8 am
Credit cards	Visa, MasterCard, and Amex
Style	Coffee bar

"Legend George Howell does high volume."
—Josh Littlefield

RENDER

563 Columbus Avenue
South End
Boston
Massachusetts 02118
United States
+1 6172624142
www.render.coffee

Opening hours	Mon–Fri from 7 am, Sat–Sun from 8 am
Credit cards	Visa, MasterCard, and Amex
Style	Coffee bar

"I had a great visit at Render."—Donald Niemyer

1369 COFFEE HOUSE

1369 Cambridge Street
Cambridge
Massachusetts 02139
United States
+1 6175761369
www.1369coffeehouse.com

Opening hours	Mon–Fri from 7 am, Sat–Sun from 8 am
Credit cards	Cash only
Style	Coffee bar

CREMA CAFE

27 Brattle Street
Cambridge
Massachusetts 02138
United States
+1 6178762700
www.cremacambridge.com

Opening hours	Mon–Fri from 7 am, Sat–Sun from 8 am
Credit cards	Visa and MasterCard
Style	Coffee bar

BARISMO

364 Broadway
Cambridge
Massachusetts 02139
United States
+1 6177145536
www.barismo.com

Opening hours	Mon–Fri from 7 am, Sat–Sun from 8 am
Credit cards	Visa, MasterCard, and Amex
Style	Coffee bar

"The guys are knowledgeable, serious, and roast great coffee."—Josh Littlefield

SIMON'S COFFEE SHOP

1736 Massachusetts Avenue
Cambridge
Massachusetts
02138 United States
+1 6174977766
www.simonscoffeeshop.com

Opening hours	Mon–Fri from 7 am, Sat–Sun from 8 am
Credit cards	Visa and MasterCard
Style	Coffee bar

"PUSHING BOUNDARIES WITH THE RESTAURANT TEAM AND ENCOURAGING THE SAME WITH GUESTS IS NO EASY FEAT AND ELEVEN MADISON PARK MANAGES THIS WITH ENTHUSIASM, FUN, AND A GENTLENESS FOR COFFEE."

JAMIE JESSUP P.295

NEW YORK CITY

"THE BEST FILTER COFFEE I'VE BEEN SERVED IN A CAFE IN RECENT MEMORY—IT WAS CLEAN, ARTICULATE, BALANCED, JUICY, SWEET: PRETTY MUCH EVERYTHING YOU COULD EVER WANT IN A CUP OF FILTER COFFEE." SAMUEL LEWONTIN P.295

"ONE OF MY FAVORITE FILTER COFFEES EVER WAS AT JOE PRO, WHICH SERVES A GREAT SELECTION OF COFFEES THAT ARE DIFFICULT TO FIND IN THE STATES."

CAMILA RAMOS P.294

"I STILL REMEMBER BEING BLOWN AWAY BY AN ESPRESSO THEY SERVED A FEW YEARS BACK."

ANDY SPRENGER P.294

NEW YORK CITY

MANHATTAN UPTOWN

N̂   SCALE

0   290   580   870

yd.

1. BLUE BOTTLE (HIGH LINE) (P. 294)
2. CAFÉ GRUMPY (P. 294)
3. INTELLIGENTSIA MINI-BAR (P. 294)
4. JOE PRO SHOP (P. 294)
5. ELEVEN MADISON PARK (P. 295)
6. LITTLE COLLINS (P. 295)

"SMITH CANTEEN HAD A 'THUNDERBOLT': HOMEMADE LEMONADE TOPPED WITH A BRIGHT YIRGACHEFFE COFFEE FROM COUNTER CULTURE. I WAS BLOWN AWAY AT HOW DELICIOUS, BALANCED, AND REFRESHING IT WAS."

CAMILA RAMOS P.295

NEW YORK CITY

"VOYAGER IS A WONDERFUL SURPRISE: A FUN, THOUGHTFUL, SHARPLY EXECUTED COFFEE BAR WITH A PERSONALITY UNLIKE ANY OTHER IN NEW YORK, AND LOCATED JUST WHERE YOU'D LEAST EXPECT IT." SAMUEL LEWONTIN P.297

"THIS CAFE FEELS LIKE A COMMUNITY ANCHOR AND IMMEDIATELY MADE ME AS A TRAVELER FEEL LIKE A PARTICIPANT IN A COMMUNITY."

KEATON RITCHIE P.297

"SOME OF THE MOST MEMORABLE ESPRESSOS I'VE HAD."

KALLE FREESE P.298

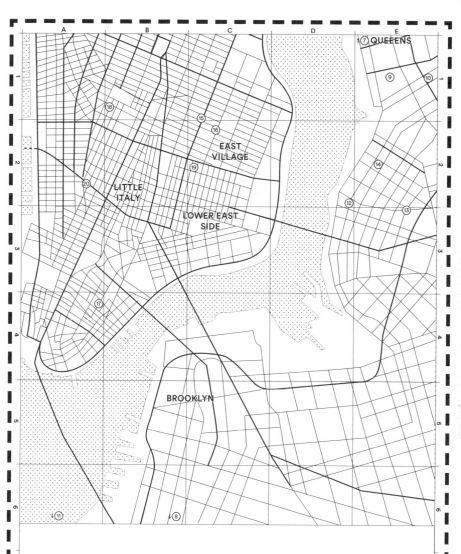

NEW YORK CITY

MANHATTAN DOWNTOWN, BROOKLYN & QUEENS

N̂   SCALE

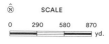

0   290   580   870
yd.

7. SWEETLEAF (P. 297)
8. SMITH CANTEEN (P. 295)
9. BUDIN (P. 295)
10. CAFÉ GRUMPY(GREENPOINT) (P. 296)
11. FORT DEFIANCE (P. 296)

12. DEVOCIÓN CAFE (P. 296)
13. PARLOR COFFEE (INSIDE PERSONS
    OF INTEREST BARBERSHOP) (P. 296)
14. REYNARD (P. 296)
15. ABRAÇO (P. 297)

16. AMOR Y AMARGO (P. 297)
17. VOYAGER ESPRESSO (P. 297)
18. THIRD RAIL (P. 298)
19. EL REY (P. 298)
20. EVERYMAN ESPRESSO (P. 298)

BLUE BOTTLE (HIGH LINE)

10th Avenue and West 16th Street
Chelsea
New York 10014
United States
+1 5106533394
www.bluebottlecoffee.com

Opening hours..Daily from 9 am
Credit cards.............................Visa, MasterCard, and Amex
Style..Coffee bar

"Innovative food pairings."—Cora Lambert

CAFÉ GRUMPY

224 West 20th Street
Chelsea
New York 10011
United States
+1 2122555511
www.cafegrumpy.com

Opening hours...Mon–Fri from 7 am,
Sat–Sun from 7:30 am
Credit cards.............................Visa, MasterCard, and Amex
Style..Coffee bar

"I think of Café Grumpy when I'm in New York City. I still
remember being blown away by an espresso they served
a few years back. It was a coffee from Colombia that one
of their baristas was using in competition. I remember
raspberry being one of the tasting notes, and they nailed it.
So sweet and complex and tasty."—Andy Sprenger

INTELLIGENTSIA MINI-BAR (OUTSIDE THE HIGH LINE HOTEL)

180 10th Avenue
Chelsea
New York 10011
United States
+1 2129339736
www.intelligentsiacoffee.com

Opening hours...Daily from 8 am,
weather permitting
Credit cards.............................Visa, MasterCard, and Amex
Style...Coffee truck

"The truck outside is nice at the hotel. Coffee outside is
always really fun."—Aaron Ultimo

JOE PRO SHOP

131 West 21st Street
Chelsea
New York 10011
United States
+1 2129247400
www.joenewyork.com

Opening hours...Mon–Fri from 8 am,
Sat–Sun from 9 am
Credit cards.............................Visa, MasterCard, and Amex
Style..Coffee bar

"One of my favorite filter coffees ever was served to me
at Joe Pro, which serves a great selection of coffees that
are difficult to find in the States."—Camila Ramos

This is not your average Joe coffee shop. This tiny spot in
Chelsea is the only Joe coffee shop that serves coffee from
around the world. Their meticulously curated coffee is only
surpassed by the skilled baristas pouring it. There is a bench
outside and just a few stools inside, so you will likely be
taking your coffee to go.

ELEVEN MADISON PARK

11 Madison Avenue
Flatiron District
New York 10010
United States
+1 2128890905
www.cafefoamy.ca

Opening hours.............................Mon–Wed from 5:30 pm,
Thu–Sat from noon and 5:30 pm,
Sun from 5:30 pm
Credit cards............................Visa, MasterCard, and Amex
Style..Fine dining

"The energy the staff has for the service of coffee (a coffee cart delivered to your table, where the coffee is brewed to order) in a setting like Eleven Madison Park is incredibly inspiring. Pushing boundaries with the restaurant team and encouraging the same with guests is no easy feat and Eleven Madison Park manages this with enthusiasm, fun, and a gentleness for coffee."—Jamie Jessup

LITTLE COLLINS

667 Lexington Avenue
Midtown East
New York 10022
United States
+1 2123081969
www.littlecollinsnyc.com

Opening hours...Mon–Fri from 7 am,
Sat–Sun from 8 am
Credit cards............................Visa, MasterCard, and Amex
Style...Coffee and food

"The best filter coffee I've been served in a cafe in recent memory was a Kalita Wave of Finca Kilimanjaro, brewed using the Modbar machine at Little Collins in New York. It was clean, articulate, balanced, juicy, sweet: pretty much everything you could ever want in a cup of filter coffee."
—Samuel Lewontin

SMITH CANTEEN

343 Smith Street
Carroll Gardens
Brooklyn
New York 11231
United States
+1 3472940292
www.smithcanteen.com

Opening hours...Daily from 7 am
Credit cards............................Visa, MasterCard, and Amex
Style...Coffee and food

"Smith Canteen had a 'Thunderbolt': homemade lemonade topped with a bright Yirgacheffe coffee from Counter Culture. I was blown away at how delicious, balanced, and refreshing it was."—Camila Ramos

BUÐIN

114 Greenpoint Avenue
Greenpoint
Brooklyn
New York 11222
United States
+1 3478449639
www.budin-nyc.com

Opening hours...Mon–Fri from 7 am,
Sat–Sun from 8 am
Credit cards............................Visa, MasterCard, and Amex
Style...Coffee and bar

"Best filter coffee."—Josh Littlefield

"Best espresso."—Esther Shaw

CAFÉ GRUMPY

193 Meserole Avenue
Greenpoint
Brooklyn
New York 11222
+1 7183497623
www.cafegrumpy.com

Opening hours..Mon–Fri from 7 am,
Sat–Sun from 7:30 am
Credit cards.............................Visa, MasterCard, and Amex
Style...Coffee bar

FORT DEFIANCE

365 Van Brunt Street
Red Hook
Brooklyn
New York 11231
United States
+1 3474536672
www.fortdefiancebrooklyn.com

Opening hours..Mon–Fri from 10 am,
Sat–Sun from 9 am
Credit cards.............................Visa, MasterCard, and Amex
Style...Restaurant

"Small restaurant doing great pour-over."—Steve Mierisch

DEVOCIÓN CAFÉ

69 Grand Street
Williamsburg
Brooklyn
New York 11249
United States
+1 7182856180
www.devocion.com

Opening hours..Mon–Fri from 7 am,
Sat–Sun from 8 am
Credit cards.............................Visa, MasterCard, and Amex
Style..Roastery cafe

"This Colombian roaster retailer is flying over green coffee
direct from origin for their incredible storefront roastery
cafe. The baristas there have served up some delicious filter
expressions of selected microlot coffees of late that really
make you stop and consider the coffees themselves and the
craftsmanship of the baristas serving them."—John Moore

PARLOR COFFEE (INSIDE PERSONS OF INTEREST BARBERSHOP)

82–84 Havemeyer Street
Williamsburg
Brooklyn
New York 11211
United States
+1 7182189100
www.parlorcoffee.com

Opening hours.......................................Mon–Fri from noon,
Sat–Sun from 11 am
Credit cards.............................Visa, MasterCard, and Amex
Style..Coffee and haircuts

"I still remember being delighted the first time I visited
Parlor Coffee's retail space. Pairing an espresso bar and a
barber shop still makes very little sense to me, but that
tidy little postage stamp of a bar is so completely charming,
and the hospitality and coffee that I've gotten there so
consistently on point that I can't help but love it."
—Samuel Lewontin

REYNARD

80 Wythe Avenue
Williamsburg
Brooklyn
New York 11249
United States
+1 7184608000
www.reynardnyc.com

Opening hours...Daily from 7 am
Credit cards.............................Visa, MasterCard, and Amex
Style...Boutique hotel restaurant

"It seems maybe too obvious, but I had an absolutely stellar
cup from Reynard in Brooklyn. An El Salvador from George
Howell. It blew me away. I probably had two or three cups
and I rarely finish one. I think great coffee is never a mistake
or a random occurrence. It can be unexpected."
—Ben Kaminsky

SWEETLEAF

10-93 Jackson Avenue
Long Island City
Queens
New York 11101
United States
+1 9178326726
www.sweetleafcoffee.com

Opening hours...Mon–Fri from 7 am,
Sat–Sun from 8 am
Credit cards............................Visa, MasterCard, and Amex
Style..Coffee bar

"This cafe feels like a community anchor and immediately made me as a traveler feel like a participant in a community. The first time I stepped into the original Sweetleaf in Long Island City I felt like I was joining a secret club."
—Keaton Ritchie

"For espresso, Sweetleaf really hits the sweet spot with what I look for in a shot."—Anthony Rue

ABRAÇO

86 East 7th Street
East Village
New York 10003
United States
www.abraconyc.com

Opening hours...Tue–Sat from 8 am,
Sun from 9 am
Credit cards...Cash only
Style...Coffee and baked goods

"Pretty essentially New York City for me . . . tiny, bustling, and great pastries."—Ryan Fisher

"Abraço I think summarizes what is cool about New York City. Superraw and practical, but they hustle and get it done right."—Samuel James

AMOR Y AMARGO

443 East 6th Street
East Village
New York 10009
United States
+1 2126146818
www.amoryamargony.com

Opening hours...Mon–Fri from 5 pm,
Sat–Sun from 3 pm
Credit cards............................Visa, MasterCard, and Amex
Style...Coffee and cocktails

"Top marks for drinks and coffee would have to go to the folks at Amor y Amargo and their Double Buzz Sundays. I've never had coffee/drink pairings like this before, and I love the way their bottled iced coffee is nestled among bottles of spirits and used as an ingredient like any other component in a cocktail. It's like coffee is hanging out with the cool kids rather than being pushed in a fridge with the sticky bottles of presqueezed grapefruit juice."—Zachary Carlsen

"The coffee-based cocktails at the Double Buzz weekend service at Amor y Amargo in New York are consistently excellent and consistently combine the flavors of specific coffees and specific spirits in interesting and compelling ways."—Samuel Lewontin

VOYAGER ESPRESSO

110 William Street
Financial District
New York 10038
United States
+1 6468856792
www.voyagerespresso.com

Opening hours...Mon–Fri from 7:30 am
Credit cards............................Visa, MasterCard, and Amex
Style..Coffee bar

"Voyager is a wonderful surprise: a fun, thoughtful, sharply executed coffee bar with a personality unlike any other in New York, and located just where you'd least expect it."
—Samuel Lewontin

For a coffee shop to do something truly different in design or conception is unusual nowadays, but there's nothing usual about Voyager Espresso. It is stowed away in a downstairs subway-access corridor (near the 2/3 trains) in the Financial District (you may get lost trying to find it!) and operates without much in the way of even a sign. You'll first notice the shop by its unusual round, metallic bar, minimal menu, and gaggle of happy, in-the-know patrons. There is a vague Carl Sagan theme and a quarterly rotation of elite roasters; it's one of the best coffee spots going—in one of the city's most unlikely places.

THIRD RAIL

240 Sullivan Street
Greenwich Village
New York 10012
United States
www.thirdrailcoffee.com

Opening hours	Mon–Fri from 7 am, Sat–Sun from 8 am
Credit cards	Cash only
Style	Coffee bar

"Best Chemex."—Alice Quillet

EL REY

100 Stanton Street
Lower East Side
New York 10002
United States
+1 2122603950
www.elreynyc.com

Opening hours	Mon–Fri from 7 am, Sat–Sun from 8 am
Credit cards	Visa, MasterCard, and Amex
Style	Coffee bar, wine bar, luncheonette

EVERYMAN ESPRESSO

301 West Broadway
SoHo
New York 10013
United States
+1 2122262362
www.everymanespresso.com

Opening hours	Mon–Fri from 8 am, Sat–Sun from 9 am
Credit cards	Visa, MasterCard, and Amex
Style	Coffee and waffles

"Best espresso."—Alex Bernson

"They always seem to be playing with different mixed concoctions."—JoEllen Depakakibo

"Some of the most memorable espressos I've had."
—Kalle Freese

"They served me one of the sweetest (unsweetened) cappuccinos I've ever had. The ambience is clean, hip, and intimate, and the service is on point. The (often) tiki-themed signature beverages are innovative and delicious (as are the doughnuts), and the coffee never disappoints."—Jess Steffy

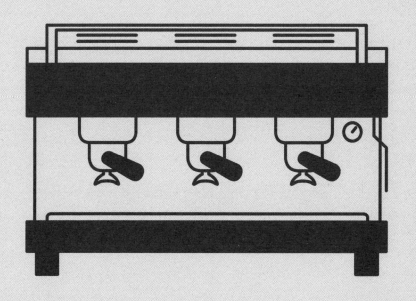

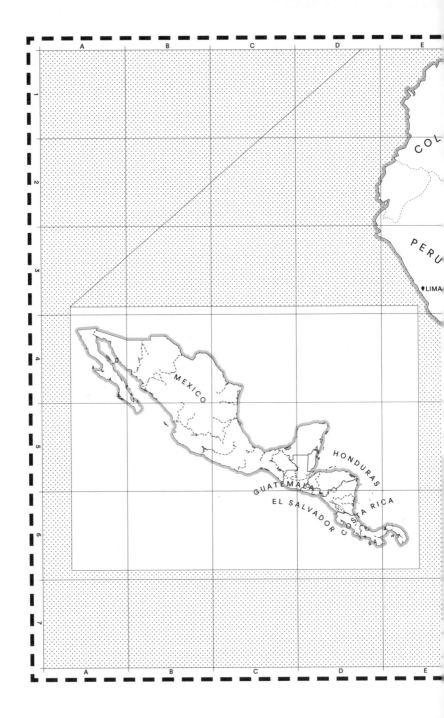

F G H I J

1

A

2

BRAZIL

3

BOLIVIA

4

CHILE

SÃO PAULO ◆

5

CENTRAL
& SOUTH
AMERICA

6

N̂ SCALE

0   300   600
mi.

7

F G H I J

"THERE IS LOTS OF PEDIGREE IN THIS GROUP WITH MULTI-TIME GUATEMALA AND WORLD BARISTA CHAMPIONS PUTTING THEMSELVES ON THE LINE FOR QUALITY COFFEE AND SOURCING."

SCOTT CONARY P.304

CENTRAL AMERICA

"GREAT COFFEE AT ORIGIN IS ALWAYS AMAZING, AND VIVA NAILS IT."

STEPHEN LEIGHTON P.304

"ALL THE COFFEE FOR THE CAFE IS ROASTED AT THE FARM IN HUEHUE ON A DIEDRICH COFFEE ROASTER."

ROBERT DAN GRIFFIN P.305

"ON A HOT DAY YOU CAN ENJOY AN ICED COFFEE OUTSIDE AT A COURTYARD TABLE, WHILE TAKING IN THE SPANISH-STYLE ARCHITECTURE OF THE HISTORIC CHURCH ACROSS THE STREET."

SCOTT CONARY P.306

CENTRAL
AMERICA

SCALE

0   75   150 mi.

MEXICO

MEXICO CITY P. 308

GUATEMALA

EL SALVADOR

HONDURAS

COSTA RICA

CAFÉ DON MAYO

Contiguo a Walmart
Mango Plaza
Alajuela
San José 12850-1000
Costa Rica
+506 25199205
www.cafedonmayo.com

Opening hours...Daily from 9 am
Credit cards...........................Visa, MasterCard, and Amex
Style...Coffee and food

CAFÉ BRUMAS DEL ZURQUÍ

San Francisco, San Isidro, Heredia
Faro del Caribe
Heredia
San José 40604
Costa Rica
+506 40312375
www.cafebrumasdelzurqui.com

Opening hours..Vary
Credit cards...Cash only
Style...Coffee bar

"The people who run the Brumas del Zurquí farm near my
aunt's house in Heredia, Costa Rica, also have a small cafe
tucked behind a gas station in an unassuming strip mall.
I went there and had an incredible Chemex of their Gesha
varietal that the barista prepared at the table. Watching the
familiar steps in the barista's careful preparation really gave
me a new admiration for what has grown out of the third
wave. It was a great cup and everything a Gesha promises."
—Jim Saborio

4 MONKEYS COFFEE SHOP

Final Avenida Albert Einstein Pasaje 11 #1
Colonia La Sultana II
Antiguo Cuscatlán
La Liberdad CP 1502
El Salvador

Opening hours...Daily from 9 am
Credit cards...........................Visa, MasterCard, and Amex
Style...Coffee bar

"There is lots of pedigree in this group with multi-time
Guatemala and World Barista Champions putting
themselves on the line for quality coffee and sourcing."
—Scott Conary

EL ZONTE S-COOL

503 El Zonte
El Zonte
La Libertad
El Salvador
+503 70558201
www.facebook.com/El-zonte-s-
cool-138422989588584

Opening hours...Vary
Credit cards...Cash only
Style...Educational tours and coffee

"S-Cool mainly serves as an info spot for tours and serves
coffee as a means to get customers to come in. It really only
serves French-press coffee, but that coffee is well prepared.
I found out later the coffee was from a small high-quality
producer and roasted by the producer himself."
—Bronwen Serna

VIVA ESPRESSO

Plaza Futura, 87A Avenida Norte, Calle del Mirador
Colonia Escalón
San Salvador CP 1101
El Salvador
+503 22641597
www.facebook.com/vivaespresso.es

Opening hours.....................................Mon–Fri from 7 am,
Sat–Sun from 8:30 am
Credit cards...........................Visa, MasterCard, and Amex
Style...Coffee and food

"A visit to Viva Espresso is always special. Great coffee
at origin is always amazing, and Viva nails it."
—Stephen Leighton

"They really push hard for the specialty market in an origin
country!"—Fabrizio Sención Ramírez

"Federico Bolaños has become synonymous with quality
and a pursuit of perfection in the barista craft. He has
trained the World Barista Champions from El Salvador.
Going to their cafe, you always get a good coffee and a
nice smile."—Kris Schackman

CRAFTERS

Avenida Dr Alvarez
Colonia Médica
San Salvador CP 1101
El Salvador

Opening hours..Mon–Sat from 7 am
Credit cards............................Visa, MasterCard, and Amex
Style..Coffee bar

"Past El Salvador barista champion William Hernandez has put his neck on the line with a great new shop. Having worked with some of the best coffee minds in the country and beyond, he put together a concept that blends the progressive future and the coffee community in El Salvador. Here you can count on delicious coffee, carefully sourced and roasted, and small bites to accompany."—Scott Conary

CAFÉ DIVINO

4 Avenida 14-10, Zona 10 Local 01
C. C Las Mercedes
Guatemala City 01010
Guatemala
+502 54572364
www.facebook.com/pg/cafedivinoguatemala/about/

Opening hours..Mon–Sat from 7 am
Credit cards..Cash only
Style..Coffee bar

"Located in the upscale Zona 10 in Guatemala City, Divino would be considered a true hole-in-the-wall. It is a one-entrance space within a larger building, but Teco (the owner's nickname, which is short for owl in Spanish) has made the bar and area outside the entrance very comfy, with large electrical pool tables and pour-over equipment sitting on a handmade bar. In the back is a small cupping/roasting space where he roasts the coffee you are going to enjoy—and you are going to enjoy it! His precision from being a national champion shows through, and every cup or espresso is carefully prepared. It's a great place to meet friends or grab your first cup of the day."—Scott Conary

THE ROOM

3A Avenida 17-52 Zona 14
Edificio Gaudi
Guatemala City 1014
Guatemala
+502 25088074
www.facebook.com/theroom.coffeeandteastudio

Opening hours..Mon–Sat from 9 am
Credit cards..Visa and MasterCard
Style..Coffee and food

"The Room is owned by two sisters, Nancy and Diana. They both worked in design and industrial design, so the space is really cute. All of the furniture was designed by the sisters or friends of theirs from school. There is a really pretty mural of macaws on the back wall. They serve coffee roasted by Mayaland Coffee, and a lot of the farmers that Mayaland works with go there for coffee. You can go there and run into Josue Morales, who roasted the beans, and the farmer who grew the coffee. Obviously this is very cool!"—Robert Dan Griffin

EL INJERTO CAFÉ

9th Calle 15-15, Zona 13
Guatemala City 1013
Guatemala
+502 23629787
www.fincaelinjerto.com

Opening hours...Mon–Sat from 8 am,
Sun from 9 am
Credit cards............................Visa, MasterCard, and Amex
Style..Coffee and food

"Finca El Injerto is one of the most famous and amazing farms in all of Central America. The farm is located in Huehuetenango and is gorgeous. All the coffee for the cafe is roasted at the farm in Huehue on a Diedrich coffee roaster. Naturally they feature some of their best coffees in the cafe, where you can get coffee brewed to order on a variety of brewers. I had a great cup of single-varietal Pacamara!"—Robert Dan Griffin

CAFÉ MUSEO

4 Calle 7-40 Zona 1
Huehuetenango 13001
Guatemala
+502 77641101
www.facebook.com/cafemuseo.huehue

Opening hours..Daily from 7 am
Credit cards..Visa
Style...Coffee and food

"The facade of the cafe is very nondescript. Once you walk in, it's pretty typical, until the cafe opens up into a beautiful courtyard—it's some serious alfresco dining! They roast coffee on-site in an ancient coffee roaster that most roasters in the States would have no idea how to work. The courtyard and cafe are full of old coffee-processing equipment, including depulpers; devices for removing pergamino, or parchment; and rakes for moving coffee around on drying patios. The courtyard is awesome, and you could easily pass a day hanging out there with friends. The food was really good, typical Guatemalan fare, and the coffee was nice and freshly brewed in a French press."
—Robert Dan Griffin

BELLA VISTA COFFEE

6a Avenida Norte #1
Antigua
Sacatepequez 3001
Guatemala
+502 78325568
www.bellavistacoffee.com

Opening hours..Daily from 7 am
Credit cards...Visa and MasterCard
Style...Coffee bar

"Bella Vista Coffee has a very, very friendly staff, an amazing roof deck with a view of Antigua and the volcanoes, and a barista exchange program with baristas from other countries. They also have one of the best mills in Guatemala."—David Nigel Flynn

KALDI'S COFFEE

Costado Sur de la Catedral
Santa Rosa de Copan
Copán 41101
Honduras
+504 26626202
www.cafeoamy.ca

Opening hours...................................Mon–Sat from 10 am,
Sun from 11:30 am
Credit cards..Cash only
Style...Coffee and food

"Drawing from local farms and utilizing multiple brewing methods, this husband-and-wife duo show their passion for the coffee grown around them in the western Honduran mountains. You can enjoy a range of flavors while being surrounded by testimonials of international customers and coffee bags from various roasters. On a hot day you can drink an iced coffee outside at a courtyard table, while taking in the Spanish-style architecture of the historic church across the street, right off the Parque Central. If you're lucky, owner Salomé Cardoza will offer up a song, as she is also an accomplished singer. The owners are consistent supporters of coffee competitions, as competitors, judges, and sponsors. A great representation of delicious Honduran coffee."—Scott Conary

EL DORAO

Carretera Salida al Mochito
Peña Blanca
Cortés
Honduras
+504 26500170
www.cafefoamy.ca

Opening hours...Daily from 7 am
Credit cards...Cash only
Style..Coffee bar

"The first time I visited some of our coffee producers in Honduras, I was excited to find out that our friend Benjamin Paz from Beneficio San Vicente owned a cafe in town called El Dorao. My favorite part of the day, after visiting farms and cupping coffee, would be to sit in El Dorao and drink a cappuccino. There are bags of coffee from roasters around the world on display on a shelf, jute coffee bags on the wall, and other coffee-processing decorations. But what is remarkable about the space is abstract—the feeling that you get when you are traveling and you find something that makes you feel at home." —Caroline Bell

"Typically, all the great coffee in coffee-producing countries is exported and the coffee consumed by locals tends to be what wasn't good enough for export. El Dorao is an exception. Benjamin Paz and his family run El Dorao, in addition to exporting some of the best coffees in the world through their mill and exporting company, San Vicente. El Dorao has coffees from the Santa Barbara region roasted under the El Dorao brand, but during the harvest season they offer a rotating cast of guest coffees that were left by the green buyers visiting farmers in the surrounding region. Often this means you can get a cup of Koppi, Kaffa, Tim Wendelboe, or even Belleville in a small town (ten thousand people) next to the mountains of the Santa Barbara region of Honduras."—David Nigel Flynn

AROMA CAFE

Colonia Modelo
Marcala
La Paz
Honduras
+504 97414415

Opening hours...Daily from 7 am
Credit cards...Cash only
Style..Coffee and bar

In Honduras is a small cafe in Marcala that I do not know the name of, but everyone calls it Nancy's coffee shop. Nancy Hernandez is also a small coffee producer—they always have consistently amazing French-press coffee, without using scales, measurements, and brew ratios." —Sasa Sestic

CAFFE SOSPESO

Joaquín Clausell 10312
Zona Río
Tijuana
Baja California 22010
Mexico
+52 6646343184
www.caffesospeso.com

Opening hours.......................................Mon–Fri from 7 am,
Sat from 8:30 am, Sun from 2 pm
Credit cards...Visa
Style..Coffee bar

"Best filter coffee."—Fabrizio Sención Ramírez

CAFÉ PASSMAR
Mercado Lazaro Cardenas
Coll del Valle Nte
Mexico City
Federal District
3100
Mexico
+52 5556691994
www.cafepassmar.com

Opening hours.................................Mon–Sat from 7:30 am
Credit cards..Visa and MasterCard
Style...Coffee bar

"Nowhere else in the world have as many national barista champions gone on to start extraordinary, supersuccessful coffee businesses. Café Passmar (owned by former barista champion Salvador Benitez and his wife, Alelí Labastida, a former latte art and barista champion) is perhaps the most famous of these." —Sarah Allen

BUNA 42
Orizaba 42
Colonia Roma
Mexico City
Federal District 6700
Mexico
+52 67245578
www.bunamx

Opening hours.................................Mon–Fri from 7:30 am,
                                                                  Sat–Sun from 8 am
Credit cards............................Visa, MasterCard, and Amex
Style...Coffee bar

"How often do we accidentally stumble upon a place and fall in love? As I was walking through the historical district of La Roma, a very clean, modern, and bright design caught my eye. The minimal design, paired with an obvious attention to the tiniest details, made this shop stand up visually to any of the top shops I've seen across the world. As I began peeking in, I saw all the initial signs of 'This could be good': Modbar espresso components, Mahlkonig K30 and EK43 grinders, and a set of Kalita pour-over brewers. Since I was in Mexico, it seemed appropriate to order a Oaxacan coffee. I got my espresso—it was extracted nicely, layered in syrupy sweetness, and quite lovely! It was a great way to start off my trip in Mexico. I'll be going back." —Ryan Knapp

> "PEDRO AND HIS STAFF ARE INCREDIBLY EARNEST, AND THE SPACE AND NEIGHBORHOOD BOTH HAVE SUCH A VIBRANT, MULTICULTURAL LIFE TO THEM."

JARED LINZMEIER P.315

SOUTH AMERICA NORTH

> "AMONG FILTER COFFEES, THERE ARE A FEW THAT STAND OUT FOR ME, BUT ONE IN PARTICULAR WAS AT AZAHAR CAFÉ."

SEANNA FOREY P.315

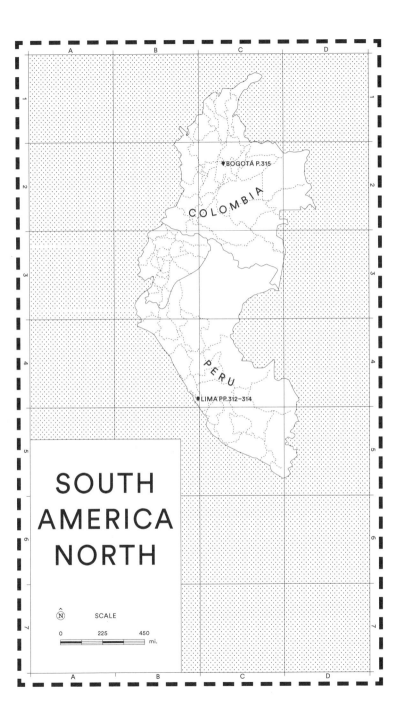

A
B
C
D

1

2

BOGOTÁ P.315

COLOMBIA

3

4

PERU

LIMA PP.312–314

5

SOUTH
AMERICA
NORTH

6

7

N

SCALE

0   225   450
mi.

"THEY ARE ALWAYS LOOKING FOR GREAT COFFEE, THE ATMOSPHERE IS GREAT, AND THEY PUT IN A LOT OF ATTENTION TO DETAIL TO MAXIMIZE THE EXPERIENCE OF DRINKING PERUVIAN SPECIALTY COFFEES."

HARRYSSON NEIRA P. 314

LIMA

"THE BARISTAS POUR BEAUTIFUL DRINKS, AND THERE'S A REALLY NICE GARDEN IN THE BACK TO SIT IN." SCOUT ROSE P. 314

"THE BARISTA'S GRANDFATHER OWNS THE FARM THAT THEY BOUGHT THE COFFEE FROM, AND THAT FAMILY HAS BEEN MAKING COFFEE ON THAT FARM SINCE THE 1800S." SCOUT ROSE P. 314

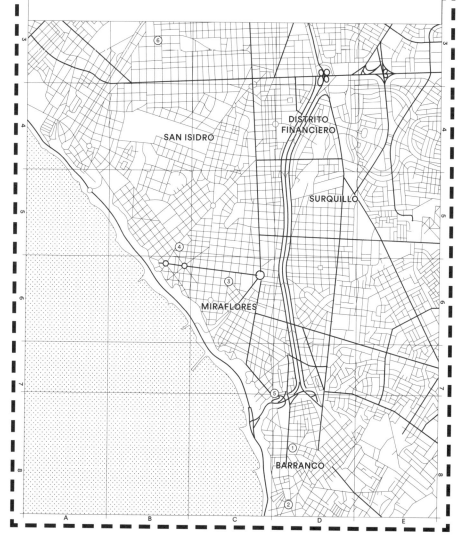

LIMA

N

SCALE

0   620   1238   1855
yd.

1. FINCA LA CAMPIÑA (P. 314)
2. TOSTADURIA BISETTI (P. 314)
3. ARABICA (P. 314)
4. CAFÉ VERDE (P. 314)
5. EL CAFÉ DE HARRY (P. 314)
6. THE COFFEE ROAD (P. 314)

SAN ISIDRO

DISTRITO
FINANCIERO

SURQUILLO

MIRAFLORES

BARRANCO

FINCA LA CAMPIÑA

Avenida Nicolas de Pierola #110
Barranco
Lima 15063
Peru
+51 12567572
www.lacampina.fr

Opening hours	Mon–Sat from 10 am
Credit cards	Visa
Style	Roastery cafe

"I got a Chemex at Finca la Campiña. The barista's grandfather owns the farm that they bought the coffee from, and that family has been making coffee on that farm since the 1800s. It was delicious. They make AeroPress, Chemex, and some other brew methods, and they have a full espresso bar."—Scout Rose

TOSTADURIA BISETTI

Avenida Pedro de Osma 116
Barranco
Lima
Lima 15063
Peru
+51 12474399
www.cafebisetti.com

Opening hours	Mon–Fri from 8 am, Sat from 9 am, Sun from 2 pm
Credit cards	Visa, MasterCard, and Amex
Style	Coffee and breakfast

"The baristas pour beautiful drinks, and there's a really nice garden in the back to sit in."—Scout Rose

ARABICA

Calle Gral Recavarren 269
Miraflores
Lima 15074
Peru
+51 14470904

Opening hours	Mon–Fri from 8 am, Sat from 10 am, Sun from 2 pm
Credit cards	Visa and MasterCard
Style	Full service

CAFÉ VERDE

Avenida Santa Cruz 1305
Miraflores
Lima 15073
Peru
+51 16527682
www.cafeverdeperu.com

Opening hours	Mon–Fri from 7 am, Sat from 8 am
Credit cards	Visa and MasterCard
Style	Coffee bar

EL CAFÉ DE HARRY

Avenida Armendáriz 546
Miraflores
Lima 15074
Peru

Opening hours	Daily from 8 am
Credit cards	Visa, MasterCard, and Amex
Style	Coffee bar

THE COFFEE ROAD

Avenida Guillermo Prescott 378-380
San Isidro
Lima 15076
Peru
+51 16372028

Opening hours	Mon–Fri from 7:30 am, Sat from 9 am, Sun from 1 pm
Credit cards	Visa, MasterCard, and Amex
Style	Coffee bar

"They are always looking for great coffee, the atmosphere is great, and they put in a lot of attention to detail to maximize the experience of drinking Peruvian specialty coffees."
—Harrysson Neira

CAFÉ PERGAMINO

Carrera 37 8A, 37 Via Primavera
Zona Rosa
Medellín
Antioquia
Colombia
+57 42686444
www.pergamino.co

Opening hours..Mon–Fri from 8 am,
Sat from 9 am
Credit cards.............................Visa, MasterCard, and Amex
Style...Coffee bar

"Pedro and his staff are incredibly earnest, and the space
and neighborhood both have such a vibrant, multicultural
life to them."—Jared Linzmeier

AMOR PERFECTO

Carrera 4 #66, 46 Bogotá
Chapinero
Bogotá
Colombia
+57 0312484658
www.cafeamorperfecto.com

Opening hours...Mon–Sat from 8 am
Credit cards.............................Visa, MasterCard, and Amex
Style...Coffee bar

AZAHAR CAFÉ

Carrera 14 #93A-48
Parque de la 93
Bogotá
Colombia
+57 17034799
www.azaharcoffee.com

Opening hours...Mon–Sat from 7 am,
Sun from 1 pm
Credit cards...............................Visa, MasterCard, Amex,
and Diners Club
Style...Coffee bar

"Among filter coffees, there are a few that stand out for me,
but one in particular was at Azahar Café. I honestly don't
remember which of their coffees it was, but they serve only
Colombians, and it tasted and smelled like a small wedge
of mandarin dipped in honey. It was divine."
—Seanna Forey

"MELDS THE TRENDY DESIGN AND FASHION SCENE OF THE CITY WITH THE MOST PROGRESSIVE COFFEE PRODUCER."

KRIS SCHACKMAN P.322

"IN BRAZIL, THE COFFEE LAB OF ISABELA RAPOSEIRAS WINS HANDS DOWN FOR COFFEE PAIRING AND SUPERB DRINKS."

JONATHAN HUTCHINS P.323

SOUTH AMERICA SOUTH

"SANTO GRÃO IS ONE OF MY FAVORITE CAFES ON EARTH." DOUG ZELL P.322

"IN LA PAZ, I TURNED A CORNER OFF THE BEATEN TRACK AND HAD AN AMAZING SHOT, AND THEY WERE ALSO MAKING DELICIOUS CHEMEX."

STEPHEN LEIGHTON P.318

"IN THE MIDDLE OF THE BUSINESS DISTRICT IN SANTIAGO, CHILE, THERE WAS A YOUNG GUY DOING POUR-OVERS FROM A TRICYCLE CART, WHICH HE BUILT HIMSELF."

SEANNA FOREY P.318

A B C D

1

B R A Z I L

2

LA PAZ P.318 ♥

3

♥ SÃO PAULO PP.320–323

CURITIBA P.318 ♥

CHILE

4

SANTIAGO
P.318 ♥

5

SOUTH
AMERICA
SOUTH

6

N̂

SCALE

0   350   700

mi.

7

ROASTER BOUTIQUE

Calle Gabriel René Moreno E20
San Miguel
La Paz 5912
Bolivia
+591 22147234
www.roasterboutique.com

Opening hours	Daily from 7:30 am
Credit cards	Visa and MasterCard
Style	Coffee bar

"In La Paz, I turned a corner off the beaten track and had an amazing shot, and they were also making delicious Chemex. Roaster Boutique is a must-visit."—Stephen Leighton

LUCCA CAFÉS ESPECIAIS

Alameda Presidente Taunay, 40 Batel
Batel
Curitiba
Paraná 80420-180
Brazil
+55 4130166675
www.luccacafesespeciais.com

Opening hours	Mon–Fri from 8 am, Sat from 9 am, Sun from noon
Credit cards	Visa, MasterCard, and Amex
Style	Coffee and burgers

"Lucca Cafés Especiais has the most welcoming atmosphere of any cafe I've visited, and it's a staple of coffee quality not only in that town but in all of Brazil."—Josue Morales

RAUSE CAFÉ E VINHO

Alameda Dr. Carlos de Carvalho, 696
Centro
Curitiba
Paraná 80430-180
Brazil
+55 4130240696
www.rausecafe.com.br

Opening hours	Mon–Fri from 9 am, Sat from noon
Credit cards	Visa and MasterCard
Style	Coffee and wine

"Rause is a fantastic cafe whose staff's dedication to coffee doesn't compromise their identical dedication to the delicious small plates of food and dessert they offer or the excellent selection of beer and wine. Owner Juca Esmanhoto is a passionate coffee professional who is always trying to increase the quality of your experience through training and practice. He works hard to find amazing local coffee to pair with the delightful atmosphere of the shop."—Scott Conary

São Paulo, see pages 320–323

CAFÉ TRICICLO (MOBILE; VARIOUS LOCATIONS)

Santiago
Santiago Metropolitan Region
Chile
+56 995430623
www.cafetriciclo.cl

Opening hours	Vary
Credit cards	Cash only
Style	Mobile cart

"In the middle of the business district in Santiago, Chile, there was a young guy doing pour-overs from a tricycle cart, which he built himself. He calls it Café Triciclo and takes it around Santiago educating people on specialty coffee. He was so passionate and energetic about coffee, it was really quite inspiring, plus he served wonderful coffees."—Seanna Forey

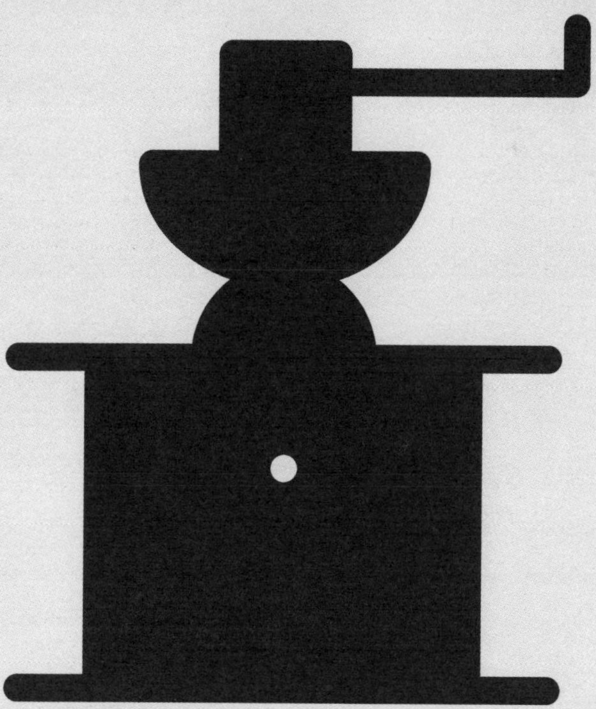

"REALLY GOOD COFFEE AND A GREAT AND DIVERSE MENU AS WELL AS SOME AMAZING SCENERY A LA SÃO PAULO."

DOUG ZELL P.322

"THE MENU MIX IS A VIRTUAL CATALOG OF COFFEE EXPERIMENTATION OFFERED AS ENUMERATED 'RITUALS.'"

JOHN MOORE P.323

SÃO PAULO

"EVERYTHING ABOUT THE SPACE IS DEDICATED TO THE SENSORY EXPERIENCE OF COFFEE AND THE INTERACTION BETWEEN THE BRILLIANTLY TALENTED BARISTAS WHO WORK THERE AND THE GUESTS."

JOHN MOORE P.323

"CHANGING THE WAY BRAZILIANS THINK ABOUT AND ENJOY COFFEE."

TIM WENDELBOE P.323

SÃO PAULO

Ñ   SCALE

0   300   605   910
━━━━━━━━━━━ yd.

1. ISSO É CAFÉ (P. 322)   4. OCTAVIO CAFÉ (P. 322)
2. SANTO GRÃO (P. 322)   5. COFFEE LAB (P. 323)
3. SUPLICY CAFE (P. 322)

PERDIZES

HIGIENÓPOLIS

CONSOLAÇÃO

VILA MADALENA

BELA VISTA

PINHEIROS CENTRO

JARDIM PAULISTA

JARDINS

ISSO É CAFÉ

Rua Carlos Comenale
Bela Vista
São Paulo 01332-020
Brazil
+55 1138625833
www.issoecafe.com

Opening hours	Tue–Sun from 10 am
Credit cards	Visa, MasterCard, and Amex
Style	Coffee bar

"Isso é Café is above the exit off a highway tunnel and it's a really cool place to hang out. It melds the trendy design and fashion scene of the city with the most progressive coffee producer."—Kris Schackman

SANTO GRÃO

R Jerônimo da Veiga, 179
Itaim Bibi
São Paulo 04536-000
Brazil
+55 1130713169
www.santograo.com.br

Opening hours	Mon from 9 am, Tue–Sun from 7:30 am
Credit cards	Visa, MasterCard, and Amex
Style	Coffee and food

"Santo Grão is one of my favorite cafes on earth. I'm usually there a few times during any visit to Brazil. It reflects perfectly the Jardins District's beauty and energy and is busy from 7 am until midnight. It offers really good coffee and a great and diverse menu as well as some amazing scenery á la São Paulo." —Doug Zell

SUPLICY CAFÉS ESPECIAIS

Alameda Lorena 1430
Jardim Paulista
São Paulo 01424-001
Brazil
+55 1130713169
www.suplicycafes.com.br

Opening hours	Mon–Fri from 7:30 am, Sat from 8 am, Sun from 8:30 am
Credit cards	Visa, MasterCard, and Amex
Style	Coffee and food

OCTAVIO CAFÉ

Avenida Brigadeiro Faria Lima, 2996
Jardim Paulistano
São Paulo 01451-000
Brazil
+55 1130740110
www.octaviocafe.com

Opening hours	Mon–Fri from 7 am, Sat–Sun from 8:30 am
Credit cards	Visa, MasterCard, and Amex
Style	Coffee and food

"I love the grandiose nature of Octavio Café."—John Moore

COFFEE LAB

Rua Fradique Coutinho, 1340
Vila Madalena
São Paulo 05416-001
Brazil
+55 1133757400
www.coffeelab.com.br

Opening hours..Daily from 7 am
Credit cards............................Visa, MasterCard, and Amex
Style...Coffee bar

"In Brazil, the Coffee Lab of Isabela Raposeiras wins hands down for coffee pairing and superb drinks."
—Jonathan Hutchins

"Everything about the space is dedicated to the sensory experience of coffee and the interaction between the brilliantly talented baristas who work there and the guests. Make no mistake, these are not customers—they are truly guests. And the very fact that there is no queue and you essentially walk into the kitchen to stand next to working baristas says it all. The menu mix is a virtual catalog of coffee experimentation offered as enumerated 'rituals.' Guests are served these rituals by well-versed coffee professionals who are totally devoid of arrogance."
—John Moore

"Hand brewing happens at the table. She only can roast Brazilian coffee, so it's interesting to see what she can accomplish with a relatively small selection of beans."
—Kris Schackman

"Coffee Lab is run by the extremely creative and talented Isabela Raposeiras. Although she is limited by import restrictions to work only with Brazilian coffees in her shop, I am always amazed by the quality and diversity of coffee flavor she is putting out. I think the restrictions have made her more creative and forced her to think differently when it comes to how she offers coffee. She also has the impossible task of changing the way Brazilians think about and enjoy coffee. In a country that is the biggest coffee producer in the world and already has a very traditional and established coffee culture, that is an intimidating task. But Coffee Lab and Isabela have made a huge impact already, and she is now considered one of the most influential people in gastronomy in Brazil. That is a huge effort for a coffee person, to be considered in the same league as famous chefs." —Tim Wendelboe

THE CONTRIBUTORS

KHALID AL MULLA
Khalid Al Mulla is the founding director of the Coffee Museum of Dubai and director of green coffee and equipment importers Easternmen & Co. He is based in Dubai.

CHRISTOPHER ALAMEDA
While his roots in New York informed his love of baseball, his upbringing in Seattle, Washington, set Christopher Alameda on a path toward coffee with no turning back. He is the owner and head barista of Menotti's Coffee Stop in Venice, California, and an accomplished latte artisan.

NICO ALARY
A world-traveling food and coffee enthusiast, Nico Alary is the cofounder and barista at Paris breakfast hot spot Holybelly, which he owns with his partner, chef Sarah Mouchot.

SARAH ALLEN
Editor and cofounder of Portland, Oregon–based *Barista Magazine* (baristamagazine.com), Sarah Allen has been highlighting the work of exceptional coffee professionals worldwide since 2007.

TRACY ALLEN
A long-standing fixture of the coffee competition circuit, World Barista Championship head judge, and past president of the Specialty Coffee Association of America, Tracy Allen is CEO and founder of coffee consultancy Brewed Behavior. He lives in Kansas City, Missouri.

BODIN AMORNPAHT-THANAKUN
Manager of *Coffee, Tea & Ice Cream Magazine*, Bodin Amornpahtthanakun is based in Bangkok, Thailand.

CORY ANDREEN
Cory Andreen is an American expat working to provide the people of Berlin with great coffee at Café CK, Berlin. He was previously the owner of Mockingbird Hill cafe in Washington, DC, and also works as a consultant.

CHARLES BABINSKI
Cofounder of busy Los Angeles cafes G&B (he's the B) and Go Get Em Tiger along with business partner Kyle Glanville, Charles Babinski is the 2015 United States Barista Champion and the creator of Cold Brew by Babinski.

CHRIS BACA
Chris Baca is cofounder of the Cat & Cloud coffee company (catandcloud.com), podcast, and experience alongside longtime collaborator Jared Truby. He lives in California.

ANDREW BARNETT
A former restorer of carousel horses who grew up on the South Side of Chicago, Andrew Barnett discovered a passion for coffee while living in Northern California in the 1990s. He is a longtime Cup of Excellence judge, was a founder of Santa Rosa's Centro Espresso and acclaimed roastery Ecco Caffe, and is currently the owner of San Francisco's Linea Caffe, a waffle and coffee bar located in the Mission District.

MARCOS BARTOLOMÉ
Though the name may be misleading, Marcos Bartolomé is the true owner of hidden Barcelona cafe Satan's Coffee Corner.

CAROLINE BELL
Along with partner Chris Timbrell, Caroline Bell is co-owner and founder of popular New York City roastery and coffee shop chain Café Grumpy.

ANTHONY BENDA
British Columbia native Anthony Benda operates Café Myriade and Pikolo Espresso Bar in Montreal.

ALEX BERNSON
Currently acting as marketing manager for the many competitions and events hosted by World Coffee Events, Alex Bernson is also a coffee journalist and the founder of Wesleyan University's Espwesso cafe in Connecticut.

JOANNE BERRY
Based in Oslo, Norway, native South African Joanne Berry works as director of coffee for green sourcing company Nordic Approach.

MARCUS BONI
Marcus Boni is vice president of retail for Intelligentsia Coffee and chair of World Coffee Events. He lives in Chicago.

GABRIEL BOSCANA
Longtime roaster and coffee consultant Gabriel Boscana is the founder of Máqina Coffee, based in eastern Pennsylvania.

ANNA BRONES

Travel writer and outdoor-coffee-brewing expert Anna Brones (annabrones.com) is a regular columnist for coffee website sprudge.com and is the author of *Paris Coffee Revolution* and *Fika: The Art of the Swedish Coffee Break*.

JENNI BRYANT

Former lacrosse coach Jenni Bryant is general manager at Market Lane Coffee in Melbourne, Australia.

ZAC CADWALADER

Zac Cadwalader is editor and writer for a popular coffee website Sprudge (sprudge.com) news channel.

KATIE CARGUILO

Katie Carguilo was the 2013 United States Barista Champion. She works as head of West Coast Quality Control for Counter Culture Coffee in Emeryville, California.

ZACHARY CARLSEN

Zachary Carlsen is cofounder of the coffee news website Sprudge (sprudge.com).

JORDAN CHAMBERS

Based in Atlanta, Georgia, Jordan Chambers is the Southeast wholesale educator for Intelligentsia Coffee and Kilogram Tea.

CHAN KWUN HO (DAWN CHAN)

Dawn Chan is a two-time barista champion of Hong Kong and works there at the Cupping Room.

NICHOLAS CHISTYAKOV

Nicholas Chistyakov oversees roasting, sourcing, and quality control at Camera Obscura Coffee in Moscow.

NICHOLAS CHO

Nicholas Cho is an active online coffee personality and the cofounder of Wrecking Ball Coffee Roasters in San Francisco.

NICOLAS CLERC

Nicolas Clerk is a barista and manager at Paris cafe Télescope.

SCOTT CONARY

Scott Conary is a coffee consultant and World Barista Championship judge; he is also the owner of Caffee Driade, Open Eye Café, and Carrboro Coffee Roasters—all in North Carolina.

FELIPE CROCE

Felipe Croce is the owner of Fazenda Ambiental Fortaleza (FAF) farm and FAF Coffees green exporting, both based in Mococa, Brazil, as well as Isso é Café roastery cafe, based in São Paulo.

JAY CUNNINGHAM

Artist and skateboarder Jay Cunningham spends his working hours at Intelligentsia Coffee in Chicago, where he is a green coffee buyer and wholesale sales representative.

GWILYM DAVIES

Gwilym Davies is a certified World Coffee Events judge, founder of Prufrock Coffee, London, and director of the Coffee Training Centre in Prague. He is the 2009 World Barista Champion.

JOELLEN DEPAKAKIBO

JoEllen Depakakibo fell in love with coffee while working at Intelligentsia Coffee in Chicago and Blue Bottle Coffee in San Francisco, before opening her own cafe, Pinhole Coffee, in San Francisco's Bernal Heights.

JAY DEROSE

Jay DeRose owns and operates MiddleState Coffee, a roasting company, and Little Owl Coffee, a coffee bar, in Denver, Colorado.

SHANE DEVERAUX

Shane Deveraux is the founder of Habit Coffee, which operates two cafes in Victoria, British Columbia.

CHARLIE EISENSTAT

An Ohio coffee pioneer, Charlie Eistenstat brings internationally renowned coffees to the Rust Belt at his shop, Pour Cleveland.

TUMI FERRER

Tumi Ferrer is the 2011 Icelandic Barista Champion, the Icelandic Brewers Cup Champion, and head trainer at Te & Kaffi in Reykjavík.

RYAN FISHER

A coffee lover drawn equally by the hospitality and the beverage, Ryan Fisher is an avid coffee ambassador and barista competitor. He leads retail operations and wholesale training for Commonwealth Coffee Roasters in Denver, Colorado.

DAVID NIGEL FLYNN

American expat David Flynn is a founder of Belleville Brûlerie and La Fontaine de Belleville in Paris.

SEANNA FOREY

Seanna Forey is an owner and barista at Little Owl Coffee in Denver, Colorado.

BRENT FORTUNE

A former cafe owner and current consultant, cat advocate Brent Fortune is also a longtime certified competition judge and is the founder of Coffee Common.

KALLE FREESE

Former barista champion of Finland and founder of the short-lived Freese Coffee Company in Helsinki, Kalle Freese is the director of instant coffee project Sudden Coffee.

EVAN GILMAN

Evan Gilman is the creative director at Royal Coffee Importers and writes about Southeast Asia coffee culture for Sprudge (sprudge.com).

PETER GIULIANO
Coffee industry leader and beloved storyteller Peter Giuliano is the former director of Counter Culture Coffee and is senior director of symposium at the Specialty Coffee Association of America. He is originally from Encinitas, California.

KYLE GLANVILLE
The 2008 United States Barista Champion, Kyle Glanville is the cofounding "G" in Los Angeles cafe G&B, as well as co-owner of the sister cafes Go Get Em Tiger.

PHIL GOODLAXSON
Phil Goodlaxson is an owner and green coffee buyer at Corvus Coffee Roasters, in Denver, Colorado.

JOHN GORDON
Former UK barista champion John Gordon is director of Framework Coffee in Auckland, New Zealand.

SONJA BJÖRK GRANT
Globe-trotting Sonja Björk Grant, a longtime World Coffee Events staff member, is recognized as an ambassador to coffee worldwide. She was a founder of Reykjavík's Kaffismiðja Íslands and is co-owner of Kaffibrugghúisð, also in Reykjavík, Iceland.

ROBERT DAN GRIFFIN
Longtime barista and coffee enthusiast Dan Griffin currently works as U.S. relationship manager for TG Lab coffee, based in Guatemala City, Guatemala.

CAGATAY GULABIOGLU
Based in Istanbul, Turkey, Cagatay Gulabioglu is founder of Kronotrop and co-owner of Probador Colectiva, a coffee roaster, training, and consulting company.

METTE-MARIE HANSEN
Mette-Marie Hansen is a coffee trader based in Kenya.

COLIN HARMON
Former investment finance worker Colin Harmon took his first coffee job across the street from his old employer's office tower. He is now a four-time barista champion of Ireland, the founder of Dublin's 3fe cafe, and the author of *What I Know About Running Coffee Shops*.

BEN HELFEN
Ben Helfen works for Counter Culture Coffee in Durham, North Carolina.

ANDREW HETZEL
Andrew Hetzel is a coffee supply chain and trade consultant based in Hawaii.

JOSH HOCKIN
Josh Hockin travels internationally as a green coffee buyer for Transcend Coffee in Edmonton, Alberta.

KARINA HOF
New Jersey native Karina Hof is a freelance journalist living in Amsterdam, where she covers the Netherlands coffee scene for website Sprudge (sprudge.com).

JAMES HOFFMANN
Cofounder and director of Square Mile Coffee in London, former musician James Hoffmann is the 2007 World Barista Champion and author of *The World Atlas of Coffee*.

GEORGE HOWELL
George Howell holds one of the industry's most respected palates and is the founder of the George Howell Coffee Company in Acton, Massachusetts. He is also the inventor of the Frappuccino.

ELLIE HUDSON
A resident of Traverse City, Michigan, Ellie Hudson serves as the director of professional development for the Specialty Coffee Association of America.

JONATHAN HUTCHINS
Jonathan Hutchins is owner, roaster, and coffee buyer at Williams & Sons Coffee in Porto Alegre, Rio Grande do Sul, Brazil.

YUKO ITOI
Kyoto, Japan's Yuko Itoi has been working with coffee shops, roasters, and direct trade relationships with coffee farms for more than thirty years. She is a Cup of Excellence judge and vice president of the International Women's Coffee Alliance chapter in Japan.

HIDENORI IZAKI
The 2014 World Barista Champion, Hidenori Izaki celebrated a long career at Maruyama Coffee before founding his own business, Samurai Coffee Experience, a worldwide coffee training and consulting business. He is based in Kamakura, Japan.

HELLE JACOBSEN
Helle Jacobsen is an operator of Copenhagen Coffee Lab, a mobile coffee truck and stationary cafe, located in Lisbon, Portugal.

SAMUEL JAMES
Former model Sam James is founder of the Toronto-based Sam James Coffee Bar cafes and their sister roasting operation, Cut Coffee.

JAMIE JESSUP
Jamie Jessup is former partnership manager at World Coffee Events. She lives in London.

DREW JOHNSON
Drew Johnson is an owner of Bows & Arrows Coffee Roasters in Victoria, British Columbia, where he also roasts the coffee.

JESSICA JOHNSTON
A founder of the Prairie Coffee Collective, Jessica Johnston is a Canadian barista competition head judge and freelance barista and consultant. She is based outside of Calgary, Alberta.

BEN KAMINSKY

Three-time United States Cup Tasters champion Ben Kaminsky is a coffee consultant based in San Francisco, California.

EILEEN P. KENNY

Founder of print magazine *Birds of Unusual Vitality*, Eileen P. Kenny is green coffee buyer for Small Batch Roasting Co. in Melbourne, Australia.

MOHAMMAD KHANI

Mohammad Khani is managing director of the Iranian Barista Guild. He lives in Tehran.

BK KIM

BK Kim is a cofounding coffee roaster, green coffee buyer, and a barista at Fritz Coffee Company in Seoul.

RYAN KNAPP

Ryan Knapp is co-owner and cofounder of Madcap Coffee, where he also serves as the director of coffee. He is based in Grand Rapids, Michigan.

RANUT KONG-PICHAYANOND

Coffee enthusiast Ranut "Big" Kongpichayanond formerly worked at Kopplin's Coffee in St. Paul, Minnesota. These days he roasts coffee at Bubble Café in Bangkok, Thailand.

ANDRÉ KRÜGER

André Krüger is a founder of the Third Wave Wicheln project (thirdwavewicheln.com), an annual international secretly selected holiday gift exchange for lovers of specialty coffee. He is based in Hamburg, Germany.

BJÖRG BREND LAIRD

Björg Brend Laird is the company culture director at AKA Coffee in Oakland, California.

CORA LAMBERT

Cora Lambert is a coffee professional based in Chicago, Illinois, and was the founder/owner of Box Kite in New York City.

DEREK LAMBERTON

London-based Derek Lamberton is the publisher and editor of the London's Best Coffee app and the London Specialty Coffee map, along with apps and paper maps for Paris, New York, and Berlin, plus the London Brutalist Map.

DAVID LATOURELL

Former barista David Latourell is a coffee consultant based in Williamsburg, Virginia.

MATT LEE

Matt Lee is the owner of Manic Coffee in Toronto.

STEPHEN LEIGHTON

Stephen Leighton is the managing director of Has Bean Coffee based in Birmingham, England.

SAMUEL LEWONTIN

Beverage aficionado Samuel Lewontin is general manager at New York City's Everyman Espresso. He is the four-time fourth-place U.S. barista champion.

PETE LICATA

Pete Licata is based in a Kansas City, Missouri, and is the 2013 World Barista Champion; he also formed Licata Coffee Consultants to coach competitors and founded the website Roast Ratings (roastratings.com).

JAY LIJEWSKI

Jay Lijewski is a coffee consultant based in Tacoma, Washington.

HENGTEE LIM

Writer Hengtee Lim helms the Tokyo news desk for coffee website Sprudge (sprudge.com).

JARED LINZMEIER

Native Wisconsinite Jared Linzmeier is the owner of Ruby Coffee Roasters in Nelsonville, Wisconsin.

JOSH LITTLEFIELD

Josh Littlefield is a traveling coffee professional and founder of the the website Great American Coffee Tour (greatamericancoffeetour.com).

JIAYING LOU (ECHO LOU)

Echo Lou is the editor of *Coffee, Tea & Ice Cream Magazine*, based in Shanghai, China.

SCOTT LUCEY

Scott Lucey is the manager of Kickapoo Coffee's flagship cafe in Milwaukee, Wisconsin. He is also the inventor of the coffee drink Liquid Swords.

CYNTHIA LUDVIKSEN

Cindy Ludviksen is the managing director of World Coffee Events, overseeing the World Barista Championship and other international events. She lives in Durham, North Carolina.

CANDICE MADISON

Candice Madison is a certified Q sensory instructor and coffee consultant, splitting her time between London and New York City.

POUL MARK

Poul Mark is the founder and CEO of Transcend Coffee, based in Edmonton, Alberta, in Canada.

JOE MARROCCO

Based in Minneapolis, Minnesota, Joe Marrocco is a senior sales associate and the director of education for Café Imports.

JORDAN MICHELMAN

Jordan Michelman is the cofounder and editor of world coffee website Sprudge (sprudge.com).

STEVE MIERISCH
Texan-Nicaraguan Steve Mierisch is the founder of Pulley Collective, a shared coffee roasting incubation space with locations in Brooklyn, New York, and Oakland, California.

ANDREW MILSTEAD
Andrew Milstead is the owner of Seattle, Washington, coffee bar Milstead & Co., where he is also a barista.

JOHN MOORE
John Moore is a senior coffee trader for Volcafe Specialty Coffee, based in New York City.

JOSUE MORALES
Josue Morales is master roaster at Mayaland Coffee in Guatemala City, Guatemala, and director of TG Lab.

STEPHEN MORRISSEY
Stephen Morrissey is a former barista champion of Ireland and the 2008 World Barista Champion. He works as a coffee consultant and is senior creative advisor for the Specialty Coffee Association of America. He lives in Chicago.

ERIC MULLINS
Eric Mullins is a founder of Hyperion Coffee Roasters in Ypsilanti, Michigan.

NATHAN MYHRVOLD
Nathan Myhrvold is the founder of the Modernist Cuisine team. He is the lead author of all of their titles, including the upcoming 5-volume book *Modernist Bread*, on sale in 2017.

HARRYSSON NEIRA
Harrysson Neira is the 2014 World Barista Champion and founder of El Cafe de Harry in Lima, Peru.

ANTOINE NÉTIEN
Antoine Nétien is CEO and co-founder of Coutume Cafe in Paris, France.

DONALD NIEMYER
Don Niemyer is a partner and owner of Story Coffee Company, a cafe in a tiny house in Colorado Springs, Colorado.

BRIAN Ó CAOIMH (BRIAN O'KEEFFE)
Brian Ó Caoimh is the 2015 Irish Brewers Cup Champion and the owner of Meet Me in the Morning cafe in Dublin.

EMILY OAK
Emily Oak is state manager of operations and sales for Sensory Lab and St. Ali coffee in New South Wales, Australia.

MASAHIRO ONISHI
Masahiro Onishi is the owner of Switch Coffee, a roaster and coffee stand in Tokyo, Japan.

NIK OROSI
Nik Orosi is the director, roaster, and barista at Eliscafe in Zagreb, Croatia.

DOUG PALAS
Doug Palas is the director of tea and head tea buyer for Kilogram Coffee and Tea, in Chicago.

JENNIFER PARK
Jennifer Park is the owner of Diesel Café, Bloc11 Café, and Forge Baking Company, all based in Somerville, Massachusetts.

SANG HO PARK
Sang Ho Park is head of roasting and quality at Square Mile Coffee Roasters in London.

MATT PERGER
A partner in Melbourne's Sensory Lab, Matt Perger is a two-time barista champion of Australia, 2012 World Brewer's Cup Champion, and 2014 Coffee in Good Spirits World Champion. He is the founder of Barista Hustle (baristahustle.com).

LORENZO PERKINS
Lorenzo Perkins is co-owner of Fleet Coffee in Austin, Texas.

MICHAEL PHILLIPS
Michael Phillips is the 2010 World Barista Champion and was a founding partner of Handsome Coffee Roasters. He is currently the director of training for Blue Bottle Coffee's worldwide operations and is based in Los Angeles.

VINCE PICCOLO
Vince Piccolo is the owner of 49th Parallel Coffee Roasters just outside Vancouver, British Columbia.

WILL PRATT
Will Pratt is co-owner of Tandem Coffee Roasters in Portland, Maine.

BENJAMIN PUT
Ben Put is a three-time barista champion of Canada. He is a cofounder of Monogram Coffee in Calgary, Alberta, in Canada.

ALICE QUILLET
Based in Paris, France, Alice Quillet is a chef and owner at Ten Belles coffee shop and Le Bal Café.

FABRIZIO SENCIÓN RAMÍREZ (FABRIZIO SEED)
Multiple-time barista champion of Mexico, Fabrizio Seed is the founder of Cafeteria 5pm in Mexico City and co-owner of Café Sublime Coffee Roasters.

CAMILA RAMOS
Camila Ramos is the owner of ALL DAY coffee in Miami, Florida.

SCOTT RAO
Longtime cafe owner, consultant, and coffee science expert, Scott Rao is the author of *The Professional Barista's Handbook*, *Everything but Espresso*, and *The Coffee Roaster's Companion*.

ISABELA RAPOSEIRAS
Coffee roaster and educator Isabela Raposeiras is owner of Coffee Lab in São Paulo, Brazil.

SANTIAGO RIGONI
Santiago Rigoni is owner and barista at Toma Café in Madrid.

EILEEN HASSI RINALDI
Eileen Hassi Rinaldi owns and operates Ritual Coffee in San Francisco.

KEATON RITCHIE
Keaton Ritchie is found most often in Montreal, where he performs a variety of beverage and service roles and is de facto commissar at Café Myriade.

RAÚL RODAS
Raúl Rodas is the 2012 World Barista Champion and is a barista, roaster, and coffee sourcer based in Guatemala City, Guatemala. He is the owner and founder of Paradigma Coffee Roasters and Paradigma Café.

STEPHEN ROGERS
Stephen Rogers is the founder of Pipe & Tabor Roasting, as well as a pop-up barista. He lives in Brooklyn, New York.

CLANCY ROSE
Clancy Rose is a coffee roaster and cofounder of Wild Gift Coffee in Austin, Texas.

SCOUT ROSE
Scout Rose is visual and branding manager at Joe Coffee in New York City and Philadelphia, Pennsylvania.

TRISH ROTHGEB
Trish Rothgeb, the director of Q Grader and educational programs with the Coffee Quality Institute, is the cofounder of Wrecking Ball Coffee Roasters in San Francisco.

JONATHAN RUBINSTEIN
Former talent agent Jonathan Rubinstein is co-owner of Joe Coffee Company based in New York City and Philadelphia.

ANTHONY RUE
Anthony Rue is a co-owner and working barista at Volta Coffee in Gainesville, Florida, and a United States Barista Championship–certified sensory judge.

ZAK RYE
Ypsilanti, Michigan, native Zak Rye is the co-owner of Gaslight Coffee Roasters in Chicago.

JIM SABORIO
Jim Saborio is the owner of Comet Coffee in Ann Arbor, Michigan.

KRIS SCHACKMAN
Kris Schackman is the founder and roastmaster at Five Elephant in Berlin.

JASON SCHELTUS
Jason Scheltus is director at Market Lane Coffee in Melbourne, Australia.

ANYA SEREDA
Based in Adelaide, Australia, Anya Sereda is a coffee consultant and former barista.

BRONWEN SERNA
Bronwen Serna is a world-traveling coffee educator and barista and the 2004 United States Barista Champion. She currently lives in Singapore.

SASA SESTIC
Sasa Sestic is the managing director at Ona Café in Canberra, Australia, and is the 2015 World Barista Champion.

JON SHARP
Jon Sharp is a barista champion based in Edinburgh, Scotland, and operates these coffee shops there: Kilimanjaro Coffee, Wellington Coffee, Press Coffee, Project Coffee, Blackwood Coffee, and Thomas J. Walls.

ESTHER SHAW
Esther Shaw is a green coffee buyer, roaster, and coffee educator based in Astoria, Oregon. She is co-owner of Coptic Light Coffee.

KYONGHEE SHIN
Kyonghee Shin is events administrator for World Coffee Events. She lives in San Francisco.

MARK SMESRUD
Mark Smesrud is head roaster and director of organization for Purple Door Coffee in Denver, Colorado.

ANDY SPRENGER
Andy Sprenger is the 2011 and 2012 United States Brewers Cup Champion and the owner of Sweet Bloom Coffee Roasters in Denver, Colorado.

PAUL STACK
Paul Stack is operations director at Marco Beverage Systems in Dublin, Ireland, and is the president of the Specialty Coffee Association of Europe.

JESS STEFFY
Jess Steffy is owner of Square One Coffee in Philadelphia and Lancaster, Pennsylvania.

DAN STREETMAN
You can't take the Texas out of Dan Streetman, who currently works as director of coffee and vice president at Irving Farm Coffee Roasters in New York City.

FLEUR STUDD
Fleur Studd is director of Market Lane Coffee, Melbourne, Australia, and of Melbourne Coffee Merchants.

MARCO SUPLICY
Marco Suplicy is the founder of Suplicy Cafés Especiais S.A., based in São Paulo, Brazil.

SEBASTIAN SZTABZYB
Sebastian Sztabzyb is cofounder of Phil & Sebastian Coffee Roasters in Calgary, Alberta, in Canada.

KLAUS THOMSEN
Klaus Thomsen is the 2006 World Barista Champion and is one of the founding owners of the Coffee Collective in Copenhagen.

ALEX TRAN
Alex Tran is a founder of Capital Espresso in Toronto, Canada.

JARED TRUBY
(TIMOTHY JARED TRUBY)
Jared Truby is cofounder of the Cat & Cloud coffee company (catandcloud.com), podcast, and experience alongside longtime collaborator Chris Baca. He lives in Santa Cruz, California.

AARON ULTIMO
Aaron Ultimo is a United States Barista Championship–certified judge and the owner of Ultimo Coffee, a café and roastery business in Philadelphia.

MICHAEL VACLAV
Michael Vaclav is CEO and a cofounder of Caffé Medici, in Austin, Texas.

TIM VARNEY
Tim Varney is cofounder of the World AeroPress Championship and of the Bureaux Collective, a shared coffee roasting space in Melbourne, Australia.

TAMARA VIGIL
Tamara Vigil was born and raised in coffee, and currently works as trainer and lead barista at Cultiva Coffee in Lincoln, Nebraska.

TYLER J. WELLS
Coffee consultant to the stars and nonstars, Tyler Wells was a cofounder of Handsome Coffee Roasters and is an owner of Blacktop Coffee. He lives in Los Angeles.

TIM WENDELBOE
Tim Wendelboe, the 2004 World Barista Champion, is the owner and founder of Tim Wendelboe in Oslo, Norway, and co-founder of the Nordic Approach coffee sourcing company.

LAILA GHAMBARI WILLBUR
Raised in a coffee family in a coffee city, Laila Ghambari Willbur is the director of coffee at Cherry Street Coffee in Seattle, Washington.

RYAN WILLBUR
Ryan Willbur is a market development specialist for coffee equipment manufacturer La Marzocco. He is based in Seattle, Washington.

GÖKÇE YILDIRIM
Gökçe Yildirim is an Istanbul-based contributor to coffee website Sprudge (sprudge.com).

WILLE YLI-LUOMA
Finnish-born Wille Yli-Luoma is co-owner of Heart Coffee Roasters in Portland, Oregon.

MIKE YUNG
Mike Yung is the head of coffee development for Pacific Coffee based in Hong Kong. He also sits on the board of World Coffee Events.

DOUG ZELL
Doug Zell is the cofounder and CEO of Chicago, Los Angeles, New York, and San Francisco–based company Intelligentsia Coffee.

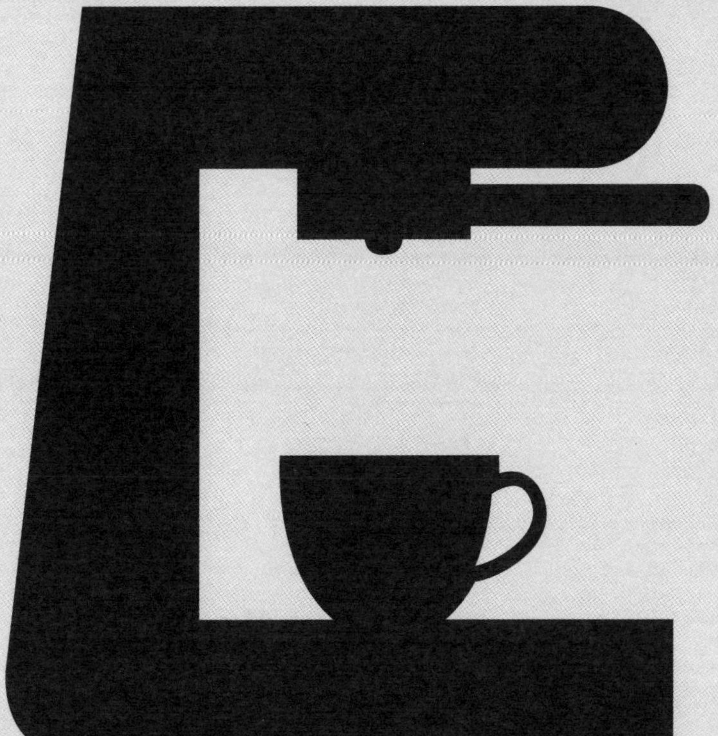

INDEX BY CONTRIBUTOR

AL MULLA, KHALID
Elbgold...150
Kaffee, Espresso Und Barista..............142
Kaffeemuseum...................................150
Tom & Serg......................................191

ALAMEDA, CHRISTOPHER
Arise Coffee Roasters.....................68–9
Espresso Vivace...............................254
Zig Zag Café....................................257

ALARY, NICO
Duchess of Spotswood........................33
Market Lane Coffee............................33

ALLEN, SARAH
Café Passmar...................................308

ALLEN, TRACY
St. Ali...32

AMORNPAHT THANAKUN, BODIN
Brave Roasters..................................60
Roast Coffee & Eatery.........................60

ANDREEN, CORY
Association Coffee.............................106
Father Carpenter...............................147
Five Elephant..................................146
Harbinger Coffee...............................217

BACA, CHRIS
Barista...242
Menotti's Coffee Stop........................228

BARNETT, ANDREW
The Coffee Collective...........................90

BARTOLOMÉ, MARCOS
Coutume...133
El Rey..298
Fragments..132
Karma Coffee Roasters.........................155

BELL, CAROLINE
Espresso Vivace...............................254

BENDA, ANTHONY
49th Parallel Coffee Roasters............205
Prufrock Coffee.................................107

BERNSON, ALEX
Chromatic Coffee...............................216
Everyman Espresso.............................298
Taglio..178
Tim Wendelboe...............................98–9

BERRY, JOANNE
Bulldog Edition.................................109
Espresso Lab Microroasters..............184
Factory Café....................................184
Father Coffee...................................184
Rosetta Roastery...............................184
Workshop (Clerkenwell)........................107

BONI, MARCUS
Bar Francis......................................220
Second Best Coffee.............................263

BOSCANA, GABRIEL
Algorithm Coffee Co...........................232
Bartavelle Coffee & Wine Bar..............232
Mazarine...234
Ritual Coffee Roasters........................235
Stumptown Coffee Roasters..............244
Timeless Coffee Roasters.....................232

BRONES, ANNA
Café Bretelles..................................128
Café Lomi.......................................134
Coava Coffee Roasters.........................242
Cream..135
Headfirst Coffee Roasters.....................124
Holybelly.......................................133
Honor Cafe......................................133
Kaffeverket/Snickarbacken 7...............85
Kale'i Kaffebar..................................86
KB Cafeshop....................................133
Loustic..132
Seniman Coffee Studio.........................56
Syster Marmelad.................................86
Viktors Kaffe.....................................86

BRYANT, JENNI
Amass...90
Ritual Coffee Roasters........................235

CADWALADER, ZAC
Amethyst Coffee................................238
Cherry Espresso Bar.............................277
Mercantile Dining & Provisions..........238

CARGUILO, KATIE
Ultimo Coffee...................................283

CARLSEN, ZACHARY
Scandinavian Embassy..........................124
Trouble Coffee Co...............................234

CHAMBERS, JORDAN
City and State...................................278

CHAN, DAWN
18 Grams..48
Barista Caffe.....................................49
Barista Jam.......................................48
Coco Espresso 701 Concept Store.......48
Hazel & Hershey..................................48
Sweet Bloom Coffee Roasters...........239

CHISTYAKOV, NICHOLAS
Café del Parco...................................174
Chernyi Cooperative............................174
Coffeemania.....................................175
Drop Coffee.......................................85
Ema..154
Les...175
Nomad..138
Tailor Made......................................160
The Underdog....................................160
Wakeup Café......................................174

CHO, NICHOLAS
Scout Coffee.....................................215

CLERC, NICOLAS
G&B Coffee.......................................225
Mocca...99

CONARY, SCOTT
4 Monkeys Coffee Shop................304
Bard Coffee................................282
Café Divino...............................305
Crafters...................................305
Kaldi's Coffee............................306
Rause Café e Vinho......................318
Ugly Duckling Coffee Bar................52
Unlimited Coffee Bar.....................70

CROCE, FELIPE
Black Oak Coffee Roasters..............216
Good Life Coffee...........................84
Sightglass Coffee........................235

CUNNINGHAM, JAY
Astro Coffee..............................260

DAVIES, GWILYM
Bar Termini..............................109
Filtry Dobra Kawa........................155
Kavarna Prazirna.........................154
Kofi Brand................................156
Machhörndl Kaffee........................142
Tesla Coffee..............................175

DEPAKAKIBO, JOELLEN
Everyman Espresso........................298
Linea Caffe...............................233

DEROSE, JAY
Crema Coffee House.......................238
The Ristretto Coffee Lounge.............217

DEVERAUX, SHANE
Bows & Arrows.............................198
Elysian Coffee............................204
Parlour...................................199
Ratio Coffee & Pastry....................198
Stumptown.................................257

EISENSTAT, CHARLIE
Collective Espresso.......................265
Fox in the Snow...........................265
Mission...................................266

FERRER, TUMI
Kaffibrugghúisd............................94

FISHER, RYAN
Palace Coffee Company.....................218
Prufrock Coffee...........................107
Slate Coffee Bar..........................256

FLYNN, DAVID NIGEL
Bella Vista Coffee........................306
El Dorao..................................307
Java..99
Revolver Coffee...........................204

FOREY, SEANNA
Azahar Café...............................315
Café Triciclo
  (mobile, various locations).............318
Caffè Terzi...............................178
Workshop (Marylebone)....................108

FORTUNE, BRENT
Alpine Modern Café........................217
Mecca......................................23
Patricia Coffee Brewers...................31
Salvage Coffee.............................22

FREESE, KALLE
Everyman Espresso........................298
Workshop (Fitzrovia).....................108

GILMAN, EVAN
ABCD (A Bunch of Caffeine Dealers)....56
Arbor.....................................232
Mangsi.....................................56
Modern Coffee.............................232
Revolver...................................56

GIULIANO, PETER
Bar Pasticceria Elisa.....................179

GLANVILLE, KYLE
Patricia Coffee Brewers...................31
Saint Frank...............................234

GOODLAXSON, PHIL
Verve Coffee Roasters.....................216

GORDON, JOHN
Colonna & Smalls..........................102
Ona Coffee.................................18

GRANT, SONJA BJÖRK
Auction Rooms..............................31
Bragginn-Clay and Coffee..................84
The Coffee Collective...................90, 91
Ditta Artigianale.........................179
Fumbally Cafe.............................116
Kaffihús Vesturbæjar......................95
Kaffislippur...............................94
Pallett Kaffikompaní......................84
Viva Sara Kaffée..........................120

GRIFFIN, ROBERT DAN
49th Parallel Coffee Roasters...........205
Café Museo................................306
The Coffee Collective.....................90
El Injerto Café...........................305
Go Get Em Tiger...........................226
The Room..................................305

GULABIOGLU, CAGATAY
Norm Coffee...............................168

HANSEN, METTE-MARIE
Café Ubuntu...............................184
Paramount Coffee Project..................22
Supreme Roastworks........................98

HARMON, COLIN
Kaph......................................117
Love Supreme..............................117
Proper Order..............................116
Roasted Brown Coffee Company..........117

HELFEN, BEN
Café Dulce................................227
Chattahoochee Coffee......................275
Crema Coffee..............................279
G&B Coffee................................225
Intelligentsia............................228

HETZEL, ANDREW
Caffè Artigiano...........................204
La Colombe (Fishtown)....................283
Unlimited Coffee Bar.......................70

HOCKIN, JOSH
Boxcar Social.............................209
Gravity Espresso & Wine Bar.............197
Monogram Coffee...........................196
Phil & Sebastian..........................196

HOF, KARINA
Man Met Bril Koffie.......................120
White Label Coffee........................125

HOFFMANN, JAMES
Caffè del Doge............................179
The Plan..................................103
Simon Says................................120

HUDSON, ELLIE
Barista...................................244
BLK MRKT..................................262
Madcap Coffee.............................261
Proud Mary.................................31

HUTCHINS, JONATHAN
Coffee Lab..............323
Single Origin Roasters..............23

ITOI, YUKO
Café Phalam..............64
Sentido..............64

IZAKI, HIDENORI
Auction Rooms..............31
Glitch Coffee..............68
The Local Coffee Stand..............70
Sarutahiko Coffee Atelier Senagwa.....68

JACOBSEN, HELLE
Bettina & Niccolò Corallo..............138

JAMES, SAMUEL
Abraço..............297
Bud's Coffee Bar..............209
Jacked Up.
 (mobile café, locations vary)..........208
Jason's Coffee Shop..............208

JESSUP, JAMIE
Dill..............94
Eleven Madison Park..............295
Fritz Coffee Company..............77
Maruyama Coffee..............69

JOHNSON, DREW
The Birds & The Beets..............204

JOHNSTON, JESSICA
Analog Coffee..............196
Bows & Arrows..............198
Elm Café..............197
Habit Coffee..............198
Hey Happy..............199
Little Sister Coffee Maker..............199
Make Coffee + Stuff..............199
Monogram Coffee..............196
Phil & Sebastian..............196
Rosso Coffee Roasters..............197
Thom Bargen..............200
Transcend..............197

KAMINSKY, BEN
G&B Coffee..............225
Reynard..............296
Saint Frank..............234
Tim Wendelboe..............98–9

KENNY, EILEEN P.
Bunker Coffee..............26
The Coffee Collective..............91
Exchange Specialty..............18
Merriweather Cafe..............26
Strauss FD..............26

KHANI, MOHAMMAD
Lamiz..............191
Mahtab Café..............190
Roberto Café..............190
Saraye Ameriha Boutique Café..........190
Street Lounge Café..............190
V Café..............190

KIM, BK
Bohemian..............78

KNAPP, RYAN
Buna 42..............308

KONGPICHAYANOND, RANUT
The Cupping Room..............49
Knock Box Coffee..............48

KRÜGER, ANDRÉ
Bonanza..............147
Coffee Nerd..............142
Companion Coffee..............146
Stockholm Espresso Club..............150

LAIRD, BJÖRG BREND
Café Europa 1989..............90

LAMBERT, CORA
Blackberry Market..............260
Blue Bottle (High Line)..............294
Go Get Em Tiger..............226
Intelligentsia..............228

LAMBERTON, DEREK
The Barn..............147
Browns of Brockley..............106
Chapter One..............146
Coffee Profilers..............146
Companion Coffee..............146
Curator's Coffee Studio..............106
Five Elephant..............146
Kontakt..............154
Lyle's..............109
Nano Kaffee..............147

LATOURELL, DAVID
Koppi..............85
Solberg & Hansen Konseptbutikk........98
Tim Wendelboe..............98–9

LEE, MATT
Be a Good Neighbor..............71
Go Get Em Tiger..............226

LEIGHTON, STEPHEN
Bold Street..............102
Caravan Roasters..............106
Kaffeine..............107
Roaster Boutique..............318

LEWONTIN, SAMUEL
Amor y Amargo..............297
Barista..............242
Little Collins..............295
Milstead & Co..............256
Parlor Coffee (inside Persons of.
 Interest barbershop)..............296
Voyager Espresso..............297

LICATA, PETE
49th Parallel Coffee Roasters..........205
Boxcar Coffee..............239
Parisi Artisan Coffee..............263
Tanamera..............56

LIJEWSKI, JAY
G&B Coffee..............225
Street Bean..............254

LIM, HENGTEE
Arise Coffee Roasters..............68–9
Café Les Jeux..............69
Switch Coffee..............69

LINZMEIER, JARED
Café Pergamino..............315
Either/Or..............243
Good Coffee..............243
Milstead & Co..............256
Sqirl..............227
Volta Coffee, Tea & Chocolate..........274

LITTLEFIELD, JOSH
Angelina's............................284
Blacktop Coffee....................224
Bolt Coffee (at the Dean Hotel)..........284
Buðin..................................295
Barismo................................289
George Howell Coffee................288
Le Pista Café Montréal.
(mobile café, locations vary)..........201
Seven Stars Bakery...................284
The Shop...............................284
Swings.................................279

LOU, ECHO
Café Bintino..........................42
Café Mingqian........................43
Mondoli Studio.......................43
Real Coffee...........................42
Rose Cafe.............................42
Uni-Uni................................42
Voyage Coffee........................42

LUCEY, SCOTT
Bradbury's............................266
Colectivo Coffee.....................267
Five Watt..............................263
Four Barrel Coffee...................233
Java...................................99
Madcap Coffee........................261

LUDVIKSEN, CYNTHIA
5 Brewing.............................76
Café del Volcán......................43
Club Espresso........................76
Coffee Libre..........................76
Coffee Seed...........................77
Seesaw Coffee.........................43

MADISON, CANDICE
5 Brewing.............................76
46B Espresso Hut.....................108
Colonna & Smalls.....................102
Koppi.................................85

MARROCCO, JOE
The Coffee Ethic.....................263
Kaldi's Coffee........................263
Ruby Coffee Roasters................267

MICHELMAN, JORDAN
All That Is Coffee....................112
Assembly.............................30
Avenue Coffee........................112
Café du Monde........................277
Customs...............................36
Everyday Coffee......................31
Flight Coffee.........................37
Heart Coffee Roasters...............243
Kokako Organic Coffee...............36
Koko Coffee & Design................124
Laboratorio..........................112
Papercup Coffee Company............112
Peña..................................112
Scandinavian Embassy................124
Stardust Video & Coffee.............275

MIERISCH, STEVE
Fort Defiance.........................296

MILSTEAD, ANDREW
Canlis................................255
Garage Auto Hero.....................220
Heart Coffee Roasters...............243
Lava Java.............................221
Olympia Coffee Roasters.............220
Vif....................................256

MOORE, JOHN
Coffee Lab............................323
Devoción Café........................296
Octavio Café.........................322

MORALES, JOSUE
Elixr Coffee Roasters...............283
Gabee.................................52
Lucca Cafés Especiais...............318
Tiago Coffee Bar + Kitchen.........226

MORRISSEY, STEPHEN
Elysian Coffee........................204
Leila's Shop..........................109

MULLINS, ERIC
Comet Coffe..........................260

MYHRVOLD, NATHAN
Bear Pond Espresso..................69
Espresso Vivace......................254
Sant'Eustachio il Caffè.............178
Tim Wendelboe.......................98–9
Zombie Runner.......................214

NEIRA, HARRYSSON
The Coffee Road......................314

NÉTIEN, ANTOINE
Seven Seeds..........................30

NIEMYER, DONALD
21st Street Coffee & Tea............284
Brash Coffee..........................278
Coffee Commissary...................226
The Commonplace Coffee Co....283
Constellation Coffee.................283
The Lab by Alchemy Coffee.........279
Onyx Coffee Lab......................274
Render................................288
Stone Creek Coffee Roasters........267
Tandem Coffee Roasters.............282
Timeless Coffee Roasters...........232

CAOIMH, BRIAN Ó
3fe....................................116
Fragments............................132
Vice (inside Wigwam)................117

OAK, EMILY
Bar 9.................................19
Dandelion & Driftwood..............26
Five Senses...........................19
Gauge.................................26
Intelligentsia........................227
Pourboy...............................26
Tim Wendelboe.......................98–9

ONISHI, MASAHIRO
About Life Coffee Brewers..........70
Market Lane Coffee..................33

OROSI, NIK
Bistro 75..............................164
Mak Na Konac........................164
Pržionica D59B.......................160

PALAS, DOUG
G&B Coffee...........................225

PARK, SANG HO
Fritz Coffee Company...............77

PERGER, MATT
Fika Fika.............................52
Fritz Coffee Company...............77
Nylon.................................57

PERKINS, LORENZO
Blue Bottle Coffee...................234
Cuvee Coffee Bar....................249
Flat Track Coffee....................249
Houndstooth Coffee.................250
Patricia Coffee Brewers.............31

PHILLIPS, MICHAEL
Dead River Coffee...............................261

PICCOLO, VINCE
Lighthouse Roasters...........................255

PRATT, WILL
Blue Bottle Coffee.............................234

PUT, BENJAMIN
The Coffee Collective..........................90
Little Sister Coffee Maker................199
Parlour...199
Phil & Sebastian..............................196
Thom Bargen....................................200

QUILLET, ALICE
Télescope...132
Third Rail...298

RAMÍREZ, FABRIZIO SENCIÓN
Caffe Sospeso...................................307
The Coffee Collective..........................90

RAMOS, CAMILA
Go Get Em Tiger................................226
Joe Pro Shop....................................294
Smith Canteen..................................295
Sólo Espresso...................................276
Verve Coffee Roasters.......................224

RAO, SCOTT
Bayleaf Cafe.......................................18
Be Speciality......................................36
Bread & Sons Bakery.........................200
Clandestino Roasters...........................18
Ditta Artigianale................................179
Edition Coffee Roasters.......................22
Go Get Em Tiger................................226
Harry's..22
Irons and Craig..................................18
Kopplin's Coffee................................263
Můjšálek Kávy...................................154
Scout & Co.......................................285
Shaker Dam Coffeehouse..................282
Timberyard UK (Seven Dials)..............108
Typika Artisan Roasters.......................19
Vanguard Speciality Coffee Co...........36

RIGONI, SANTIAGO
Climpson & Sons..............................108
Satan's Coffee Corner.......................138
Verve Coffee Roasters.......................216

RINALDI, EILEEN HASSI
Analog Coffee...................................254
Café Evoke.......................................266
Ten Belles...134

RITCHIE, KEATON
Pikolo Espresso Bar..........................201
Pinecone..200
Sam James Coffee Bar.......................209

RODAS, RAÚL
Coffeemania.....................................175

ROGERS, STEPHEN
Anthracite..76
Fritz Coffee Company..........................77
Hell Cafe..78

ROSE, SCOUT
Finca La Campiña..............................314
Tostaduria Bisetti..............................314

RUBINSTEIN, JONATHAN
Bird Rock Coffee Roasters.................215
Pour Cleveland.................................265

RUE, ANTHONY
All Day...275
Brew Five Points...............................274
Empire State South...........................275
Sweetleaf...297
Workshop (Clerkenwell)....................107

RYE, ZAK
Caffe Streets.....................................270
Caffe Vita...257
Cultivate Coffee and Tap House........262
Hyperion Coffee................................262
Ipsento...270
Metric Coffee....................................270
Victrola Coffee Roasters...................255
The Wormhole...................................271

SABORIO, JIM
Café Brumas del Zurquí.....................304

SCHACKMAN, KRIS
Coffee Lab..323
Isso é Café..322
Nobelhart & Schmutzig.....................147
Seesaw Coffee....................................43
Tazza d'Oro......................................178
Viva Espresso....................................304

SCHELTUS, JASON
Ritual Coffee Roasters.......................233

SEREDA, ANYA
Elementary Coffee...............................18
Monday's Coffee Store.........................19
Sensory Lab.......................................30

SERNA, BRONWEN
Café de L'Ambre..................................68
El Zonte S-Cool.................................304
Espressamente Illy............................178
Nanyang Old Coffee............................57
Vif..256

SESTIC, SASA
Aroma Cafe.......................................307
The Maling Room.................................30

SHARP, JON
Artisan Coffee...................................102
Fortitude Coffee................................103

SHAW, ESTHER
Arise Coffee Roasters........................68–9
Budin..295
Fika Fika...52
Intelligentsia (Chicago).....................270
Peloso Coffee Roasters........................53

SHIN, KYONGHEE
Coffee Seed..77
Coffee Temple.....................................77
Fika Fika...52
Fritz Coffee Company..........................77

SMESRUD, MARK
Archetype Coffee...............................264
Corvus Coffee...................................239
Dogwood Coffee................................262
Fireflour Pizza...................................265
Sweet Bloom Coffee Roasters...........239
Two Rivers Craft Coffee Company......216
Water Avenue Coffee.........................242
Zoka Coffee......................................256

SPRENGER, ANDY
Café Grumpy.....................................294
Ceremony Coffee Roasters................277

STACK, PAUL
Coffeeangel (SAS).............................116
Tamp and Stitch................................117
Top Paddock.......................................32

STEFFY, JESS
The Daily Press ... 277
Everyman Espresso ... 298

STREETMAN, DAN
Caffé Medici ... 250
Wrecking Ball Coffee Roasters ... 233

STUDD, FLEUR
Altius ... 31
Coffee Alchemy ... 22

SZTABZYB, SEBASTIAN
Espresso Vivace ... 254
Prufrock Coffee ... 107
Tim Wendelboe ... 98–9

THOMSEN, KLAUS
Patricia Coffee Brewers ... 31
Reykjavík Roasters ... 94
Scandinavian Embassy ... 124

TRAN, ALEX
Boxcar Social ... 209
Manic Coffee and Gelato ... 208
Reunion Island Coffee ... 208
Sam James Coffee Bar ... 209
Tokyo Smoke Found ... 208

TRUBY, JARED
Menotti's Coffee Stop ... 228

ULTIMO, AARON
Coava Coffee Roasters ... 242
Intelligentsia Mini-Bar
(outside the High Line Hotel) ... 294
Jubala ... 278
Sightglass Coffee ... 235

VACLAV, MICHAEL
Fleet Coffee ... 249

VARNEY, TIM
Small Batch ... 32
Tim Wendelboe ... 98–9

VIGIL, TAMARA
Archetype Coffee ... 264

WELLS, TYLER J.
Barista ... 242
Espresso Embassy ... 155
The Kettle Black ... 32

WENDELBOE, TIM
Coffee Lab ... 323
Eliscaffe ... 164

WILLBUR, LAILA GHAMBARI
G&B Coffee ... 225
Good Coffee ... 243
Sam Café ... 191
Vif ... 256

WILLBUR, RYAN
Ditta Artigianale ... 179
Heart Coffee Roasters ... 243
Holybelly ... 133
The Seed ... 274
Télescope ... 132
Workshop (Clerkenwell) ... 107

YILDIRIM, GÖKÇE
Kronotrop ... 168
Mandabatmaz ... 168
Petra Roasting Co. ... 168
Şark Kahvesi (at the Grand Bazaar) ... 169

YLI-LUOMA, WILLE
49th Parallel Coffee Roasters ... 205

YUNG, MIKE
Colonna & Smalls ... 102
Da Matteo ... 86
Fuglen ... 70

ZELL, DOUG
Panther Coffee ... 275
Santo Grão ... 322

INDEX BY COUNTRY

AUSTRALIA
Bar 9......................................19
Elementary Coffee....................19
Exchange Specialty..................19
Monday's Coffee Store..............19
Brisbane
Bunker Coffee.........................26
Dandelion & Driftwood..............26
Gauge....................................26
Merriweather Cafe....................26
Pourboy.................................26
Strauss FD.............................26
Byron Bay
Bayleaf Cafe...........................18
Canberra
Ona Coffee.............................18
Melbourne
Altius....................................31
Assembly...............................30
Auction Rooms........................31
Duchess of Spotswood.............33
Everyday Coffee......................31
The Kettle Black.......................32
The Maling Room......................30
Market Lane Coffee..................33
Patricia Coffee Brewers............31
Proud Mary.............................31
St. Ali....................................32
Sensory Lab............................30
Seven Seeds...........................30
Small Batch............................32
Top Paddock...........................32
Noosa
Clandestino Roasters................18
Perth
Typika Artisan Roasters.............19
Rockingham
Five Senses............................19
Sydney
Coffee Alchemy.......................22
Edition Coffee Roasters.............22
Harry's..................................22
Mecca...................................23
Paramount Coffee Project..........22
Salvage Coffee........................22
Single Origin Roasters..............23
Yamba
Irons and Craig........................18

BELGIUM
Ghent
Simon Says............................120
Kortrijk
Viva Sara Kaffée......................120

BOLIVIA
La Paz
Roaster Boutique.....................318

BRAZIL
Curitiba
Lucca Cafes Especiais..............318
Rause Café e Vinho..................318
São Paulo
Coffee Lab.............................323
Isso é Café.............................322
Octavio Café...........................322
Santo Grão.............................322
Suplicy Café...........................322

CANADA
Calgary
Analog Coffee.........................196
Gravity Espresso & Wine Bar......197
Monogram Coffee.....................196
Phil & Sebastian......................196
Rosso Coffee Roasters.............197
Edmonton
Elm Café................................197
Transcend..............................197
Halifax
Two If By Sea..........................200
Hamilton
Pinecone................................200
Jasper
Grémio...................................198
Montreal
Café Myriade..........................201
Pikolo Espresso Bar.................201
Le Pista Café Montréal.
(mobile café, locations vary)......201
Ottawa
Bread & Sons Bakery................200
Red Deer
Dose.....................................198
Saskatoon
Collective Coffee.....................201
Museo....................................201

Toronto
Jacked Up.
(mobile café, locations vary)......208
Vancouver
49th Parallel Coffee Roasters.....205
The Birds & The Beets...............204
Boxcar Social.........................209
Bud's Coffee Bar.....................209
Caffè Artigiano........................204
Elysian Coffee.........................204
Jason's Coffee Shop.................208
Manic Coffee and Gelato...........208
Prado Café.............................205
Reunion Island Coffee..............208
Revolver Coffee.......................204
Sam James Coffee Bar..............209
Timbertrain Coffee Roasters.......205
Tokyo Smoke Found..................208
Vernon
Ratio Coffee & Pastry................198
Victoria
Bows & Arrows........................198
Habit Coffee...........................198
Hey Happy..............................199
Winnipeg
Little Sister Coffee Maker...........199
Make Coffee + Stuff..................199
Parlour..................................199
Thom Bargen..........................200

CHILE
Santiago
Café Triciclo.
(mobile, various locations)..........318

CHINA
Beijing
Real Coffee.............................42
Voyage Coffee..........................42
Dailan
Café Bintino.............................42
Guangzhou
Rose Cafe...............................42
Hong Kong
18 Grams................................48
Barista Caffe...........................49
Barista Jam.............................48
Coco Espresso 701 Concept Store...48
The Cupping Room.....................49

Hazel & Hershey...............48
Knock Box Coffee.............48
Nanjing
Uni-Uni..............................42
Shanghai
Café del Volcán................43
Café Mingqian..................43
Seesaw Coffee.................43
Sichuan
Mondoli Studio.................43

COLOMBIA
Bogotá
Amor Perfecto..................315
Azahar Café.....................315
Medellín
Café Pergamino...............315

COSTA RICA
San José
Café Brumas del Zurquí....304
Café don Mayo.................304

CROATIA
Zagreb
Bistro 75..........................164
Eliscaffe..........................164
Express Bar......................164
Mak Na Konac..................164

THE CZECH REPUBLIC
Prague
Ema.................................154
Kavarna Prazirna..............154
Můjšálek Kávy...................154

DENMARK
Aarhus
La Cabra..........................84
Copenhagen
Amass..............................90
Café Europa 1989.............90
The Coffee Collective........90
Democratic Coffee............91
Forloren Espresso.............91
Prolog Coffee Bar.............91
Frederiksberg
The Coffee Collective........91

EL SALVADOR
Antiguo Cuscatlán
4 Monkeys Coffee Shop.....304
El Zonte
El Zonte S-Cool................304

San Salvador
Crafters...........................305
Viva Espresso...................304

FINLAND
Helsinki
Good Life Coffee...............84
Kahvila Siili......................84

FRANCE
Bordeaux
Alchimiste........................128
Blacklist...........................128
Lille
Tamper Espresso Bar........128
Lyon
La Boîte à Café.................128
Paris
Café Lomi........................134
Coutume..........................133
Cream..............................135
La Fontaine de Belleville....134
Fragments........................132
Hexagone Café.................134
Holybelly.........................133
Honor Cafe.......................133
KB Caféshop....................133
Loustic............................132
Télescope........................132
Ten Belles........................134
Strasbourg
Café Bretelles...................128

GERMANY
Berlin
The Barn..........................147
Bonanza...........................147
Chapter One.....................146
Coffee Profilers.................146
Companion Coffee.............146
Father Carpenter...............147
Five Elephant....................146
Nano Kaffee......................147
Nobelhart & Schmutzig......147
Hamburg
Elbgold............................150
Kaffeemuseum..................150
Speicherstandt Kafferösterei...150
Stockholm Espresso Club...150
Heidelberg
Coffee Nerd......................142
Munich
Kaffee, Espresso Und Barista...142
Nuremberg
Machhörndl Kaffee............142

GREECE
Athens
Tailor Made.......................160
The Underdog....................160

GUATEMALA
Antigua
Bella Vista Coffee.............306
Guatemala City
Café Divino.......................305
El Injerto Café...................305
The Room.........................305
Huehuetenango
Café Museo.......................306

HONDURAS
Marcala
Aroma Cafe.......................307
Peña Blanca
El Dorao...........................307
Santa Rosa de Copan
Kaldi's Coffee...................306

HUNGARY
Budapest
Espresso Embassy.............155
Kontakt............................154
My Little Melbourne...........155

ICELAND
Hafnarfjördur
Pallett Kaffikompaní...........84
Hrunamannahreppur
Bragginn Clay and Coffee...84
Reykjavík
Dill..................................94
Kaffibrugghúisd.................94
Kaffihús Vesturbæjar..........95
Kaffislippur......................94
Reykjavík Roasters............94

INDONESIA
Bali
Denpasar
Mangsi.............................56
Kuta
Revolver...........................56
Ubud
Seniman Coffee Studio.......56

JAKARTA
ABCD (A Bunch..................
of Caffeine Dealers)...........56
Tanamera..........................56

IRAN
Kashan
Saraye Ameriha Boutique Café......190
Shiraz
Street Lounge Café...........190
Tehran
Lamiz...........191
Mahtab Café...........190
Roberto Café...........190
Sam Café...........191
V Café...........190

ITALY
Bologna
Caffè Terzi...........178
Florence
Ditta Artigianale...........179
Lucca
Bar Pasticceria Elisa...........179
Milan
Taglio...........178
Rome
Sant'Eustachio il Caffè...........178
Tazza d'Oro...........178
Trieste
Espressamente Illy...........178
Venice
Caffè del Doge...........179

JAPAN
Kyoto
Café Phalam...........64
Sentido...........64
Tokyo
About Life Coffee Brewers...........70
Arise Coffee Roasters...........68–9
Be a Good Neighbor...........71
Bear Pond Espresso...........69
Café de L'Ambre...........68
Café Les Jeux...........69
Fuglen...........70
Glitch Coffee...........68
The Local Coffee Stand...........70
Maruyama Coffee...........69
Sarutahiko Coffee...........
Atelier Senagwa...........68
Switch Coffee...........69
Unlimited Coffee Bar...........70

KENYA
Nairobi
Café Ubuntu...........184

MALAYSIA
Kuala Lumpur
VCR...........56

MEXICO
Mexico City
Buna 42...........308
Café Passmar...........308
Tijuana
Caffe Sospeso...........307

THE NETHERLANDS
Amsterdam
Headfirst Coffee Roasters...........124
Koko Coffee & Design...........124
Scandinavian Embassy...........124
White Label Coffee...........125
Maastricht
Maison Blanche Dael...........120
Rotterdam
Man Met Bril Koffie...........120

NEW ZEALAND
Auckland
Be Speciality...........36
Kokako Organic Coffee...........36
Dunedin
Vanguard Speciality Coffee Co........36
Wellington
Customs...........36
Flight Coffee...........37

NORTHERN IRELAND
Belfast
Established Coffee...........103

NORWAY
Oslo
Java...........99
Mocca...........99
Solberg & Hansen Konseptbutikk....98
Supreme Roastworks...........98
Tim Wendelboe...........98–9

PERU
Lima
Arabica...........314
Café Verde...........314
The Coffee Road...........314
El Café de Harry...........314
Finca La Campiña...........314
Tostaduria Bisetti...........314

POLAND
Kraków
Karma Roasters...........155
Warsaw
Filtry Dobra Kawa...........155
Kofi Brand...........156
Ministerstwo Kavy...........156
Relaks Kawiarnia...........156

PORTUGAL
Lisbon
Bettina & Niccolò Corallo...........138
Fábrica Coffee Roasters...........138

REPUBLIC OF IRELAND
Dublin
3fe...........116
Coffeeangel (SAS)...........116
Fumbally Cafe...........116
Kaph...........117
Love Supreme...........117
Proper Order...........116
Roasted Brown Coffee Company.....117
Tamp and Stitch...........117
Vice (Inside Wigwam)...........117

THE RUSSIAN FEDERATION
Moscow
The Burger Brothers...........175
Café del Parco...........174
Chernyi Cooperative...........174
Coffeemania...........175
Double B...........174
Good Enough Coffee...........175
Les...........175
The Man and the Steamboat...........174
Wakeup Café...........174
Yekaterinburg
Tesla Coffee...........175

SCOTLAND
Edinburgh
Artisan Coffee...........103
Fortitude Coffee...........103
Glasgow
All That is Coffee...........112
Avenue Coffee...........112
Laboratorio...........112
Papercup Coffee Company...........112
Peña...........112

SERBIA
Belgrade
Kofein...........160
Pržionica D59B...........160

SINGAPORE
Nanyang Old Coffee..........................57
Nylon..57

SOUTH AFRICA
Cape Town
Espresso Lab Microroasters............184
Rosetta Roastery...............................184
Durban
Factory Café.......................................184
Johannesburg
Father Coffee.....................................184

SOUTH KOREA
Seoul
2ffect Coffee.......................................78
5 Brewing...76
Anthracite..76
Bohemian...78
Club Espresso....................................76
Coffee Libre.......................................76
Coffee Seed..77
Coffee Temple....................................77
Fritz Coffee Company........................77
Hell Cafe...78

SPAIN
Barcelona
Nomad...138
Satan's Coffee Corner.....................138

SWEDEN
Gothenburg
Alkemisten..87
Da Matteo..86
Kale'i Kaffebar...................................86
Syster Marmelad................................86
Viktors Kaffe.......................................86
Skåne
Koppi...85
Stockholm
Drop Coffee...85
Johan & Nystrom Concept Store....85
Kaffeverket/Snickarbacken 7...........85

TAIWAN
Keelung
Homerun Roasters..............................44
Taichung
Café Lulu...44
Retro/Mojocoffee...............................44
Taipei City
Coffee Lover's Planet.........................52
Fika Fika..52
Gabee..52
Peloso Coffee Roasters.....................53

Rahdesign Café..................................52
Ugly Duckling Coffee Bar.................52
WOW (Woolloomooloo Out West)..53

THAILAND
Bangkok
Brave Roasters...................................60
Ceresia Coffee....................................60
Gallery Drip Coffee............................60
Phil Coffee Company.........................60
Roast Coffee & Eatery.......................60

TURKEY
Istanbul
Kronotrop..168
Mandabatmaz...................................168
Norm Coffee......................................168
Petra Roasting Co.............................168
Şark Kahvesi
(at the Grand Bazaar)....................169

UNITED ARAB EMIRATES
Dubai
The Sum of Us..................................191
Tom & Serg..191

UNITED KINGDOM
Belfast
Established Coffee............................102
Bath
Colonna & Smalls.............................102
Cardiff
The Plan...103
Edinburgh
Artisan Coffee...................................102
Fortitude Coffee................................103
Glasgow
All That Is Coffee..............................112
Avenue Coffee...................................112
Laboratorio.......................................112
Papercup Coffee Company.............112
Peña...112
Liverpool
Bold Street..102
London
46B Espresso Hut.............................108
Association Coffee............................106
Bar Termini.......................................109
Browns of Brockley..........................106
Bulldog Edition.................................109
Caravan Roasters.............................106
Climpson & Sons..............................108
Craft...106
Curator's Coffee Studio...................106
Dose Espresso...................................106

Kaffeine...107
Leila's Shop.......................................109
Lyle's..109
Prufrock Coffee.................................107
Timberyard UK (Seven Dials).........108
Workshop (Clerkenwell)...................107
Workshop (Fitzrovia)........................108
Workshop (Marylebone)...................108
Stansted
Harris and Hoole...............................102

UNITED STATES OF AMERICA
Alabama
Birmingham
Seeds Coffee Co...............................274
Arizona
Jerome
The Flatiron.......................................214
Phoenix
Cartel Coffee Lab.............................214
Arkansas
Bentonville
Onyx Coffee Lab...............................274
California
Berkeley
Algorithm Coffee Co.........................232
Bartavelle Coffee & Wine Bar........232
Clovis
Kuppa Joy...214
Los Angeles
Blacktop Coffee.................................224
Café Dulce...227
Coffee Commissary..........................226
Cognoscenti Coffee..........................224
G&B Coffee.......................................225
Go Get Em Tiger (Hancock Park).....226
Go Get Em Tiger (Los Feliz)............227
Intelligentsia (Silver Lake)..............227
Intelligentsia (Venice).....................228
Menotti's Coffee Stop.......................228
Proof Bakery.....................................224
Sqirl..227
Tiago Coffee Bar + Kitchen............226
Verve Coffee Roasters.....................224
Oakland
Arbor..232
Modern Coffee..................................232
Timeless Coffee Roasters...............232
Palo Alto
Zombie Runner..................................214
San Diego
Bird Rock Coffee Roasters..............215
San Francisco
Blue Bottle Coffee............................234
Four Barrel Coffee............................233

Linea Caffe..................................233
Mazarine.....................................234
Ritual Coffee Roasters.....................
   (Mission District)......................233
Ritual Coffee Roasters.....................
   (Western Addition).....................235
Saint Frank.................................234
Sightglass Coffee..........................235
Trouble Coffee Co..........................234
Wrecking Ball Coffee Roasters.....233
San Luis Obispo
Scout Coffee................................215
Santa Barbara
The French Press...........................215
Santa Clara
Chromatic Coffee...........................216
Santa Cruz
Cat & Cloud Coffee Co....................216
Verve Coffee Roasters...................216
Ukaiah
Black Oak Coffee Roasters.............216
Colorado
Arvada
Two Rivers Craft Coffee...................
   Company..................................216
Boulder
Alpine Modern Café.......................217
Denver
Amethyst Coffee...........................238
Boxcar Coffee...............................239
Corvus Coffee..............................239
Crema Coffee House.......................238
Mercantile Dining & Provisions.....238
Novo Coffee.................................238
Fort Collins
Harbinger Coffee...........................217
Lakewood
Sweet Bloom Coffee Roasters......239
Steamboat Springs
The Ristretto Coffee Lounge..........217
Florida
Boca Raton
The Seed.....................................274
Gainesville
Volta Coffee, Tea & Chocolate......274
Jacksonville
Bold Bean Coffee Roasters............274
Brew Five Points...........................274
Miami
All Day.......................................275
Miami Beach
Panther Coffee.............................275
Orlando
Stardust Video & Coffee................275
Georgia
Atlanta

Chattahoochee Coffee...................275
Empire State South........................275
Spiller Park..................................276
Savannah
The Florence................................276
Perc...276
Idaho
Post Falls
Doma..218
Illinois
Chicago
Caffe Streets................................270
Intelligentsia (Chicago).................270
Ipsento.......................................270
Metric Coffee...............................270
The Wormhole..............................271
Glen Ellyn
Blackberry Market.........................260
Kansas
Topeka
PT's Coffee..................................260
Kentucky
Louisville
Gralehaus....................................276
Louisiana
New Orleans
Café du Monde.............................277
Cherry Espresso Bar......................277
Sólo Espresso..............................276
Maine
Portland
Bard Coffee.................................282
Tandem Coffee Roasters...............282
Maryland
Annapolis
Ceremony Coffee Roasters...........277
Massachusetts
Boston
George Howell Coffee....................288
Pavement Coffeehouse..................288
Render..288
Cambridge
1369 Coffee House........................289
Crema Café..................................289
Barismo......................................289
Simon's Coffee Shop.....................289
West Stockbridge
Shaker Dam Coffeehouse..............282
Michigan
Ann Arbor
Comet Coffee...............................260
Detroit
Astro Coffee.................................260
Grand Rapids
Madcap Coffee..............................261
Rowster.......................................261

Marquette
Dead River Coffee..........................261
Traverse City
BLK MRKT....................................262
Ypsilanti
Cultivate Coffee and Tap House..262
Hyperion Coffee............................262
Minnesota
Lutsen
Fika..262
Minneapolis
Dogwood Coffee............................262
Five Watt.....................................263
St. Paul
Kopplin's Coffee............................263
Missouri
Clayton
Kaldi's Coffee...............................263
Kansas City
Parisi Artisan Coffee......................263
Second Best Coffee.......................263
St. Louis
Blueprint Coffee............................264
Olio...264
Sump Coffee.................................264
Springfield
Brick & Mortar Coffee....................264
The Coffee Ethic...........................263
Nebraska
Omaha
Archetype Coffee...........................264
Nevada
Las Vegas
Publicus......................................218
New Hampshire
Nashua
Pressed Café................................282
New York
Ithaca
Gimme! Coffee..............................282
New York City
Brooklyn
Budin..295
Café Grumpy................................296
Devoción Café..............................296
Fort Defiance...............................296
Parlor Coffee (inside Persons ....
   of Interest barbershop)..............296
Reynard.......................................296
Smith Canteen..............................295
Manhattan
Chelsea
Blue Bottle (High Line)...294
Café Grumpy................................294
Intelligentsia Mini-Bar....................
   (outside the High Line Hotel)....294

Joe Pro Shop.................................294
East Village
Abraço...297
Amor y Amargo...........................297
Financial District
Voyager Espresso.........................297
Flatiron District
Eleven Madison Park....................295
Greenwich Village
Third Rail....................................298
Lower East Side
El Rey...298
Midtown East
Little Collins...............................295
SoHo
Everyman Espresso.....................298
Queens
Sweetleaf....................................297
North Carolina
Charlotte
The Daily Press...........................277
Not Just Coffee...........................277
Raleigh
Jubala...278
North Dakota
Bismarck
Fireflour Pizza.............................265
Ohio
Cincinnati
Collective Espresso.....................265
Cleveland
Pour Cleveland...........................265
Columbus
Fox in the Snow..........................265
Mission.......................................266
Oklahoma
Edmond
Café Evoke..................................266
Oregon
Corvallis
Tried & True Coffee.....................218
Portland
Barista (Alberta).........................242
Barista..244
Coava Coffee Roasters................242
Either/Or....................................243
Good Coffee...............................243
Heart Coffee Roasters.................243
Stumptown Coffee Roasters........244
Water Avenue Coffee...................242
Pennsylvania
Philadelphia
La Colombe (Fishtown).................283
Elixr Coffee Roasters...................283
Ultimo Coffee.............................283
Pittsburgh

21st Street Coffee & Tea.................284
The Commonplace Coffee Co......283
Constellation Coffee.....................283
Rhode Island
Bristol
Angelina's...................................284
Providence
Bolt Coffee (at the Dean Hotel).....284
Seven Stars Bakery.....................284
The Shop....................................284
South Carolina
Charleston
City Lights Coffee.........................278
Travelers Rest
Travelers Rest.............................278
South Dakota
Sioux Falls
Coffea Roasterie.........................266
Tennessee
Chattanooga
Brash Coffee...............................278
Memphis
City and State..............................278
Nashville
Crema Coffee..............................278
Texas
Amarillo
Palace Coffee Company...............218
Austin
Caffé Medici................................250
Cenote..248
Cuvee Coffee Bar........................249
Figure 8 Coffee Purveyor............248
Flat Track Coffee.........................249
Fleet Coffee................................249
Houndstooth Coffee.....................250
Once Over Coffee Bar..................248
Patika Wine and Coffee...............250
Thunderbird Coffee.....................248
Coppell
Zenzero Kitchen.........................218
Dallas
Cultivar Coffee Bar......................219
Davis Street Espresso.................218
Fort Worth
Avoca..219
Brewed......................................219
Houston
Blacksmith..................................219
Boomtown Coffee........................219
Southside Espresso.....................219
San Antonio
Local Coffee...............................220
Waco
Dichotomy Coffee & Spirits..........220
Vermont

Burlington
Brio Coffeeworks.........................285
Maglianero..................................285
Scout & Co..................................285
Virginia
Alexandria
Swings..279
Floyd
Black Water Loft..........................279
Richmond
The Lab by Alchemy Coffee.........279
Washington
Everett
Garage Auto Hero........................220
Olympia
Bar Francis..................................220
Olympia Coffee Roasters.............220
Ridgefield
Lava Java....................................221
Seattle
Analog Coffee..............................254
Caffe Vita....................................257
Canlis...255
Espresso Vivace..........................254
Lighthouse Roasters.....................255
La Marzocco Cafe and Showroom......
at KEXP...................................255
Milstead & Co..............................256
Slate Coffee Bar..........................256
Street Bean.................................254
Stumptown..................................257
Victrola Coffee Roasters..............255
Vif..256
Zig Zag Café...............................257
Zoka Coffee................................256
Wenatchee
Café Mela...................................221
Wisconsin
Madison
Bradbury's..................................266
Milwaukee
Colectivo Coffee..........................267
Kickapoo Coffee..........................267
Stone Creek Coffee Roasters........267
Nelsonville
Ruby Coffee Roasters..................267

INDEX BY VENUE

2ffect Coffee.....77
3fe.....116
4 Monkeys Coffee Shop.....304
5 Brewing.....76
18 Grams.....48
21st Street Coffee & Tea.....284
46B Espresso Hut.....108
49th Parallel Coffee Roasters.....205
1369 Coffee House.....289

A

ABCD (A Bunch of Caffeine Dealers).....56
About Life Coffee Brewers.....70
Abraço.....297
Alchimiste.....128
Algorithm Coffee Co......232
Alkemisten.....87
All Day.....275
All That Is Coffee.....112
Alpine Modern Café.....217
Altius.....31
Amass.....90
Amethyst Coffee.....238
Amor Perfecto.....315
Amor y Amargo.....297
Analog Coffee (Calgary).....196
Analog Coffee (Seattle).....254
Angelina's.....284
Anthracite.....76
Arabica.....314
Arbor.....232
Archetype Coffee.....264
Arise Coffee Roasters.....68–9
Aroma Cafe.....307
Artisan Coffee.....102
Assembly.....30
Association Coffee.....106
Astro Coffee.....260
Auction Rooms.....31
Avenue Coffee.....112
Avoca.....219
Azahar Café.....315

B

Bar 9.....19
Bar Francis.....220
Bar Pasticceria Elisa.....179
Bar Termini.....109
Bard Coffee.....282
Barista (Alberta, Portland).....242

Barista (Portland).....244
Barista Caffe.....49
Barista Jam.....48
The Barn.....147
Bartavelle Coffee & Wine Bar.....232
Bayleaf Cafe.....18
Be a Good Neighbor.....71
Be Speciality.....36
Bear Pond Espresso.....69
Bella Vista Coffee.....306
Bettina & Niccolò Corallo.....138
Bird Rock Coffee Roasters.....215
The Birds & The Beets.....204
Bistro 75.....164
Black Oak Coffee Roasters.....216
Black Water Loft.....279
Blackberry Market.....260
Blacklist.....128
Blacksmith.....219
Blacktop Coffee.....224
BLK MRKT.....262
Blue Bottle Coffee.....234
Blue Bottle (High Line).....294
Blueprint Coffee.....264
Bohemian.....78
La Boîte à Café.....128
Bold Bean Coffee Roasters.....274
Bold Street.....102
Bolt Coffee (at the Dean Hotel).....284
Bonanza.....147
Boomtown Coffee.....219
Bows & Arrows.....198
Boxcar Coffee.....239
Boxcar Social.....209
Bradbury's.....266
Braginn – Clay and Coffee.....84
Brash Coffee.....278
Brave Roasters.....60
Bread & Sons Bakery.....200
Brew Five Points.....274
Brewed.....219
Brick & Mortar Coffee.....264
Brio Coffeeworks.....285
Browns of Brockley.....106
Budin.....295
Bud's Coffee Bar.....209
Bulldog Edition.....109
Buna 42.....308
Bunker Coffee.....26
The Burger Brothers.....175

C

La Cabra.....84
Café de L'Ambre.....68
Café Bintino.....42
Café Bretelles.....128
Café Brumas del Zurquí.....304
Café Divino.....305
Café Dulce.....227
Café Europa 1989.....90
Café Evoke.....266
Café Grumpy.....294
Café Grumpy.....296
Café Les Jeux.....69
Café Lomi.....134
Café Lulu.....44
Café don Mayo.....304
Café Mela.....221
Café Mingqian.....43
Café du Monde.....277
Café Museo.....306
Café Myriade.....201
Café del Parco.....174
Café Passmar.....308
Café Pergamino.....315
Café Phalam.....64
Café Triciclo
(mobile, various locations).....318
Café Ubuntu.....184
Café Verde.....314
Café del Volcán.....43
Caffè Artigiano.....204
Caffè del Doge.....179
Caffé Medici.....250
Caffe Sospeso.....307
Caffe Streets.....270
Caffè Terzi.....178
Caffe Vita.....257
Canlis.....255
Caravan Roasters.....106
Cartel Coffee Lab.....214
Cat & Cloud Coffee Co......216
Cenote.....248
Ceremony Coffee Roasters.....277
Ceresia Coffee.....60
Chapter One.....146
Chattahoochee Coffee.....275
Chernyi Cooperative.....174
Cherry Espresso Bar.....277
Chromatic Coffee.....216

City and State................................278
City Lights Coffee..........................278
Clandestino Roasters.......................18
Climpson & Sons...........................108
Club Espresso................................76
Coava Coffee Roasters...................242
Coco Espresso 701 Concept Store......48
Coffea Roasterie...........................266
Coffee Alchemy.............................22
The Coffee Collective (Copenhagen)....91
The Coffee Collective
    (Frederiksberg)...........................84
Coffee Commissary.........................226
The Coffee Ethic............................263
Coffee Lab....................................323
Coffee Libre..................................76
Coffee Lover's Planet......................52
Coffee Nerd..................................142
Coffee Profilers..............................146
The Coffee Road...........................314
Coffee Seed..................................77
Coffee Temple...............................77
Coffeeangel (SAS).........................116
Coffeemania.................................175
Cognoscenti Coffee........................224
Colectivo Coffee............................267
Collective Coffee...........................201
Collective Espresso........................265
La Colombe (Fishtown)....................283
Colonna & Smalls..........................102
Comet Coffee................................260
The Commonplace Coffee Co....283
Companion Coffee..........................146
Constellation Coffee.......................283
Corvus Coffee...............................239
Coutume......................................133
Craft...106
Crafters.......................................305
Cream...135
Crema Cafe..................................289
Crema Coffee................................279
Crema Coffee House.......................238
Cultivar Coffee Bar........................219
Cultivate Coffee and Tap House........262
The Cupping Room..........................49
Curator's Coffee Studio..................106
Customs......................................36
Cuvee Coffee Bar..........................249

D
Da Matteo....................................86
The Daily Press.............................277
Dandelion & Driftwood....................26
Davis Street Espresso.....................218
Dead River Coffee.........................261
Democratic Coffee.........................91

Devoción Café...............................296
Dichotomy Coffee & Spirits..............220
Dill...94
Ditta Artigianale............................179
Dogwood Coffee...........................262
Doma..218
Dose...198
Dose Espresso...............................106
Double B......................................174
Drop Coffee..................................85
Duchess of Spotswood....................33
Barismo.......................................289

E
Edition Coffee Roasters...................22
Either/Or.....................................243
El Café de Harry............................314
El Dorao......................................307
El Injerto Café..............................305
El Rey...298
El Zonte S-Cool.............................304
Elbgold.......................................150
Elementary Coffee..........................18
Eleven Madison Park.......................295
Eliscaffe......................................164
Elixr Coffee Roasters......................283
Elm Café......................................197
Elysian Coffee...............................204
Ema..154
Empire State South........................275
Espressamente Illy.........................178
Espresso Embassy..........................155
Espresso Lab Microroasters..............184
Espresso Vivace.............................254
Established Coffee..........................102
Everyday Coffee.............................31
Everyman Espresso.........................298
Exchange Specialty.........................18
Express Bar...................................164

F
Fábrica Coffee Roasters...................138
Factory Café.................................184
Father Carpenter...........................147
Father Coffee................................184
Figure 8 Coffee Purveyor.................248
Fika..262
Fika Fika......................................52
Filtry Dobra Kawa...........................155
Finca La Campiña...........................314
Fireflour Pizza...............................265
Five Elephant................................146
Five Senses...................................19
Five Watt.....................................263
Flat Track Coffee...........................249
The Flatiron..................................214

Fleet Coffee..................................249
Flight Coffee.................................37
The Florence.................................276
La Fontaine de Belleville..................134
Forloren Espresso...........................91
Fort Defiance................................296
Fortitude Coffee............................103
Four Barrel Coffee.........................233
Fox in the Snow............................265
Fragments....................................132
The French Press...........................215
Fritz Coffee Company......................77
Fuglen..70
Fumbally Cafe...............................116

G
G&B Coffee..................................225
Gabee...52
Gallery Drip Coffee........................60
Garage Auto Hero..........................220
Gauge...26
George Howell Coffee.....................288
Gimme! Coffee..............................282
Glitch Coffee................................68
Go Get Em Tiger
    (Hancock Park, Los Angeles).........226
Go Get Em Tiger
    (Los Feliz, Los Angeles)................227
Good Coffee.................................243
Good Enough Coffee.......................175
Good Life Coffee............................84
Gralehaus....................................276
Gravity Espresso & Wine Bar............197
Grémio..198

H
Habit Coffee.................................198
Harbinger Coffee............................217
Harris and Hoole...........................102
Harry's..22
Hazel & Hershey............................48
Headfirst Coffee Roasters.................124
Heart Coffee Roasters.....................243
Hell Cafe.....................................78
Hexagone Café..............................134
Hey Happy....................................199
Holybelly.....................................133
Homerun Roasters..........................44
Honor Cafe...................................133
Houndstooth Coffee.......................250
Hyperion Coffee............................262

I
Intelligentsia (Chicago)....................270
Intelligentsia
    (Silver Lake, Los Angeles)..............227

Intelligentsia (Venice, Los Angeles)...228
Intelligentsia Mini-Bar
 (outside the High Line Hotel)..........294
Ipsento.................270
Irons and Craig................18
Isso é Café................322

J

Jacked Up
 (mobile café, locations vary)..........208
Jason's Coffee Shop................208
Java................99
Joe Pro Shop................294
Johan & Nystrom Concept Store........85
Jubala................278

K

Kaffee, Espresso Und Barista.............142
Kaffeemuseum................150
Kaffeine................107
Kaffeverket/Snickarbacken 7..............85
Kaffibrugghúisd................94
Kaffihús Vesturbæjar................95
Kaffislippur................94
Kahvila Siili................84
Kaldi's Coffee (Clayton)..........263
Kaldi's Coffee (Copán)..........306
Kale'i Kaffebar................86
Kaph................117
Karma Coffee Roasters..........155
Kavarna Prazirna..........154
KB Caféshop................133
The Kettle Black................32
Kickapoo Coffee................267
Knock Box Coffee................48
Kofein................160
Kofi Brand................156
Kokako Organic Coffee................36
Koko Coffee & Design................124
Kontakt................154
Koppi................85
Kopplin's Coffee................263
Kronotrop................168
Kuppa Joy................214

L

The Lab by Alchemy Coffee..........279
Laboratorio................112
Lamiz................191
Lava Java................221
Leila's Shop................109
Les................175
Lighthouse Roasters..........255
Linea Caffe................233
Little Collins................295
Little Sister Coffee Maker................199

Local Coffee................220
The Local Coffee Stand................70
Loustic................132
Love Supreme................117
Lucca Cafés Especiais................318
Lyle's................109

M

Machhörndl Kaffee................142
Madcap Coffee................261
Maglianero................285
Mahtab Café................190
Maison Blanche Dael................120
Mak Na Konac................164
Make Coffee + Stuff................199
The Maling Room................30
The Man and the Steamboat................174
Man Met Bril Koffie................120
Mandabatmaz................168
Mangsi................56
Manic Coffee and Gelato................208
Market Lane Coffee................33
Maruyama Coffee................69
La Marzocco Cafe and Showroom
 at Kexp................255
Mazarine................234
Mecca................23
Menotti's Coffee Stop................228
Mercantile Dining & Provisions................238
Merriweather Cafe................26
Metric Coffee................270
Milstead & Co................256
Ministerstwo Kavy................156
Mission................266
Mocca................99
Modern Coffee................232
Monday's Coffee Store................19
Mondoli Studio................43
Monogram Coffee................196
Mûjšálek Kávy................154
Museo................201
My Little Melbourne................155

N

Nano Kaffee................147
Nanyang Old Coffee................57
Nobelhart & Schmutzig................147
Nomad................138
Norm Coffee................168
Not Just Coffee................277
Novo Coffee................238
Nylon................57

O

Octavio Café................322
Olio................264

Olympia Coffee Roasters................220
Ona Coffee................18
Once Over Coffee Bar................248
Onyx Coffee Lab................274

P

Palace Coffee Company................218
Pallett Kaffikompaní................84
Panther Coffee................275
Papercup Coffee Company................112
Paramount Coffee Project................22
Parisi Artisan Coffee................263
Parlor Coffee (inside Persons of
 Interest barbershop)................296
Parlour................199
Patika Wine and Coffee................250
Patricia Coffee Brewers................31
Pavement Coffeehouse................288
Peloso Coffee Roasters................53
Peña................112
Perc................276
Petra Roasting Co................168
Phil & Sebastian................196
Phil Coffee Company................60
Pikolo Espresso Bar................201
Pinecone................200
Le Pista Café Montréal
 (mobile café, locations vary)................201
The Plan................103
Pour Cleveland................265
Pourboy................26
Prado Café................205
Pressed Cafe................282
Prolog Coffee Bar................91
Proof Bakery................224
Proper Order................116
Proud Mary................31
Prufrock Coffee................107
Pržionica D59B................160
PT's Coffee................260
Publicus................218

R

Rahdesign Café................52
Ratio Coffee & Pastry................198
Rause Café e Vinho................318
Real Coffee................42
Relaks Kawiarnia................156
Render................288
Retro/Mojocoffee................44
Reunion Island Coffee................208
Revolver................56
Revolver Coffee................204
Reykjavík Roasters................94
Reynard................296
The Ristretto Coffee Lounge................217

Ritual Coffee Roaster................................
   (Mission District, San Francisco)....233
Ritual Coffee Roasters (Western..............
   Addition, San Francisco)...................235
Roast Coffee & Eatery............................60
Roasted Brown Coffee Company........117
Roaster Boutique.................................318
Roberto Café...190
The Room...305
Rose Cafe..42
Rosetta Roastery.................................184
Rosso Coffee Roasters........................197
Rowster..261
Ruby Coffee Roasters.........................267

S
St. Ali..32
Saint Frank..234
Salvage Coffee......................................22
Sam Café..191
Sam James Coffee Bar........................209
Santo Grão...322
Sant'Eustachio il Caffè........................178
Saraye Ameriha Boutique Café...........190
Şark Kahvesi (at the Grand Bazaar)....169
Sarutahiko Coffee Atelier Senagwa.....68
Satan's Coffee Corner..........................138
Scandinavian Embassy........................124
Scout & Co...285
Scout Coffee..215
Second Best Coffee.............................263
The Seed..274
Seeds Coffee Co..................................274
Seesaw Coffee.......................................43
Seniman Coffee Studio..........................56
Sensory Lab...30
Sentido..64
Seven Seeds...30
Seven Stars Bakery..............................284
Shaker Dam Coffeehouse....................282
The Shop..284
Sightglass Coffee.................................235
Simon Says...120
Simon's Coffee Shop............................289
Single Origin Roasters...........................23
Slate Coffee Bar...................................256
Small Batch..32
Smith Canteen......................................295
Solberg & Hansen Konseptbutikk........98
Sólo Espresso......................................276
Southside Espresso..............................219
Speicherstandt Kafferösterei..............150
Spiller Park..276
Sqirl..227
Stardust Video & Coffee......................275
Stockholm Espresso Club....................150

Stone Creek Coffee Roasters.............267
Strauss FD...26
Street Bean..254
Street Lounge Café..............................190
Stumptown...257
Stumptown Coffee Roasters...............244
The Sum of Us......................................191
Sump Coffee...264
Suplicy Cafés Especiais.......................322
Supreme Roastworks.............................98
Sweet Bloom Coffee Roasters............239
Sweetleaf...297
Swings..279
Switch Coffee...69
Syster Marmelad...................................86

T
Taglio...178
Tailor Made..160
Tamp and Stitch...................................117
Tamper Espresso Bar...........................128
Tanamera...56
Tandem Coffee Roasters.....................282
Tazza d'Oro..178
Télescope...132
Ten Belles..134
Tesla Coffee...175
Third Rail..298
Thom Bargen..200
Thunderbird Coffee..............................248
Tiago Coffee Bar + Kitchen.................226
Tim Wendelboe................................98–9
Timbertrain Coffee Roasters...............205
Timberyard UK (Seven Dials)..............108
Timeless Coffee Roasters....................232
Tokyo Smoke Found.............................208
Tom & Serg...191
Top Paddock...32
Tostaduria Bisetti................................314
Transcend..197
Travelers Rest......................................278
Tried & True Coffee..............................218
Trouble Coffee Co................................234
Two If By Sea.......................................200
Two Rivers Craft Coffee Company......216
Typika Artisan Roasters.........................19

U
Ugly Duckling Coffee Bar......................52
Ultimo Coffee......................................283
The Underdog.......................................160
Uni-Uni..42
Unlimited Coffee Bar.............................70

V
V Café...190

Vanguard Speciality Coffee Co............36
VCR...56
Verve Coffee Roasters (Los Angeles)..224
Verve Coffee Roasters (Santa Cruz)...216
Vice (Inside Wigwam)..........................117
Victrola Coffee Roasters......................255
Vif..256
Viktors Kaffe...86
Viva Espresso......................................304
Viva Sara Kaffée..................................120
Volta Coffee, Tea & Chocolate...........274
Voyage Coffee..42
Voyager Espresso................................297

W
Wakeup Café..174
Water Avenue Coffee...........................242
White Label Coffee...............................125
Workshop (Clerkenwell, London).......107
Workshop (Fitzrovia, London)..............108
Workshop (Marylebone, London)........108
The Wormhole......................................271
WOW (Woolloomooloo Out West)......53
Wrecking Ball Coffee Roasters...........233

Z
Zenzero Kitchen...................................218
Zig Zag Café...257
Zoka Coffee...256
Zombie Runner.....................................214

Phaidon Press Limited
Regent's Wharf
All Saints Street
London N1 9PA

Phaidon Press Inc.
65 Bleecker Street
New York, NY 10012

phaidon.com

First published 2017
© 2017 Phaidon Press Limited

ISBN 978 0 7148 7392 3

A CIP catalogue record for this book is available from
the British Library and the Library of Congress.

As many establishments change their opening hours in
relation to the seasons or close for extended periods at
different times of the year, it is always advisable to check
opening hours before visiting. All information is correct
at the time of going to print, but is subject to change.

Commissioning Editor: Emily Takoudes
Project Editor: Olga Massov
Production Controllers: Amanda Mackie
    and Alenka Oblak
Designed by Kobi Benezri and Julia Hasting

Printed in Italy

The publisher would like to thank all the participating
contributors for their generosity, time, and insightful
recommendations; Liz Clayton and Avidan Ross for their
expertise and commitment; Vanessa Bird, Couper Cox,
Elizabeth Ellis, Domenic Etre, Jude Grant, Dorothy Irwin,
Lesley Malkin, Luísa Martelo, João Mota, Tracey Smith,
and Luc Spicer for their contributions to the making of
this book.

Illustrations from thenounproject.com, based on original
artwork by: Ali Riza Saçan (french press, p.27); Marie-
Pierre Bauduin (steam wand, p.45); Abdo (coffee beans,
p.61); Nathan Rofkahr (siphon, p.65); Edward Boatman
(demitasse spoon, p.79); Katie Schultz (portafilter, p.113);
Mark Caron (mug, p.121); Peter Carleton (latte, p.129);
chiara ardenghi (moka pot, p.139); Becca (portafilter,
p.143); Milky - Digital innovation (milk bottle, p.151);
Guvnor Co (coffee pot, p.157); Raz Cohen (espresso
tamper, p.161); Andrey Vasiliev (ibrik, p.164); William
Woods (coffee pot, p.185); Thomas Helbig (coffee cup,
p.229); L Recker (Chemex, p.245); Guvnor Co (coffee
dripper, p.251); Gabriela Muñiz (espresso machine,
p.299); AMMAR BADR (coffee bean scoop, p.309);
Ralf Schmitzer (manual coffee grinder, p.319);
Bakunetsu Kaito (espresso machine, p.331).

About the authors

Liz Clayton is one of the world's foremost coffee writers.
She is editor at Sprudge, writer for Twitchy, and author
of *Nice Coffee Time*. She lives in Brooklyn, New York.

Avidan Ross is the founding partner of Root Ventures
and an inventor, glassblower, and coffee connoisseur.
He lives in Los Angeles, California.

Author acknowledgments

For their invaluable, above-and-beyond legwork in
their regions of expertise, without which I would have
been completely lost, I owe tremendous thank-yous
to Nicholas Chistyakov, Jessica Johnston, BK Kim,
Mohammad Khani, and Echo Lou. Thank you also
to Peter's friend Vanessa for going above and beyond
the call of duty in Lucca, Italy. For patience and
encouragement, and for bringing me coffee in bed
on weekend mornings, thanks and love to Eduardo Gil.
—Liz Clayton

To my decaf-drinking wife Elizabeth Ross, and my
milk-drinking son, Ezra Ross, thank you for the love
and support. —Avidan Ross